Complete Guide to Trees & Shrubs

Meredith® Books
Des Moines, Iowa

Complete Guide to Trees & Shrubs

The Right Plant for the Right Purpose   6

The Right Plant for the Right Place   22

Planting and Care   30

The Art and Science of Pruning   50

Tree Selection and Growing Guide **88**

Shrub Selection Guide **142**

Selecting Woody Vines **196**

The Right Plant
FOR THE RIGHT PURPOSE

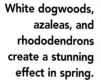

**White dogwoods,
azaleas, and
rhododendrons
create a stunning
effect in spring.**

Trees and shrubs are the building blocks of the landscape. They bring beauty in foliage, flower, and form, and they also provide function by organizing space and making living areas more comfortable. They work together and apart to create unique yards that still blend neatly into neighborhoods and towns.

The value of trees and shrubs

Trees have layers of meaning and use. Their impact on the landscape transcends their size and stature. Trees root communities with their continuity; they assure that what has been before us will be here long after. They bring communities together in neighborhood plantings and in lightings of the town tree at Christmas. Trees are planted in memory of friends and family and as a link with the past. Trees mark the seasons of the year and are steady companions, lasting for lifetimes, generations, and in some cases, millennia.

Landscapes, when planted with trees, become more comfortable; with shade in summer and wind protection in winter. Trees structure outdoor space and shape it into rooms and hallways. Their trunks are walls; their spreading boughs are ceilings.

Like living works of art, they add color, form, and allegory to our gardens. And trees are fun: In a child's heart, no play equipment will ever replace an old climbing tree or a rope swing.

Shrubs alone can make a garden. They are the garden's backbone, bringing beauty, comfort, and pleasure to the landscape by adding structure to the outdoors. Shrubs create a transition from the house to the environment that surrounds it, whether that world consists of eastern forests, Midwestern prairies, or western dry lands. Before you purchase another plant for the garden, consider investing in shrubs. They offer years of low-maintenance satisfaction, often at a minimal price. Shrubs can change how you feel about being outside. They can create a sense of privacy and psychological comfort by hiding unsightly views and provide physical comfort by altering wind, light, and noise pollution. As long as you select the proper site and shrubs, nature will keep them healthy and full.

How to use this book

This book will guide you on your quest to find the right trees and shrubs (and even a few vines) and help you care for and protect the ones you have in your landscape.

In the first chapter, you will learn about design considerations that explain the hard work trees and shrubs can perform in your landscape: how they can make outdoor living more comfortable and enjoyable, how they can shape your yard into usable space, how you can combine trees and shrubs for beautiful visual effects, and how you can achieve the most rapid results.

The second chapter helps you choose and place trees and shrubs in the right location for optimum health and most successful growth. You are guided through regional considerations as well as the particulars of your yard regarding soil, light, moisture, and microclimates.

The third chapter leads you through acquiring, planting, and caring for new trees and shrubs, tending established trees and shrubs, and controlling common pests that may affect your woody plants.

The fourth chapter shows you how to train and prune trees and shrubs and gives all the tricks and techniques

you'll need to keep your plants not only looking their best but also healthy and strong.

The fifth and sixth chapters are selection and growing guides to more than 250 of the best trees and shrubs for North American yards and gardens.

Evergreen screening provided by American arborvitae encloses this patio year-round.

Combine ground covers with colorful foliage for a dramatic effect.

A pair of sugar maples catches the evening light.

The final chapter is a bonus. It includes information on growing 21 of the most common woody vines to complement your trees and shrubs.

Make Your Yard More Comfortable

American arborvitae are used instead of a fence to create a tall screen.

Trees and shrubs can make you feel comfortable both indoors and out. In summer, they create cooling shade and welcome relief from the glare of the hot sun. Long, curved plantings of shrubs or certain trees—set diagonally in the wind's path—can bend the breeze toward you, evaporating perspiration and leaving you cool and content. In winter, dense evergreen shrub plantings can protect the inside of your house from icy gusts by breaking them up before they reach the exterior walls.

Erosion, a slow, natural process often speeded up by contemporary construction practices, can be tempered by trees and shrubs. The leafy, twiggy top growth and spreading roots create a perfect antidote for the pounding rains and ravaging winds that can strip away precious topsoil.

A sense of peace, privacy, and tranquility in your home's landscape is important. Trees and shrubs can offer this.

They can shield you from annoying activity in the surrounding neighborhood. Trees and shrubs with hairy leaves help keep the air clean by capturing airborne dirt and pollen on their surfaces. Trees and shrubs also purify the environment through photosynthesis, a process in which they remove carbon dioxide from the atmosphere in sunlight and restore oxygen to the air.

Cooling the air

Trees are efficient at cooling the air. Working somewhat like an evaporative air conditioner, a tree pumps water vapor from its leaves (a process called transpiration), and the air cools as the moisture evaporates. This is why it feels cool and fresh under a tree even on a hot day. The combination of shade and transpiration can reduce the air temperature by 5° to 10° F.

BEST SHADE TREES

Red maple (*Acer rubrum*)
Sugar maple (*Acer saccharum*)
Horsechestnut (*Aesculus* spp.)
Yellowwood (*Cladrastis* spp.)
Gum tree (*Eucalyptus* spp.)
European beech (*Fagus sylvatica*)
White ash (*Fraxinus americana*)
Ginkgo (*Ginkgo biloba*)
Sweet gum (*Liquidambar styraciflua*)
Tulip tree (*Liriodendron tulipifera*)
Plane tree (*Platanus* spp.)
White oak (*Quercus alba*)
Northern red oak (*Quercus rubra*)
Redmond linden (*Tilia americana* 'Redmond')
Sawleaf zelkova (*Zelkova serrata*)

WHERE TO PLANT A TREE FOR MAXIMUM SHADE

Both deciduous trees (those that lose their leaves each year) and evergreens (those that keep their leaves) provide shade. However, you'll get maximum shade in the summer and maximum winter sun from a tall deciduous tree with a broad canopy of dense leaves. The temperature beneath a leafy tree can be 10° F cooler than in the open, and this cooling can be passed on to the inside of your house. By reducing the amount of hot sun against your house, your cooling bills may be lowered as well. For the most effective shading, place trees on the southwest, west, or northwest sides of the area or building to be shaded. These are the sides where the hot afternoon sun strikes in summer. The sun is highest in the early afternoon, so plant the tallest trees on the southwest side. Three well-placed shade trees can reduce your cooling costs by as much as 35 percent.

BEST EVERGREEN TREES FOR WINDBREAKS

White fir *(Abies concolor)*
Leyland cypress *(Cupressocyparis leylandii)*
Eastern red cedar *(Juniperus virginiana)*
Norway spruce *(Picea abies)*
Colorado spruce *(Picea pungens)*
Austrian pine *(Pinus nigra)*
Eastern white pine *(Pinus strobus)*
Scotch pine *(Pinus sylvestris)*
Douglas fir *(Pseudotsuga menziesii)*

Paper birch provides the kind of dappled shade desired in summer for a patio or deck.

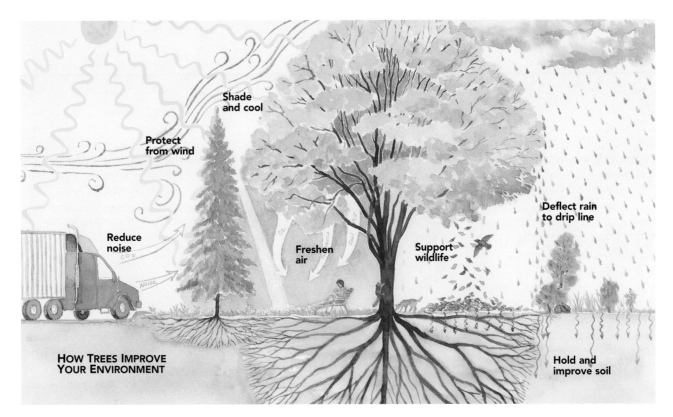

Shade and cool

Protect from wind

Deflect rain to drip line

Reduce noise

Freshen air

Support wildlife

HOW TREES IMPROVE YOUR ENVIRONMENT

Hold and improve soil

Make Your Yard More Comfortable
(continued)

Shrubs envelop this small garden, creating a cool and shady retreat.

Blocking the wind

You can reduce your annual heating bill by up to 20 percent if you plant a windbreak on the windward side of your house to deflect prevailing winter winds. Evergreen trees or shrubs with low-growing branches and dense winter foliage are the best choice. For maximum protection, they should be planted close together and should be located no farther than twice their mature height from the house. Remember that snowdrifts develop on the downwind side, so plant trees a good distance away from driveways and walks.

Trees and shrubs can also cool your environment by steering summer breezes your way. They can also reduce air turbulence by filtering the wind through their leaves, branches, and limbs.

Moreover, shrubs or a dense hedge planted on a wall's windward side can help reduce turbulence on both sides of the wall. When planting a windbreak, place shrubs beyond the width of the actual space that you want to protect because wind can travel around the sides of the windbreak.

Controlling erosion and improving soil

Erosion occurs when heavy rains or harsh winds carry away topsoil. This happens frequently on slopes, which may also be exposed to wind and broiling sun.

To combat soil loss, select shrubs that can be densely planted and have spreading surface-root systems to hold the soil in place. The shrubs should also have dense, twiggy, horizontal top growth, rough bark, and profuse needles or leaves to break up wind and rain. Mulch newly planted shrubs to help them get established. Shrubs also are useful as ground covers in areas where growing and mowing grass are difficult.

Even below the ground, trees and shrubs do beneficial things for the landscape. Tree roots anchor the tree in the ground and soak up water and nutrients from the soil. They support an underground universe of beneficial insects and microorganisms. These, in turn, keep the soil around them healthy and teeming with life. The roots of some trees, such as honeylocust, Japanese pagoda tree, and alder, even "fix" nitrogen into the soil, actually adding to the soil's fertility.

Tall, arching shrubs, such as cotoneaster or witch hazel, can create a low canopy that reduces glare and provides shade.

A thick hedge of mixed deciduous and evergreen shrubs reduces traffic noise.

Plant prostrate shrubs on slopes to serve as a ground cover and prevent erosion.

A hedge of shrubs makes an effective windbreak by slowing and diverting wind, not stopping it.

Buffering noise

Though it's a quality often overlooked, trees and shrubs have an impressive ability to muffle noise. Their leaves and small branches act as baffles, absorbing and deflecting sound. You'll get maximum noise protection from plants with dense leaves, rather than open, lacy leaves.

A combination of evergreens, deciduous trees, and dense shrubs is the best sound-absorption solution. For optimum results, trees and shrubs reaching at least 15 feet high should be spaced closely together in a bed at least 15 feet from front to back. Planting on a raised bed, high mound, or berm helps to deflect sound overhead as well as provide the additional barrier of soil.

The best sound barriers also employ a solid wall made of masonry or wood. Although shrubs and narrow plantings by themselves cannot completely control noise, a hedge 6-feet tall can hide the source of noise, creating a psychological barrier. Falling water or the songs of birds can mask unpleasant noise, so a fountain, a small waterfall, or bird-attracting shrubs can be added to moderate noise.

Directing light

Depending on their density, height, and placement, trees and shrubs can soften or block glare and reflection. For example, a tall hedge can cool you on a hot afternoon by screening the sun's rays and reducing the glare from nearby water or pavement. Evergreen plants work well for year-round protection from direct or reflected sunlight. In winter, however, you may want warm, cheerful sunshine streaming into the house from the south or east. Deciduous trees and shrubs allow sunlight to penetrate the house in winter. When leafed out in spring and summer, they block direct solar radiation and shade the walls and roof of the house.

Cleaning the air

Like living filters, trees are nature's purifiers. Through openings (stomates) in their leaves, trees absorb pollutants. Each leaf dissolves sulfur and nitrogen, breaks down ozone, and metabolizes other compounds so the tree can use them. After processing all the chemicals, trees release water and oxygen into the air.

The combined chemistry of the thousands of leaves on each tree eliminates an enormous volume of pollutants from the air. The U.S. Forest Service estimates that in one year, the trees growing in the city of Chicago can remove 6,145 tons of air pollutants. Trees also physically remove particles such as soot and dust from the atmosphere. The particles stick to the leaves and are washed away by rain.

SHRUBS FOR WINDBREAKS

Barberry (*Berberis* spp.)
Siberian peashrub (*Caragana arborescens*)
Escallonia (*Escallonia* spp.)
Burning bush (*Euonymus alatus*)
Inkberry (*Ilex glabra*)
Privet (*Ligustrum* spp.)
Dwarf mountain pine (*Pinus mugo*)
Arrowwood viburnum (*Viburnum dentatum*)

Plants Shape Outdoor Space

Adaptable and trouble-free, privet is also tolerant of shearing.

Trees and shrubs are the bones of any design; they shape spaces and add structure like nothing else. Your first step toward an outstanding garden is analyzing your space; your second step is defining it.

ENCLOSURE: To unify an open area, first enclose it. Think of it as putting up walls. A large, open lawn becomes a welcoming space when bordered by trees or tall shrubs. The classic choice for this is evergreens, which have the added plus of working year-round, but you can use a mixed border or even a staggered grove of trees to get the same effect with less of a solid feeling.

When you enclose your garden, you'll also gain privacy and shape your view out of the yard. Eyesores are easily hidden by well-placed trees and shrubs.

After you've created the larger space, break it up into smaller spaces, called outdoor rooms. These rooms invite visitors to sit and stay awhile. They create private spaces within your landscape. Make the walls of the rooms as solid or as light as you want. In and around these rooms, plant shade trees for a roof or a ceiling.

MOVEMENT: Trees and shrubs are crucial to guiding traffic within and among these rooms. They can welcome people into the backyard, announce the entrance to a garden room, or tie the house and yard together.

In a larger sense, trees and shrubs create corridors and avenues within the garden. These can be formal or informal, dense or airy, but they guide movement, so take advantage of this. Use them to show off special plantings or favorite areas.

DRAMATIC VIEWS: The corridors and rooms you've created to this point are natural settings for your favorite garden views. If you're especially proud of a particular tree or shrub, design a room around it or with an attractive view of it. Elegant columnar trees can show off a favorite vista as well as any picture frame. Use your most spectacular specimens at the end of corridors, and they will draw attention. And remember the views from your house; plan your more dramatic plantings with an eye toward the view from the house.

EXPANSION: If your space begins to feel cramped, there are ways to expand it. Make a space under the canopy of a tree to create a room without walls. Use perspective; with larger trees planted close and smaller ones farther away, the space will feel larger than it is. Or treat the garden as an expansion of the house, and it will make the house seem that much larger.

DEFINE BOUNDARIES
An enclosure can be as solid as a dense wall of evergreens or as suggestive as a single tree or shrub. Trees and shrubs in staggered groves contain space while retaining openness.

BLOCK VIEWS
Trees and shrubs can protect your privacy and screen unsightly views. Such screens are usually walls of thick foliage.

DEVELOP CORRIDORS
The trunks and foliage mass of trees and shrubs direct traffic and connect garden rooms together. Passageways can be wide and sweeping, or narrow and intimate. They can be straight and direct, or meandering and full of mystery.

SET FOCAL POINTS
A tree or shrub with an unusual sculptural frame, or seasonal color, draws the eye like a magnet. Tall, narrow trees attract attention from a distance. Up close, such columnar trees direct the gaze skyward. Use focal points with care; too many can simply confuse.

ENCLOSE INTIMATE ROOMS
Make large properties more intimate by dividing space into rooms. The connections between rooms become points of interest, and they encourage movement and exploration.

EXPAND SENSE OF SPACE
Placing large, overscaled trees up close and smaller plants farther away increases the sense of depth and distance.

ESTABLISH GATEWAYS
The trunks of trees and placement of shrubs establish gateways and portals between different parts of the yard. Examples are areas between the garden room and the corridor, the house and the yard, and the private backyard and the public front yard.

SPREAD CANOPIES OVERHEAD
A canopy overhead not only protects from hot sun and rain, it provides its own sense of enclosure and intimacy—a garden room without walls.

EXTEND THE INDOORS OUT
Trees or large shrubs arching over both house and yard create transitional spaces that extend indoor rooms into the yard.

FRAME VIEWS
As with looking at a framed painting, looking through a "frame" of trees sets off a view and magnifies its effect. Enhance a view out a window with a frame as simple as a single tree trunk to one side.

The Role of Style

Low border shrubs, tall screening ones, and individual specimens combine to form the basic structure of this formal garden.

Bigleaf hydrangea is restrained by a low hedge of Japanese boxwood clipped in a formal style.

Creating a garden brings up questions of style. Just as the interior of your home reflects your needs and personality, the outside of your house reveals similar insights into who you are. For example, does a four-square neo-Georgian home inspire visions of orderly hedges, or would you soften the austere contours of the house with a flowing design based on lush plantings of native shrubs? Both ideas have merit, but they demonstrate different ways of organizing outdoor space. The first, with its emphasis on symmetry and architecture, is formal style. The second, which relies on asymmetrical balance and the plants themselves for effect, is informal or naturalistic style.

The style and location of the house influence your ultimate garden style. A suburban center-hall colonial may lend itself to a symmetrical approach highlighting the architectural qualities of the house, whereas a restored farmhouse at the edge of the woods on a rocky hillside brings to mind a more naturalistic setting. Sometimes, the unique character of the site— the spirit of a place—inspires a landscape plan with formal features near the house with a transition to more naturalistic elements at a distance.

How to use geometry

Formal gardens have a central axis, meaning that the design turns on an imaginary line drawn down the middle of the plan. These gardens are symmetrically balanced so that the layout on one side of the axis mirrors the opposite side. In formal gardens, humans are the master of nature, imposing restraint and order on the growth of plants. Some shrubs become geometrical hedges through shearing or clipping. Others are sculpted into topiary, with shapes of cubes, spheres, spirals, or even fanciful animals.

Geometrical surface patterns, which work especially well on flat stretches of land, often pervade the design. Knots— herb or flower beds with a twining design created by low shrubs such as boxwood (*Buxus* spp.) or rosemary (*Rosmarinus officinalis*)— have been part of formal gardens since their birth in Tudor England. Parterres— flat, geometrically patterned beds of flowers and shrubs—

SHRUBS FOR FORMAL HEDGES

Barberry (*Berberis* spp.)
Boxwood (*Buxus* spp.)
Holly (*Ilex* spp.)
Privet (*Ligustrum* spp.)
Holly osmanthus (*Osmanthus heterophyllus*)
Nanking cherry (*Prunus tomentosa*)
Rosemary (*Rosmarinus officinalis*)
Yew (*Taxus* spp.)
Arborvitae (*Thuja* spp.)
Canadian hemlock (*Tsuga canadensis*)

A variety of woodland shrubs, such as viburnum and rhododendron, are combined for an attractive look.

In this setting worthy of Monet, shrubs provide most of the permanent plantings flanking the pond.

originated in the late 1400s and still exist today as formal design elements. Traditionally, knots and parterres were planted close to a house so their intricate patterns could be appreciated from the upper stories or during after-dinner garden strolls.

If you prefer the clean lines and architectural clarity of a formal design, a naturalistic plan may at first glance seem haphazard and spontaneous. On the other hand, if you are a romantic, the formality of meticulously pruned, spherical shrubs on neatly mulched beds is as appetizing as a plate of meatballs minus the spaghetti. Instead, you'd probably relish the long, flowing curves, contrasting textures, and variety of natural plant forms typical of the informal garden.

How to use informality

Informal gardens require considerable skill to create. Without forethought, they can end up a chaotic collection of plants. Naturalistic gardens have an asymmetrical balance achieved by contrasting groups of plants. If you draw a line down the center of a naturalistic plan, both sides are different but carry similar weight and interest. Because this kind of design is not obvious, it is more difficult for gardeners to create than a basic formal design.

The idealized version of nature experienced in naturalistic gardens has a romantic appeal. Human and nature combine as equal design partners, resulting in a greater focus on the plants themselves. Rocks, gnarly trees, and native shrubs add a feeling of rusticity; uneven ground and winding, mulched paths shaded by arching boughs and large plantings of shrubs convey elements of beauty and surprise. Although native plants may predominate in a wild or naturalistic garden, you can also use exotic plants with excellent results. Many woodland gardens, for instance, rely successfully on nonnative species of rhododendron and other flowering shrubs for marvelous spring color. The key is finding plants to suit the site in terms of hardiness, soil, and the right amount of water and light.

You may find it advantageous to combine both formal and informal design elements. That's fine—garden design is an accommodating art. If the house lends itself to a formal setting but you like the free-flowing look of a naturalistic garden, you can combine the two, with formal elements near the house and casual ones at a distance. A colorful parterre or fragrant knot works well outside French doors, whereas a tall, informal hedge of native shrubs makes an attractive backyard screen for ugly views and noise.

NATIVE SHRUBS FOR INFORMAL USE

Bottlebrush buckeye *(Aesculus parviflora)*
Carolina allspice *(Calycanthus floridus)*
Summersweet clethra *(Clethra alnifolia)*
Red-osier dogwood *(Cornus stolonifera)*
Dwarf fothergilla *(Fothergilla gardenii)*
Common witch hazel *(Hamamelis virginiana)*
Mountain laurel *(Kalmia latifolia)*
Mountain pieris *(Pieris floribunda)*
Highbush blueberry *(Vaccinium corymbosum)*

Trees in the Landscape

An allée of American beech in early spring arches over this pathway.

A grove of European white birch emulates how the trees are found growing in nature.

Trees provide the basic structure and mass of the landscape. The shapes of the trees are vitally important to this. When seen from a distance, the mass and skyline of the trees in your yard give your landscape weight and form. Rounded and spreading trees provide a horizontal mass that extends the house outward, whereas the vertical mass of columnar and pyramidal trees extends your house upward.

Overhead, the leafy canopy of spreading trees frames the view below it; the verticality of columnar trees lifts up the view almost like a tall window. Repeating these forms intensifies the effect, and varying them creates a dynamic, changing impression in the landscape.

At eye level, tree trunks can frame a view, extend the vertical lines of the house into the landscape, or send the eye off through mysterious depths of a grove. When

10 Best Columnar Trees

Columnar red maple (*Acer rubrum* 'Columnare')
Goldspire sugar maple (*Acer saccharum* 'Goldspire')
Columnar European hornbeam (*Carpinus betulus* 'Columnaris')
Columnar European beech (*Fagus sylvatica* 'Fastigiata')
Princeton Sentry® ginkgo or maidenhair tree (*Ginkgo biloba* 'Princeton Sentry')
Adirondak, Sentinel, or Red Barron crabapple (*Malus* 'Adirondak', 'Sentinel', or 'Red Barron')
Columnar sargent cherry (*Prunus sargentii* Columnaris or 'Spire')
Amanogawa Japanese flowering cherry (*Prunus serrulata* 'Amanogawa')
Capital or Chanticleer callery pear (*Pyrus calleryana* 'Capital' or 'Chanticleer')
Shawnee Brave bald cypress (*Taxodium distichum* 'Shawnee Brave™')

repeated, these trunks establish rhythms, calming if repeated uniformly and more dynamic if interspersed with different shapes. Showy trees, or trees with unusual form, interrupt such a rhythmic path and should be used sparingly.

The shapes of trees

Classifying the myriad shapes and sizes of trees into a few general forms helps you combine trees in a landscape that is unified and pleasing to the eye.

ROUNDED AND OVAL TREES offer a regular shape that is ideal for a formal statement when planted in rows and grids. Use them to create an effective corridor flanking a drive or street. Planted alone in an open yard, they tend to achieve their most perfect, regular form. In groups of three or more, their tops create a billowing mass of foliage that is pleasing to view from a distance.

SPREADING TREES provide a horizontal reach that is useful for continuing the horizontal lines of the house into the landscape. These are the trees to choose when you are looking for a canopy over a patio or sitting area. Their overarching branches are perfect to establish a powerful frame for a favorite view.

PYRAMIDAL TREES have crowns that taper toward the sky; when seen from a distance, they tend to lift the eye upward. They can be cone-shaped evergreens, such as spruce and fir, or deciduous

trees. Pyramidal Greenspire lindens or scarlet oaks are as well-suited for street tree plantings as for dramatic contrast behind rounded and spreading trees.

COLUMNAR OR FASTIGIATE TREES have a narrow, vertical form. They make dramatic sentinels that attract attention from a distance and lift the eye upward like an arrow pointed to the sky. Their narrow diameter makes them a favorite for planting in colonnades, as screens and windbreaks, and to create garden rooms with walls of foliage. Many common tree species are available in columnar form.

MULTIPLE-TRUNK TREES lend the effect of a natural grove with a single specimen, whereas a modest planting of only three or five can create the feeling of an entire forest. Their striking form makes them useful as an accent in more natural landscapes. And because they tend to arch out, they are often used at the corner of a house to soften stark architectural lines.

WEEPING TREES are the ideal accent to command attention in an important spot and seem especially effective next to water. A weeping cherry, for example, is a spectacular living sculpture. It makes a beautiful adornment for a pool or other small water feature.

10 BEST WEEPING TREES

Cutleaf Japanese maple (*Acer palmatum dissectum*)
Weeping Katsura tree (*Cercidiphyllum japonicum* 'Pendulum')
Weeping European beech (*Fagus sylvatica pendula*)
Red Jade crabapple (*Malus* 'Red Jade')
Weeping Serbian spruce (*Picea omorika* 'Pendula')
Weeping Yoshino cherry (*Prunus ×yedoensis* 'Shidare Yoshino')
Weeping Higan cherry (*Prunus subhirtella* 'Pendula')
Weeping willow (*Salix alba*)
Weeping Japanese snowbell (*Styrax japonicus* 'Pendula' or 'Carillon')
Weeping Canadian hemlock (*Tsuga canadensis* 'Sargentii')

An ancient white oak shows the broad, spreading, horizontal branching structure characteristic of oaks.

Fast-Growing vs. Permanent

A large tree creates an immediate effect, but a smaller tree might catch up quicker than you expect, and at less expense.

To many gardeners, waiting for trees to grow is frustrating. Trees just don't grow "fast enough." You may be patient but still not want to wait 30 years for a shade tree. Fortunately, there are several alternatives to the long wait.

Temporary trees give the fastest effect for your buck. Many will seem to spring up overnight, filling space quickly. That's the good news. The bad news is that almost all of these trees have problems; they are weak-wooded, or they throw lots of litter or have numerous pests. If you try one of these, be aware of its problems, and be prepared to deal with the cost of having it removed (which can be quite expensive).

Groves and groups of small trees can create a fast, strong effect. You should use only trees that grow naturally in groves, such as birches; others will not grow properly. You can even combine fast growers with slower growers that are shade-tolerant; over time, the slower trees will replace the faster ones. This option is not without its dangers, though. The top growth of trees planted in groups adjusts to its situation; that is, it grows differently than if the tree were freestanding. If you thin the group later, the upper part of the trees will look odd. And, as mentioned before, the expense and trouble of removing trees later should not be taken lightly.

Planting mature trees is the fastest option, but they have pitfalls, too. Besides being very expensive, mature trees don't take the shock of planting well, and they may die in the process. Even if they survive, it might take them a few years to get back to a healthy, growing state. In those few years, smaller trees might have already caught up to them.

Giving optimum care to the trees you really want is a good option. Many trees, when kept pest-free and disease-free, sited correctly, watered regularly, and mulched properly, will respond with faster-than-average growth. With such care, a good, slow-growth-rate

FASTEST-GROWING "TEMPORARY" TREES

Box elder *(Acer negundo)*
Silver maple *(Acer saccharinum)*
European black alder *(Alnus glutinosa)*
Leyland cypress *(×Cupressocyparis leylandii)*
Empress tree *(Paulownia tomentosa)*
White poplar *(Populus alba)*
Lombardy poplar *(Populus nigra* 'Italica')
Willows *(Salix* spp.)
Green Giant arborvitae *(Thuja* 'Green Giant')

TREES WITH MEDIUM-TO-FAST GROWTH RATE

Red maple *(Acer rubrum)*
Heritage river birch *(Betula nigra* 'Heritage')
Green ash *(Fraxinus pennsylvanica)*
Thornless honeylocust *(Gleditsia triacanthos inermis)*
London plane tree *(Platanus ×acerifolia)*
Pin oak *(Quercus palustris)*
Northern red oak *(Quercus rubra)*
Coast redwood *(Sequoia sempervirens)*
Bald cypress *(Taxodium distichum)*
Chinese elm *(Ulmus parvifolia)*

Planting a long-lived tree is a gift to the future. Sharing the occasion with a child is especially meaningful.

TREES TO PLANT FOR POSTERITY

Sugar maple (*Acer saccharum*)
Gum tree (*Eucalyptus* spp.)
Tulip tree (*Liriodendron tulipifera*)
London plane tree (*Platanus ×acerifolia*)
Sargent cherry (*Prunus sargentii*)
Bur oak (*Quercus macrocarpa*)
Northern red oak (*Quercus rubra*)
Live oak (*Quercus virginiana*)
Bald cypress (*Taxodium distichum*)

tree will grow at its best rate. Although this is not a cure-all or guarantee, and the results, especially with naturally slow-growing trees, are not usually dramatic, it works much of the time.

The best solution borrows a little from all of these strategies. First, select the highest-quality, medium-to-fast-growing trees that fit your needs and wants. Then give them the best site for their needs, and follow up with the best care you can give. Plant them carefully, tend them regularly, and pay attention to them year-round. Watch for pests and signs of disease; water them correctly and deeply; and mulch their root zone. This way, you get a quality tree and, more than likely, a good, fast effect from the tree in your landscape.

Plant for posterity

No discussion of trees would be complete without acknowledging their tremendous life spans. Some trees are nature's monuments, awesome not only in proportion but in longevity. Some California sequoias (redwoods) have lived more than 2,000 years. The bristlecone pines in the southwest mountains are the oldest living trees in the world, approaching 5,000 years old. Trees are increasingly a symbol of

endurance in our fast-paced, disposable culture.

If you want to plant a tree for your great-grandchildren, choose a long-lived genus such as the oak. Here's an old English adage: An oak takes "300 years growing, 300 years standing still, and 300 years dying." The Middleton Oak in Charleston, South Carolina, bears that out—it's 900 years old. The Bedford Oak in Bedford, New York, was alive when the U.S. Constitution was signed. Oaks (white, live, and English) and beeches (American and European) are trees for legacies. So are horsechestnut, London plane tree, and sequoia. Plant these long-lived trees in a wide-open area where they can grow unhindered for generations to come.

Given good conditions, this oak seedling will be a climbable tree within 20 years.

A heritage tree, such as this oak, was planted by someone with foresight.

Foundation Plantings

Foundation plantings appear in front of many American homes. This uniquely American landscape feature started as a cover-up for the tall, lattice-covered foundations constructed under the fashionable front porches of big Victorian houses. Yet even as the Victorian style passed into history, these voguish plantings started cropping up where foundations were low and there was no need for them.

Pink flowers of the 'Nearly Wild' rose combine with spirea and yew in this foundation planting of shrubs.

This island bed attractively combines shrubs including barberry, euonymus, honeysuckle, roses, and yew.

With careful consideration, you can create an effective foundation planting. Such a planting will not only disguise and lend visual stability to a tall foundation, it can soften the corners of a house and tie it into the surrounding landscape. Some foundation plantings enhance the style of a house. A symmetrical pattern reinforces the regularity of a four-square colonial home, whereas an asymmetrically balanced planting is in keeping with a prairie-style house. A well-designed planting focuses attention on the front door, the desired focal point of most homes.

SIZE AND PROPORTION: The key to a successful foundation planting is a sense of proportion and scale. Large shrubs often look best with a tall house of two or more stories, whereas smaller shrubs complement the lines of a one-story dwelling.

Be sure to find out the mature size of a shrub before buying it. Choose shrubs not for how they look in the nursery but for their mature size. Too many houses have windows, doors, and front steps darkened by formerly shrub-size conifers grown into giant trees. The mature height of doorway plants should be about one-third the distance from the ground to the eaves overhanging the walls and corner plants less than two-thirds the distance between

VERTICAL SHRUB FORMS

Pyramidal/conical
(*Taxus cuspidata*)
Japanese yew

Columnar
(*Thuja occidentalis*)
American arborvitae

Vase/fan-shaped
(*Hamamelis* ×*intermedia*)
Hybrid witch hazel

Arching/fountain
(*Spiraea* ×*vanhouttei*)
Vanhoutte spirea

Oval
(*Ilex cornuta*)
Chinese holly

the ground and the eaves. Corner plantings are taller because they both frame the house and create a transition to the landscape. If you have an existing, overgrown foundation planting, you may be able to prune the shrubs to fit the scale of the house, or you may have to remove them and start from scratch.

LOCATION: Place foundation plants in front of the drip line of the eaves so they will receive water when it rains and in front of the snow line so they won't be crushed when snow slides off the roof. If your house is limestone or stucco and your plants are acid-loving evergreens such as hollies or azaleas, acidify the soil; rain may wash the residue of limestone into the ground, making the soil less acidic. Finally, pay attention to safety. Overgrown shrubs near the entry give vandals or burglars an easy place to hide.

The shrub border

If you can design a shrub border, you can create a garden. Shrub borders are useful for enclosing space. Not only are they an attractive way to delineate the boundaries of your property, they can turn a yard into a garden by creating privacy and limiting views. Like hedges, shrub borders form the walls of outdoor rooms. These walls can be evergreen, deciduous, or both. They can serve as a background against which flowering annuals and perennials display their

charms, or they can make their own brilliant and harmonious color display when in flower.

Shrub borders are more than handsome groups of shrubs. Although a well-designed planting may create a place of visual interest or focal point in a landscape, its plants may be too far apart to create the massed, wall-like effect of the shrub border. In shrub borders, mature plants typically overlap by about one-third to create a sense of depth, richness, and mass.

Similarly, a shrub border differs from an island planting. The latter is designed to be seen from all sides. It can be treated as a bold landscape mass with overlapping shrubs or as a balanced but sparser group of plants. The shrub border, on the other hand, will be seen from at most three sides. The back of it is against a fence, wall, or property line.

To create an attractive shrub border, it's necessary

to understand how scale, balance, sequence, variety, emphasis, and repetition—the principles of design—affect a border's mass, line, color, and texture—the building blocks of your plan. In fact, making a shrub border is similar to playing with blocks. Some shrubs are tall and narrow, giving height and impact to a design. Some are a bit shorter and wider, creating a sense of mass and bulk. Others are little cubes, spheres, and slabs. These small blocks link the main masses of the design and enhance its depth and contrast. Both ends of a well-designed shrub border will have a large shrub or a strong, well-defined group of shrubs that anchors it. In addition to choosing plants for mass, include plants for visual interest. Attractive bark, berries, branching habit, and color and texture of leaves and flowers give seasonal character and beauty to a shrub planting.

Colors of evergreens are variable. Here are Colorado spruce, Norway spruce, and white spruce with hemlock and Scotch heather.

HORIZONTAL SHRUB FORMS

Rounded/globular
(Buxus sempervirens)
Common boxwood

Mounding
(Rhododendron spp.)
Evergreen Southern
Indica azalea

Prostrate
(Arctostaphylos uva-ursi)
Bearberry

Horizontal layered
(Viburnum plicatum f. *tomentosum)*
Double-file viburnum

Weeping
(Tsuga canadensis 'Pendula')
Weeping hemlock

The Right Plant
FOR THE RIGHT PLACE

Climate and soil are key factors determining which trees and shrubs will thrive in your region. Choose the right plants for your region, grow them with proper soil and light, and you'll save yourself endless trouble. Study the environment, and follow its dictates. Altering the surroundings to suit the plants can cause more work in the long run. See what's growing successfully in nearby gardens. Visit garden centers, and ask the staff members which trees and shrubs they recommend. Will your plants need to survive extreme periods of heat and cold? How much light and water do your potential purchases require? Will the plants you are considering for hedges thrive in the wind, or will they suffer damage if used for a windbreak?

The U.S. Department of Agriculture has published a map of plant hardiness zones, shown on page 23. These zones refer to the average annual minimum temperatures for each region of the United States. Determine your zone, then look up the range of zones that each plant tolerates in the plant selection guide. Trees or shrubs at either extreme may be borderline in their hardiness, depending upon the planting site and the relative hardiness of the rootstock, seed, or cutting.

Soil also varies from region to region, with differing proportions of clay, sand, and loam. Heavy clay soil lacks air pockets and sticks together when wet. The result is poor drainage or standing water, which can suffocate roots. On the other hand, drainage and air spaces in sandy soil are so plentiful that little moisture is retained. Loam, which combines roughly equal amounts of clay, silt, and sand, is ideal for growing many plants. (Silt is sediment and rock particles that are bigger than clay particles but smaller than sand.)

By noting the plants that flourish in your locale, you can have a beautiful, healthy, worry-free garden.

General climatic regions

COASTAL PACIFIC NORTHWEST: Mild winters and mild summers, along with moist conditions (except for two months in late summer) allow gardeners in this area to choose from a large list of native and exotic trees. Many conifers grow rapidly in the high humidity.

MEDITERRANEAN CALIFORNIA: The mild winters and warm, dry summers of the California coast are similar to those in the Mediterranean. Gardeners here also have a long list of native and exotic trees to

Pacific Northwest: A wide variety of landscape plants thrives in the mild winters and summers here.

Southern California: Warm, dry summers combined with mild winters are ideal for many Mediterranean plants.

Desert Southwest: Extreme heat and aridity limit the plant palette to those that are specifically adapted.

THE USDA PLANT
HARDINESS ZONE MAP
OF NORTH AMERICA

Range of Average Annual Minimum Temperatures for Each Zone

Zone 1: Below -50° F (below -45.6° C)
Zone 2: -50 to -40° F (-45.5 to -40° C)
Zone 3: -40 to -30° F (-39.9 to -34.5° C)
Zone 4: -30 to -20° F (-34.4 to -28.9° C)
Zone 5: -20 to -10° F (-28.8 to -23.4° C)
Zone 6: -10 to 0° F (-23.3 to -17.8° C)
Zone 7: 0 to 10° F (-17.7 to -12.3° C)
Zone 8: 10 to 20° F (-12.2 to -6.7° C)
Zone 9: 20 to 30° F (-6.6 to -1.2° C)
Zone 10: 30 to 40° F (-1.1 to 4.4° C)
Zone 11: Above 40° F (above 4.5° C)

work with for beautifying their landscapes.

SOUTHWEST: This region has extreme heat and aridity, but with irrigation, its list of useful trees is long. Currently, however, the emphasis is on drought-tolerant species and desert natives to deal with these dry conditions.

MIDWEST AND PLAINS: This inland region has winters comparable to those of the Northeast but with colder temperatures, along with hotter summers, higher winds, and less moisture.

NORTHEAST AND APPALACHIANS: This humid region has cold winters and mild, humid summers and is well-known for the colorful fall foliage of its native trees.

SOUTHEAST: This region is moist, with mild winters and long, hot summers. The geography within the region includes both swampy lowlands and drier, upland hardwood forests.

Midwest and Plains: Cold winters are similar to those in the Northeast, but summers are hotter and drier.

Northeast: Winters are long and cold, spring and fall pass quickly, and summers are humid and mild.

Southeast: Lots of moisture combines with mild winters and long, hot and humid summers.

Soil, Light, and Air

After your regional climate, the condition of your soil is the next most important factor in the success of your trees and shrubs. Soil (in addition to its organic matter) has three main ingredients— sand, silt, and clay—each made up of different-size particles, and each with very different physical properties as well.

Soil added to water and allowed to sit will in time settle into layers (from top) of organic matter, clay, silt, and sand, giving you a rough idea of your soil type.

Soil

SOIL TYPES: Sand is coarse, silt is microscopic, and clay particles are so small they are visible only with an electron microscope. Sandy soils will fall apart in your hand. Silt soils feel greasy, and clay soils clump together. Loam, which is usually the best general soil type, is roughly an equal mixture of these three types plus organic matter (decomposing organic material, such as leaf mold and duff).

But apart from this combination, plants also need the correct density of soil to allow air and water circulation. Soils that are too sandy drain too quickly and starve the tree of moisture. Clay soils, on the other hand, stick together and choke the roots. Compacted soil has very poor circulation as well. Even good, loose soil can become compacted by construction or carelessness on the part of the gardener. For example, walking on wet soil can cause some compaction.

PH BALANCE: Before you plant, it helps to know something about soil pH. Soil pH is a measure of its relative acidity or alkalinity, measured on a 14-point scale. Midway, 7 is considered neutral; lower numbers are acidic; higher numbers, alkaline. It's an important measure because pH extremes interfere with the ability of a tree to absorb nutrients. Most trees grow well in soils with a pH of 5.5 to 6.5 (slightly acidic), but many tolerate wider ranges. And acid-loving plants such as azaleas and rhododendrons need acidic soils to survive. You can test your soil pH with a simple kit purchased at your garden center. For a complete analysis, contact your local extension office.

NUTRIENTS: There are three primary nutrients (nitrogen, phosphorus, and potassium) and numerous secondary nutrients necessary for tree growth. Nitrogen fosters foliage growth and color, phosphorus promotes root development, and potassium is necessary for general health. Other elements, such as calcium, magnesium, iron, and sulfur, are just as vital but are needed in

SHRUBS THAT TOLERATE WET SOILS

Red chokeberry (*Aronia arbutifolia*)
Carolina allspice (*Calycanthus floridus*)
Summersweet clethra (*Clethra alnifolia*)
Tatarian dogwood (*Cornus alba*)
Red-osier dogwood (*Cornus stolonifera*)
Vernal witch hazel (*Hamamelis vernalis*)
Inkberry (*Ilex glabra* 'Compacta')
Common winterberry (*Ilex verticillata*)
Northern bayberry (*Myrica pensylvanica*)
European cranberrybush (*Viburnum opulus*)

TREES THAT TOLERATE WET SOILS

Red maple (*Acer rubrum*)
Silver maple (*Acer saccharinum*)
Alder (*Alnus* spp.)
River birch (*Betula nigra*)
Sweet gum (*Liquidambar styraciflua*)
Black gum (*Nyssa sylvatica*)
Plane tree (*Platanus* spp.)
Willow (*Salix* spp.)
Bald cypress (*Taxodium distichum*)

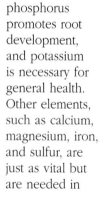

Many shrubs, such as these heaths, need acidic soil to grow well.

TREES FOR DRY, SANDY SOILS

Amur maple *(Acer tataricum ginnala)*
Box elder *(Acer negundo)*
Ohio buckeye *(Aesculus glabra)*
Common hackberry *(Celtis occidentalis)*
Green ash *(Fraxinus pennsylvanica)*
Thornless honeylocust *(Gleditsia triacanthos inermis)*
Eastern red cedar *(Juniperus virginiana)*
Black locust *(Robinia pseudoacacia)*
Chinese tallow tree *(Sapium sebiferum)*

SHRUBS FOR DRY, SANDY SOILS

Bearberry *(Arctostaphylos uva-ursi)*
California lilac *(Ceanothus* spp.)
Shore juniper *(Juniperus conferta)*
Lavender *(Lavandula* spp.)
Northern bayberry *(Myrica pensylvanica)*
Oleander *(Nerium oleander)*
Sweet olive *(Osmanthus* spp.)
Rugosa rose *(Rosa rugosa)*
Rosemary *(Rosmarinus officinalis)*

smaller amounts. Tree roots take these nutrients from the soil. Most soils already have adequate amounts.

Light

Choosing the best location for your trees and shrubs involves taking an inventory of the sun and shade patterns in your landscape. They're different at different times of the day and year. In late June, the sun rises the furthest north, is high overhead at noon, and sets in the northwest sky. In late March and September, it rises in the east, sets in the west, and is lower at noon. By late December, the sun's course is a low arc in the southern sky. The greatest heat strikes

western walls and windows in early summer and south walls and windows in winter. For summer shade, plant trees on the west side, and keep the south side open to the winter sun. A discussion of growing plants in shade can be found on pages 26–27.

Air

Often overlooked, air circulation is crucial to healthy growth. Without it, humidity favors disease-causing fungi. Give your trees enough space; plant disease-prone trees in breezy sites (or better yet, plant disease-resistant trees), and rake up infected leaves as they fall.

Air pollution can limit plant growth. Leaves absorb some pollution, but they can be damaged where levels of pollutants are heavy and constant—in highway locations, for example.

Sweet acacia is well-adapted to the dry heat of southwestern desert landscapes.

Shade patterns change through the day and through the seasons. Far left: West-facing areas are shaded in the morning and east-facing ones in the afternoon. Left: In North America, the sun is more directly overhead in summer than in winter.

Shady Gardens

Some evergreen shrubs, such as this grapeholly, grow well in shade.

SHADE-TOLERANT SHRUBS

Japanese aucuba (*Aucuba japonica*)
Winter creeper euonymus (*Euonymus fortunei*)
Gardenia (*Gardenia augusta*)
Smooth hydrangea (*Hydrangea arborescens*)
Oakleaf hydrangea (*Hydrangea quercifolia*)
Chinese holly (*Ilex cornuta*)
Kerria (*Kerria japonica*)
Drooping leucothoe (*Leucotho ×fontanesiana*)
Heavenly bamboo (*Nandina domestica*)
Japanese pittosporum (*Pittosporum tobira*)
Cherry laurel (*Prunus laurocerasus*)

A shady garden can be a magical place because shade affects the way we think about space, touching our emotions with its dark, quiet presence. Tall trees arch or buildings loom overhead like the vaults of a medieval cathedral, forming an overstory under which the low-light garden grows. Shade influences temperature, cooling the environment by blocking the sun and providing welcome relief from summer's heat.

The quality of shade varies from light to dense. Gardeners speak of full, or dense, shade as an area untouched by the sun. Dappled, or medium, shade filters sunlight through the trees. An area in partial shade has less than six hours of sunlight per day. Half shade occurs on the east and west sides of a house. On the east side, a garden has morning sun and afternoon shade, an ideal situation for many plants. On the west, a garden has morning shade and afternoon sun, which can be intensely hot. To determine the kind of shade you have, note the patterns in your garden at different seasons and times of day.

Color enriches the shady garden. Leaves of dark green, light green, purple, and variegated colors provide muted, all-season contrast. Plants with interesting foliage that tolerate shade include cut-leaf Japanese maple, Japanese aucuba, winter creeper euonymus, drooping leucothoe, and Japanese pittosporum. Variegated plants and plants with white or pastel blooms stand out in dark areas, bringing light and definition to beds. Fragrance is another way that plants touch the senses in a shady garden.

Some shrubs and small trees flourish in both sun and shade. When grown in shady conditions, these plants tend to have fewer flowers and are more delicately branched than the same cultivars grown in the full sun.

SHADE-TOLERANT TREES

Japanese maple (*Acer palmatum*)
Allegheny serviceberry (*Amelanchier laevis*)
Eastern redbud (*Cercis canadensis*)
White fringe tree (*Chionanthus virginicus*)
Flowering dogwood (*Cornus florida*)
Kousa dogwood (*Cornus kousa*)
Carolina silverbell (*Halesia tetraptera*)
American holly (*Ilex opaca*)
Sourwood (*Oxydendrum arboreum*)
Canadian hemlock (*Tsuga canadensis*)

1. North Side:
When gardening in the shade, remember that not all shade is created equal. Open shade occurs on the north side of a building with no large trees.

2. Half Shade, East Side:
Cool morning sunshine followed by afternoon shade is excellent for many shade-loving plants. Half shade occurs for only part of the day.

3. Half Shade, West Side:
Morning shade followed by afternoon sun may be too hot for many shade plants, causing them to wilt in the heat.

4. Dry Shade:
Lack of moisture, not lack of light, often proves to be the culprit when shade-loving plants fail to thrive in their preferred light conditions.

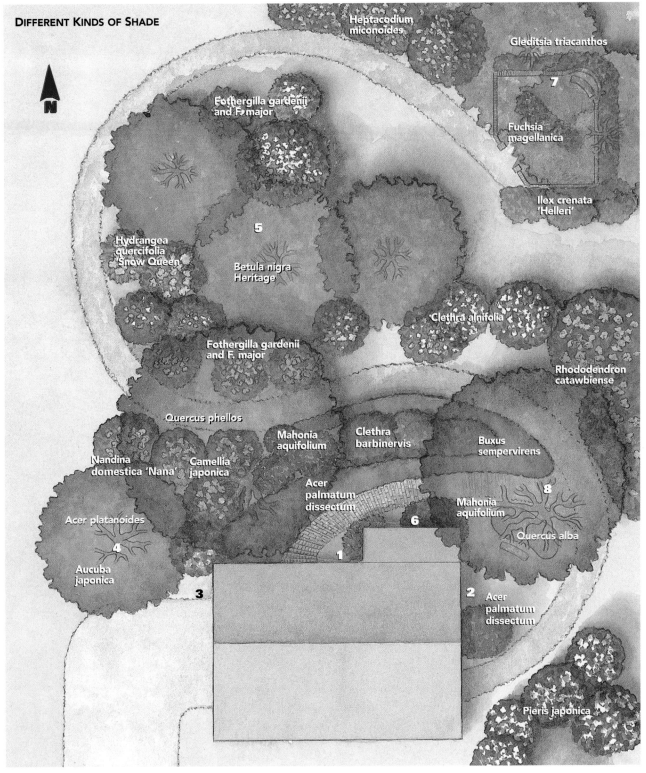

DIFFERENT KINDS OF SHADE

N

Heptacodium miconoides

Gleditsia triacanthos

Fothergilla gardenii and F. major

7

Fuchsia magellanica

Hydrangea quercifolia 'Snow Queen'

5

Betula nigra Heritage

Ilex crenata 'Helleri'

Clethra alnifolia

Fothergilla gardenii and F. major

Rhododendron catawbiense

Quercus phellos

Mahonia aquifolium

Clethra barbinervis

Buxus sempervirens

Nandina domestica 'Nana'

Camellia japonica

Acer palmatum dissectum

Mahonia aquifolium

8

Acer platanoides

4

6

Quercus alba

Aucuba japonica

1

2

Acer palmatum dissectum

3

Pieris japonica

5. Damp Shade:
Many shaded conditions are cool and damp and can be dressed up with a wide array of appropriate plants adapted to moist soils.

6. Overhang Shade:
An overhanging eave of a house may worsen a difficult location by acting as an umbrella and deflecting rain from the ground beneath, creating dry shade.

7. Dappled Shade:
Light shade or filtered shade occurs under a canopy of open-branched trees where spots of sunshine filter to the ground in a play of shadows.

8. High Open Shade:
A medium-shade environment occurs under trees that have been thinned, such as these oaks.

Small Spaces

Japanese tree lilac is a hardy flowering tree for cold climates.

A ground cover of chamomile neatly accents the brick pavers of this patio for two.

You don't need much space to have a garden. A corner of soil tucked into pavement in front of a town house, a small courtyard, or a tiny lot enclosed by a tall wooden fence behind a ground-floor condominium will do.

Many small-space gardens make excellent outdoor rooms suitable for entertaining. Whether formally or informally arranged, these little gardens depend on organization and planning. Where space is at a premium, prepare a landscape plan. For a formal town house, you can continue the decorating theme outdoors. A symmetrical design of geometrically shaped beds, neatly pruned topiary in containers, and a low-lying parterre outlined in 12-inch boxwood lend formality to a small space.

Planning is just as important for an informal design in the small garden. Angled or curved, hardscape remains a key element in the plan. For example, brick walls and a brick floor strengthen an asymmetrical arrangement of rectangular or flowing beds, sumptuous with leafy shrubs. Or a narrow, meandering path inside a walled enclosure planted with appropriate shrubs and ground covers could create a woodland effect for the smaller courtyard garden.

When landscaping the smaller garden, be aware of the ultimate size of the mature plants. The conifer that looks tidy and compact in its nursery container may one day tower over your garden, shading your entire property (and your neighbor's) and depriving other plants of necessary sunshine.

Moreover, large plants have extensive root systems that compete aggressively with those of other, smaller plants for soilborne nutrients and moisture.

Instead of buying shrubs on impulse, investigate their mature size before you purchase them. Large shrubs often have dwarf cultivars, often labeled 'Nana' or 'Compacta'. But even these terms can be misleading. *Euonymus alatus,* the popular burning bush, grows 12 to 15 feet tall. The smaller cultivar 'Compactus' grows up to 10 feet tall, still too large for many small-space gardens.

Above all else, have fun with the small-space garden. Make sure most of the plants are hard workers, providing more than a single season of interest. Contrasting textures and shapes enliven the overall design. If a bold look is what you want, don't limit the smaller garden to dwarf plants. Regularly pruning large shrubs or small trees can keep them in scale, or you can simply remove them when they grow too big for the site. But it is best to start with the right size plant.

A multitrunked amur maple provides some shade, but won't outgrow its location.

GROWING IN CONTAINERS

One solution to the challenge of a small-space garden is to grow trees and shrubs in containers. This allows you to move them around a patio or courtyard, following the sun or sheltering them from intense winds and downpours. When gardening in pots, you can change your floral display according to the season of bloom or your changing color schemes.

Shrubs in containers can look as formal or informal as the overall garden style. For example, potted topiaries and rose standards add formality to the garden, whereas unshaped lavender, rosemary, or butterfly bush have a looser look. Planters come in a variety of shapes and sizes, so it's easy to find one that supports the garden's style or theme.

Growing plants in containers allows you to grow plants intended for warmer climates. When the first frost hits, you can move the container to a sheltered spot for the winter. However, because containers sit above the ground, the plants in them are more susceptible to winter damage. If you don't intend to move the container to a protected location, choose plants that are at least one zone hardier than the area where you live.

Move your potted plants to a new location gradually. Pay special attention to containers that you're moving from a shaded to a sunny location; leaf burn may result from too much sun too quickly.

The larger the tree or shrub, the larger and stronger the container you'll need. Trees, which have naturally taller habits and are susceptible to tipping in wind, should be planted in the heaviest pots possible. Natural materials indigenous to your locale, including stone, clay, and wood, make attractive containers, especially for naturalistic gardens. Dwarf or slow-growing trees and shrubs make the best candidates for container culture.

Small-space trees

Trees that are too big for their space cause problems. Tall trees under utility lines cause serious problems. They eventually have to be pruned to keep the lines clear, and drastic pruning creates an avenue of one-sided or topless trees. Smaller trees are available that fit neatly beneath overhead lines.

TREE ROOTS: No discussion about trees and space would be complete without a warning about tree roots. Trees with aggressive or invasive roots can crack sidewalks and roads or damage sewage or drainage lines. Avoid trees with invasive roots, such as silver maple, willow, poplar, alder, pepper tree, and sweet gum near sewer lines, septic fields, wells, and drainage lines, as well as sidewalks, streets, and other paved areas. Their roots will grow into and clog the area or damage the lines, or grow under and damage the paving or concrete.

TREE LITTER: One major consideration when choosing a tree is the amount of litter it creates. If the site you've chosen doesn't need to be tidy and you have plenty of space, then it's not a worry. But for most people, this is not the case, especially with trees hanging over paving.

Tree litter includes dropped flowers, seed capsules, fruit, or even excessive leaf drop. What this means for the homeowner unlucky enough to have such a tree near the street is either constant cleaning or letting the tree litter pile up. By knowing ahead of time the habits of your potential tree, you can avoid a lot of repetitive work in the future.

Pretty Polly rose is accented by blue toadflax in this container garden.

TREES FOR SMALL SPACES AND CONTAINERS

Amur maple (*Acer tataricum ginnala*)
Japanese maple (*Acer palmatum*)
Lemon bottlebrush (*Callistemon citrinus*)
Eastern redbud (*Cercis canadensis*)
Flowering dogwood (*Cornus florida*)
Carolina silverbell (*Halesia tetraptera*)
Goldenchain tree (*Laburnum ×watereri*)
Flowering crabapple (*Malus* 'Adirondack', 'David', *M. sargentii*, or other cultivars less than 20 feet)
Amanogawa Japanese flowering cherry (*Prunus serrulata* 'Amanogawa')
Okame cherry (*Prunus* 'Okame')
Kwanzan cherry (*Prunus* 'Sekiyama')
Japanese tree lilac (*Syringa reticulata* 'Ivory Silk')

Planting and Care

Trude Webster rhododendron lights up gardens in spring.

Balled-and-burlapped trees, their trunks wrapped for protection, are ready for your garden. Getting them home safely is your first task.

You see the aboveground parts of trees and shrubs all the time, but their roots are out of sight, perhaps out of mind, and not very interesting to look at. Yet their work is essential to the survival and growth of the plant. Plant leaves convert solar energy to chemical energy as they make the food that powers both tops and roots. Roots absorb and supply the water and nutrients that are needed by the whole plant. In this way, leaves and roots depend on one another.

Just as plant tops and roots can be viewed as complementary, so can planting and care. Good soil preparation and planting give the tree what it needs to succeed. After that, plant care consists of small adjustments over time to preserve this favorable situation.

No amount of later care can fully compensate for a poor start, but careful plant selection, soil preparation, and planting can reduce the amount of aftercare that will be needed.

SOURCES: You can buy plants from garden centers, retail nurseries, or mail-order catalogs. Garden centers sell plants grown by wholesale nurseries, whereas retail nurseries grow at least some of the plants they sell and may also offer landscape design and installation services. Most mail-order firms pack and ship plants well, and at the right time for planting, and may offer plants that are not available locally, but few sell large trees. Many gardeners buy from all three.

PREPARATION FOR SALE:
Trees and shrubs are sold in different ways. Some are dug with bare roots, stored moist, and wrapped for sale. Others are dug with a soil ball, wrapped with burlap, and kept moist. Still others are dug with a soil ball, then potted in a container for sale. Finally some are grown in containers, potted as a small plant and grown in the container for a year or more. The method used depends on the age and kind of plant, the season, and the nature of the retail outlet. Some trees and shrubs have special needs. The best time to plant fleshy-rooted trees and shrubs, such as magnolia, witch hazel, and fothergilla is in midspring, just as the new leaf buds begin to unfold and new root growth begins.

SIZE: Starting with a large plant may seem like the best way to have immediate impact, but this is not always true. Smaller plants become established more easily and may outpace a larger plant started at the same time. It's more important to select for condition than size.

BARE-ROOT TREES AND SHRUBS: The best bare-root trees are young; avoid older trees with bare roots. Plant bare-root trees and shrubs while they are fully dormant—before buds begin to swell and expand into leaves. Many retailers buy bare-root trees in late winter; they may sell some bare-root and plant the rest in containers to sell later. Buy container plants after they have begun to get leaves to be sure they will grow.

BALLED-AND-BURLAPPED TREES AND SHRUBS: These are more expensive than bare-root trees, but this is the safest way to move shrubs and older trees. Even these plants lose many roots when they are dug. Some kinds of trees and shrubs are available only as balled-and-burlapped or container stock, usually for good reason.

CONTAINER-GROWN TREES AND SHRUBS: These plants are not dug, so they do not lose roots, and the transplanting risk is minimal. They can be transplanted at almost any time of year when the ground is not frozen. Remember, though, that in the nursery, these plants have received large amounts of water and nutrients to compensate for the small soil volume in the pot. After transplanting, their roots must grow enough to support the growing top under more stressful conditions. If you plant them after midsummer in the north, their roots may not grow much by autumn, so mulch them over the winter to prevent them from being heaved out of the ground by freezing and thawing cycles. If you plant them in hot, dry weather, even with normal watering they may be stressed until they have made more root growth. In the south, plant them during the cool seasons to avoid heat stress.

TRANSPORTING AND HOLDING: Carry plants in a closed vehicle so they will not lose moisture in transit. Plant them as soon as possible. Meanwhile, protect them at the planting site: Keep them in the shade, and don't let them dry out.

Look for container plants without many circling roots visible on the surface (right).

Choose plants with many small, fibrous roots (right); avoid ones with broken or cracked roots.

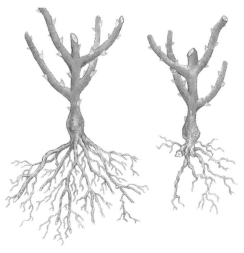

Select fully dormant, bare-root plants with many moist, fibrous roots (left).

Planting

WHEN TO PLANT: In most parts of the country, early spring (while deciduous plants are still dormant and leafless) is the best time to plant any deciduous tree and the only time you should plant bare-root trees. Leafless trees draw less water and nutrients from the roots and recover more easily from transplant shock. For the same reason, balled-and-burlapped trees should be dug from the nursery when they're dormant in early spring, late fall, or even winter (if the ground isn't frozen). They can usually be held in the nursery longer than bare-root trees and planted later in spring or early summer with reasonable success. Container-grown trees, however, can be planted successfully nearly any time of the year.

Planting in fall or winter is recommended in areas where summers are extreme and winters mild, such as the south (where summers are very hot) and the west (where summers are dry).

Trees with active, late-winter sap flow, such as birch and sugar maple, are risky choices for early spring transplanting. Wait until the sap flow ends, just as the leaf buds begin to unfold.

For spring planting of fleshy-rooted trees such as magnolia, it is best to wait until the leaves have expanded slightly.

Evergreens are best planted in early autumn, after summer heat is gone but early enough for full establishment before winter cold sets in.

You can plant trees and shrubs at almost any time, as long as you can work the soil with a spade. If possible, however, avoid planting in late spring right before hot summer weather moves in, and in late fall, when plants may not have time to establish themselves before the onset of freezing weather.

DIG THE HOLE: Dig the planting hole twice as wide and slightly shallower than the root ball because plants often sink as they settle into the earth. The root mass should sit on stable,

undisturbed soil. When the hole is deeper than the root ball, it creates a situation that can lead to crown and root rot.

AMEND THE BACKFILL SOIL: Many plants flourish in transition soil or backfill to which amendments such as compost or well-rotted manure have been added. Such organic materials help the soil hold moisture and micronutrients. Trees and shrubs planted in amended soil tend to grow better at first than shrubs planted in native soil; however, recent research shows that plants often do better in the long run when planted in unamended soil because their roots spread

deeper and wider into the surrounding area. If you decide to amend your backfill, take the soil from the planting

hole, estimate its volume, and add either compost or rotted manure. Roughly 25 percent of the final mix should be soil amendment.

REMOVE THE PLANT FROM THE CONTAINER: Most small trees and shrubs are sold in plastic containers. Before removing the plant from its pot, dampen the root ball to help it stay intact. A plant's root system may not recover from a broken or damaged root ball. To remove shrubs

from their pots, invert the pot, holding the top of the root ball (this may be a two-person job), and gently tap the edge on a bench or other solid object. A simple shake may suffice if the plant is not especially pot-bound. Trees can sometimes be tipped on their side and more easily removed from a pot (don't tug hard on the trunk; you may damage the roots). Or place a 2×4 across the rim while the plant is on its side, then strike the board with a hammer. If this doesn't dislodge the rootball, cut the pot with shears first, then remove the tree. Your nursery will usually cut the pot for you.

PLACE THE PLANT IN THE HOLE: Inspect the root ball before placing the plant in the hole. With pruners or a sharp knife, make shallow, vertical cuts along the side of the root ball, cutting any girdled, matted, or tangled roots from the root ball. Matted roots do

not readily extend into the surrounding soil. Place the plant in the hole, and work the soil around the root ball with your hands to eliminate air pockets.

FILL THE HOLE AND BUILD A BASIN: Fill the hole with the backfill to the level of the surrounding soil. Build a shallow basin around the

plant to concentrate water where it is needed most.
WATER: Thoroughly water the soil around the root zone. Apply the water slowly so it

penetrates the root ball until the soil is loose and muddy. Gently work the soil to eliminate remaining air pockets. Use the basin for watering until some roots have had a chance to expand into the surrounding soil, usually within six weeks. If dry weather conditions require continued irrigation, enlarge the basin as necessary. Be sure to break down the watering basin once the plant is established.

HOW TO PLANT BALLED-AND-BURLAPPED PLANTS: Handle the ball carefully, setting it in the hole with the wrap still on. Adjust the height of the root ball as you would with a plant from a container. If the burlap has been treated to retard rotting or if the wrap is

made of plastic or other nonbiodegradable material, remove it before planting. For burlapped plants, untie the material, and pull it away from the top of the root ball. Discard the strings if they pull away easily or, if not, let them decompose in the soil. Remove synthetic twine. Cut or fold the wrap back so that it is below the surface of the soil; exposed material wicks water out of the soil. Fill the hole and water the plant.

HOW TO PLANT BARE-ROOT PLANTS: Bare-root shrubs, which are planted while dormant, are usually acquired by mail order in the

spring. Pruning the bare roots by one-third or more results in a stronger plant. Store bare-root plants in a cool place with their roots in moist sawdust or bark. Soak them in a bucket of water for several hours before planting. Dig a hole large enough to accommodate the full span of the roots. Prune off broken or very long roots, and place the plant in the hole with the top root 1 inch below the level of the surrounding soil. Work the backfill soil between the roots with your hands to remove air pockets. Finish filling the hole and water the plant.

After Planting

Now that your trees and shrubs are safely in the ground, there are a few steps to take to provide your plants—especially trees—with further care.

Wrap the tender bark of young trees over winter to prevent trunk scald. Remove the wrap each spring.

Wrapping the trunk

Tree wrap is a crepe strip that insulates the bark against temperature fluctuations in late winter and prevents dehydration and trunk scald. It may not be necessary for some trees but is especially good for young, thin-barked varieties (a few maples, green ash, honeylocust, goldenchain tree, and cherries) the first winter after planting. Tree wrap can harbor insects and diseases, so be sure to remove it in the spring.

Staking

Staking a tree is root reinforcement; it keeps the tree from falling over or leaning until its roots are strong enough to anchor it. Most trees do not need staking, but bare-root trees, large evergreens, and top-heavy trees do. Make your staking loose enough to allow the trunk to flex both along its length and at its base. The tree will respond by developing added strength in the trunk and anchor roots. Remove the stakes after one or two growing seasons, and the tree will develop faster.

Staking deciduous trees

Avoid the materials that were once standard for staking trees: wire and garden hose. The hose constricts trunk growth. Instead, use 3-inch webbing or polyethylene strips twisted loosely at their midpoint once around the tree and attached to the stake with staples. Keep the strip as low as possible to allow the trunk to sway. Swaying is an exercise that promotes strong growth. Any tree with a trunk 3 inches or less in diameter needs only one stake, placed on the windward side, but you can use more for added stability. Larger trees should be staked in two or three directions.

Staking evergreens

Evergreen trees with branches close to the ground may not

Position stakes perpendicular to the direction of the strongest wind; set ties as low as possible.

need staking, but tall trees or those on windy sites will. Evergreens are normally staked with three guy wires attached to the trunk at the same point with webbing or polyethylene strips. The guy wires radiate in equal angles from the trunk down to the anchor stakes, which should be driven into the ground parallel to the wires. In high-traffic areas (or where children play), use tall stakes and straps looped around the trunk instead of guy wires.

Watering

During the first year after planting, water is the most important factor in new-tree and shrub survival. Deep, thorough watering done occasionally is much better than the constant shallow watering offered by sprinkler systems. Place a hose at the base of the tree, and allow a trickle of water to flow for at least 15 minutes. Shrubs can be watered for less time. Plants in sandy soils should be watered more often than trees in heavy soils. Heavy soils drain slowly, and you must allow time to elapse between waterings.

Fertilizing

Fertilize newly planted trees and shrubs if a soil test shows nutrients are necessary. Most landscape soils have enough nutrients for trees, and a young, nursery-grown tree itself is a storehouse of nutrients. It is not

Water newly planted trees and shrubs thoroughly enough to settle the soil and soak the root ball and the soil surrounding it.

Mulch after watering to slow moisture evaporation and reduce weeds.

together to make a loose mat and is not likely to float away in heavy rain. Peat moss will repel water once it dries, and may also be wind-blown.

Protecting young trees from animal damage

Deer and rabbits like young trees as much as the gardeners who planted them. They can easily bite off branches or chew bark completely off the trunk. Fortunately, there are steps you can take to prevent this. Protect young trees by enclosing them with chicken wire or wire mesh. Trunks of older trees can be protected from rodents and rabbits by ordinary tree wrap, but new, flexible plastic tree protectors, available in a variety of lengths, loosely surround the tree trunk and are better.

likely that such a tree would become nutrient-deficient while establishing itself in the landscape.

Mulching

After planting and watering, apply a 2- to 3-inch layer of mulch (never more than 4 inches) over the entire planting area. Organic mulches, such as shredded bark, conserve moisture and reduce the need for water by slowing down its evaporation from the surface. Their insulating properties help maintain more uniform soil temperatures, and that improves root growth and benefits bacteria, fungi, earthworms, and other organisms that keep the soil alive. Mulches also retard weed growth, prevent erosion, create an attractive surface, and, when used around trees, prevent lawn-mower damage to the trunks.

Types of mulch

Mulches are classified as organic or inorganic. Organic mulches include shredded bark, bark nuggets, wood chips, pine needles, and even composted leaves. Inorganic mulches are usually pea gravel or coarser aggregate. Shredded bark is a good choice because it binds

Where deer, rabbits, or other animals are abundant, protect trunks with flexible plastic tree wrap.

Caring for Established Trees and Shrubs

Maintaining a large, mulched area surrounding mature trees is one of the best ways to encourage tree health.

You can protect trees on a construction site by following the guidelines offered in Tree City, USA Bulletin No. 20 of the National Arbor Day Foundation:
1. Before construction begins, remove all trees that are not to be saved.
2. Prune low-growing limbs that may be in the way of machinery.
3. Fertilize, water, and aerate trees that will be saved.
4. Install plastic mesh fences under the drip line (the farthest reach of branches).
5. Install siltation fences to keep soil from construction areas away from root zones.
6. Do not store construction materials inside the protective drip-line fences.

Established trees and shrubs do need some attention. They are not only less stress-tolerant than younger trees, they are worth more. Established trees can add 15 to 25 percent to the value of your home, and large, mature trees are especially valuable. Watering, pruning, mulching, and root-system care can improve a tree's mature health.

Fertilizing established, healthy trees and shrubs is normally not necessary. Do not fertilize "just to be safe." Unneeded fertilizer can promote succulent new growth vulnerable to pests.

Plants with deadwood or those that exhibit declining growth, leaf size, and color are candidates for fertilization and should be fertilized in early autumn or early spring.

Watering during dry periods can help your plants, but water deeply or not at all. Add water to the root zone until at least the top 6 to 12 inches is moist (it may take longer than you expect). Then wait at least a week before watering again unless your soil is sandy. In dry-summer areas of the southwestern United States, regular watering is a necessity for survival of many nonnative trees and shrubs. Installing a drip irrigation system is the most efficient way to conserve water and keep your trees and shrubs healthy.

As long as the plants were trained properly when young, pruning established trees and shrubs is more a matter of maintenance than anything else. Pruning is covered in the next chapter.

Mulching established trees and shrubs results in better root activity and faster growth. It also keeps lawn mowers from damaging tree trunks (because you won't mow the mulch). Kill the turf with an herbicide such as glyphosate, then spread mulch on it. Be sure not to pile mulch against the trunk; it can make a home for disease-causing organisms and insect pests.

Salt damage can occur with the overuse of inorganic fertilizers or when road salt runs off into tree root zones. You'll notice that the leaves

Water-absorbing hydrogels increase the water-holding capacity of container soils.

If the grade is lowered, the opposite is done and drainage becomes excessive. To compensate, build a wall around the tree, retaining the soil, and give consideration to providing adequate water.

Caring for container plants

The gardener's main job when caring for trees and shrubs in containers is providing enough water and nutrients to keep the plants healthy. Unlike plants in the ground, the roots of container trees and shrubs are restricted. Thus, plants in containers need regular watering to keep their leaves from wilting. Give the plant enough water to run out of the drainage holes.

Watering flushes nutrients through soil in a container more quickly than from the soil around plants growing in the ground. Compensate by feeding potted plants a complete fertilizer as frequently as every two weeks in spring and summer, or use a slow-release fertilizer. You can also use liquid fertilizer, which is easy to apply.

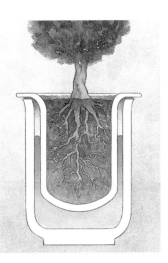

Self-watering containers maintain a reservoir of water for the roots to access as needed.

Water-absorbent silica gel doubles the water-retention capacity of potting soil. This is particularly useful in containers, where as little as a teaspoonful of gel mixed in the soil of a large pot may have significant results.

If your plant needs daily watering, transplant it to a larger container, or shave its roots, compensating for their loss by lightly pruning the top of the plant before repotting.

Move potted plants gradually from one environment to another to protect them from shock.

of affected trees have dried brown margins.

If your soil is well-drained, you may be able to wash the salts out with large volumes of water, but direct the runoff away from other trees by regrading or with barriers.

Root compaction removes the pore space that holds oxygen. If construction equipment will be operating in the area, protect tree roots by placing a fence around the root zone.

Changing grade levels can kill trees. Lowering the grade cuts off feeder roots, dries out others, and removes nutrient-rich topsoil. Raising the grade with a blanket of new soil, on the other hand, reduces the diffusion of oxygen into the root zone. Sensitive trees, such as white or red oak, can be killed by a grade change of as little as 2 inches.

To protect the tree when the grade is raised, you must create a tree well at the drip line. This protects the tree roots. Bricks or masonry retain the filled soil, and the soil must be layered with fabric and coarse gravel to allow for drainage. Also, you need to incorporate some form of pipe, usually polyvinyl chloride (PVC) pipe, to allow for drainage and soil aeration within the well.

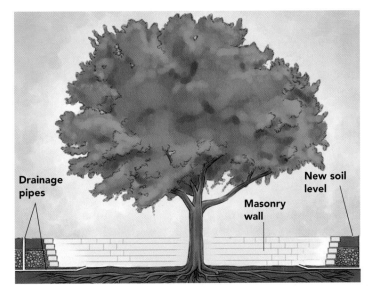

Drainage pipes

New soil level

Masonry wall

When raising the grade level around an established tree, build a tree well outside the drip line to prevent new soil from covering the roots.

Pests and Pest Control

A native tree of the southeastern United States, sweet gum is noted for its brilliant fall color.

Healthy trees and shrubs are usually low-maintenance plants with few insect or disease problems. As with all plants, though, there are exceptions to the rule. Some trees and shrubs are highly susceptible to certain pests. For example, crown gall bacterial disease and scale insects frequently attack winter creeper euonymus.

The pests that attack tree and shrub species are as diverse as the plants themselves. Among them are insects such as aphids, mites, caterpillars, and scales; powdery mildew, wilts, blights, rusts, molds, and anthracnose are common disease problems.

Controlling pests

Rarely is it possible to eliminate all pests in a landscape; instead, managing them is the key to success. One way to do that is with integrated pest management (IPM). With this approach, you coordinate cultural, physical, biological, and chemical methods of control.

Determining when to act decisively against a pest by spraying pesticides and when to apply cultural or biological controls takes time and education. Learn which pests can be problems for your trees and shrubs, the point at which natural controls no longer work, and what methods are available for managing the pests. Be aware that when using an IPM approach, you must be willing to accept the presence of some pests in your landscape.

Using IPM puts you in control. Instead of reaching for a pesticide the moment you see a problem, you first examine the circumstances, then select the most appropriate control. You realize that a few beetles chewing holes in the leaves of two or three plants may be nothing to get excited about. But if the insects are on a fourth of the bed or more, or if a fast-moving pest such as spider mites has taken hold, you know it is time to act.

Steps of IPM

The first step in IPM is to plant insect- and disease-resistant trees and shrubs, especially if your area is prone to certain pest or disease problems.

Then take time to learn about any potential problems. An extension agent can tell you what to expect in your area and the levels of damage specific plants can tolerate. The agent can point out the kind of damage a pest causes and how serious a problem it can be. The tolerance to pests varies among plant species, so ask a professional about limits and parameters. Besides knowing what the plant can take, you also need to decide how much damage to the plant you can tolerate.

Step three involves consistent monitoring. Watch for problems, and identify the cause of any that arise (disease, insect, animal, or cultural). Estimate the scope of the problem, and look for the presence of natural predators that may help control pests for you.

Step four is to choose a control. If damage reaches the point of action, a combination of control measures, from a change in cultural practices to applying pesticides to using alternative methods, helps avoid pesticide resistance and reduce predator populations. When pest populations are low, a cultural control such as increasing watering frequency may be all that is necessary. If cultural controls do not work or if the problem gets out of hand, turn to pesticides, either biological or chemical, depending on the problem.

The fifth and final step is to analyze the effectiveness of your chosen control. If your control measures seem to be working, you can relax a bit. But if not, try another approach. Again, seek advice from professionals whenever you are in doubt.

Your IPM arsenal

CULTURAL CONTROLS: One of the best defenses against pests is healthy plants, which is more of a prevention than a cure. Proper cultural practices, such as fertilizing and irrigating plants in a timely manner, can keep pests from doing major damage to plants.
PHYSICAL CONTROLS: Pruning to improve air circulation cuts down on many diseases and some insect pests.

Handpick larger pests, such as scale insects, slugs, snails, and caterpillars. Mulch to prevent water splashing on leaves; mulching helps reduce some diseases. Set out traps to snare insects, such as moths, worms, and beetles. Bait the traps with natural chemical messengers, which are based on insect pheromones. Be aware, however, that insect traps can attract pests to an area. Rather than being a control, they let you know when it's time to take action against arriving pests.

Sometimes you also have to be ruthless and remove affected plants. It's always better to toss a few diseased plants than let the disease spread through the bed. Replace them with species or varieties that are resistant to the pest.

PREDATORS: Many predator insects exist naturally in gardens. Learn to recognize these beneficial insects. Companies offer them for sale for you to release in your landscape. Among the best predators are parasitic wasps, ladybugs (or lady beetles), lacewings, predator mites, and parasitic nematodes.

Red scale parasite and black scale parasite are tiny parasitic wasps that control scale insects. They lay eggs on the scale; the larvae hatch and feed on the scale, killing it. Trichogramma wasps do the same to caterpillars. Ladybugs attack and kill a wide range of insect pests, including spider mites, small worms, aphids, and other soft-bodied insects. Lacewings feed on many of the same insect pests. Predatory mites kill the spider mites that attack plants. Parasitic nematodes, such as *Steinernema*, control ground-living insect pests, including cutworms, grubs, and weevils.

If you decide to use predators, remember that they are living organisms. You can't simply store them in the garage and pull them out when you have problems. For them to be effective, you must provide the right environment, both in storage and in the landscape when you apply them. Your supplier should be able to advise you.

BIOLOGICAL PESTICIDES: Insecticides, such as Bt *(Bacillus thuringiensis)* and neem, act against specific pests. For example, one form of the bacteria Bt kills caterpillars by attacking the lining of their stomach.

Biological insecticides usually leave the beneficial insect population intact.

Insecticidal soap reduces populations of soft-bodied insects, such as aphids and mites. Pyrethrin, rotenone, and neem are pesticides that come from plants. Like all pesticides, they can be toxic to humans, other vertebrates, and to beneficial insects.

Homemade pesticides, such as garlic sprays, act more as repellents and, as such, can keep some pests out of your planting beds. Dormant and horticultural oil sprays smother pests, such as scales and mites.

INORGANIC PESTICIDES: Chemical controls are faster-acting and more effective than biological and physical controls. Select materials labeled for your specific pest or disease problem, and follow all label directions.

Pesticides act in three ways: systemically—they are absorbed by the plant and kill pests that feed on plant tissue and sap; by contact—they kill the pests they come in contact with; and by leaving a residue on the plant's surface—they kill insects as they eat foliage, stems, and blooms.

A wide variety of sprays and dusts are available to help gardeners manage pests. Always use the least toxic spray first, and always be certain to understand and follow label directions exactly.

Solving Tree and Shrub Problems

The remainder of this chapter will help you solve the most common problems you are likely to encounter with growing trees and shrubs. It is based on *The Ortho Problem Solver,* a professional reference tool for solving plant problems. Here, you will find the experience of many experts, most of them members of research universities and cooperative extension services of various states. The photographs at the top of the page are arranged so that similar symptoms are grouped together.

Select the picture that looks most like your problem. The small map under the photograph shows how likely the problem is to affect your part of the country. If your region is colored red, the problem is commonplace or severe. If it is colored yellow, the problem is occasional or moderate. If it is white, the problem is nonexistent or minor.

The problem section describes the symptoms. The analysis section describes the organisms or cultural conditions causing the problem, including life cycles, natural processes, typical progress of the problem, and seriousness. The solution section begins by telling you what you can do immediately to alleviate the problem. Then it tells you what changes you can make in the environment or in your gardening practices to prevent the problem from returning.

In some cases, a chemical spray is recommended as an immediate solution, and a cultural change or the planting of a resistant variety as a long-range solution. Be sure the plant you want to spray is listed on the product label. Always read pesticide labels carefully, and follow label directions to the letter.

Few or no flowers

Flowerless dogwood in dark location.

Flower buds pruned off crape myrtle.

PROBLEM: Plants fail to bloom, or they bloom only sparsely and sporadically.

ANALYSIS: Plants produce few or no buds or flowers for any of several reasons. Here are the most likely:

SOLUTIONS: The numbered solutions below correspond to the numbered items in the analysis.

1. Juvenility: Plants, like people, must reach a certain age or size before they are able to reproduce. They will not develop flowers or fruit until this time.

1. Plants will eventually begin to flower if they are otherwise healthy and adapted to the area. The juvenile stage in some trees and vines may last 15 years.

2. Inadequate winter cooling: In order to produce flowers, many plants must undergo a period of cooling during the winter. The plant must be exposed for a certain number of hours to temperatures between 30° and 45° F. The number of hours varies from species to species. If the cooling requirement is not satisfied, flowering is delayed and reduced.

2. Plant trees and shrubs adapted to your area. Consult your local garden center or your extension service.

3. Improper pruning: If a plant is pruned improperly or too severely, flower and fruit production can be reduced or, in some cases, prevented. Drastic pruning, especially on young plants, stimulates a flush of green growth that inhibits flowering. Flowering is also reduced if flower buds are pruned off.

3. Prune lightly, and at a time when no flower buds are present.

4. Nutrient imbalance: Plants given too much nitrogen produce a flush of growth, sometimes inhibiting flowering.

4. Do not overfertilize plants or make a heavy application of nitrogen shortly before flowering.

5. Shade: Plants grown in inadequate light produce few or no flowers.

5. Thin out shading trees, or move plants to a sunnier area.

Buds die or drop

Drought stress.

Bud drop caused by cold injury.

Scales

Lecanium scale on redbud (life size).

PROBLEM: Many or all of the buds or flowers die or drop off.

ANALYSIS: Buds may die or drop for any of several reasons, but the following are the most common:

1. Transplant shock: Whenever a tree or shrub is transplanted, it goes through a period of shock. Even when transplanted properly, however, dormant plants may still lose some of their buds. Plants that have begun growth or are in bloom often drop many of their flower buds or flowers shortly after transplanting. Some buds may remain on the plant but not open.

2. Cold or frost injury: Flower buds or flowers may be killed by cold or freezing temperatures. Many or all of them either fail to open or drop off. Frost injury is caused by an unseasonal cold snap, in either fall or spring, which damages buds, developing flowers, and tender shoots of growing plants.

3. Drought: Flowers or flower buds dry and drop off when there is a temporary lack of moisture in the plant. This may be caused by dry soil, minor root injuries, or anything else that disrupts water movement to the top of the plant.

4. Insects: Certain insects, such as thrips and spider mites, feed on flower buds. When infestations are heavy, their feeding kills flower buds, causing them to dry and drop off. Some infested buds may open but be distorted.

SOLUTIONS: The numbered solutions below correspond to the numbered items in the analysis.

1. Whenever possible, transplant trees and shrubs while they are dormant. Avoid wounding the roots when planting, and do not let the plant dry out. Apply an antidesiccant spray to plants a few days before transplanting.

2. Plant trees and shrubs adapted to your area. Consult your local garden center or extension service. Plant tender specimens in sheltered areas. Protect shrubs and small trees from cold snaps by covering them with burlap or a plastic tent. Placing an electric lightbulb underneath the covering offers heat for additional protection.

3. Water trees and shrubs regularly. Most plants recover from minor root injuries. Frequent shallow waterings and light fertilization may speed recovery. Avoid wounding plants.

4. Identify the problem pest, then apply the least toxic chemicals first.

PROBLEM: Crusty or waxy bumps or clusters of somewhat flattened scaly bumps cover the leaves, stems, branches, or trunk. The bumps can be scraped or picked off; the undersides are usually soft. Leaves turn yellow and may drop. In some cases, a shiny or sticky substance coats the leaves. A black, sooty mold often grows on the sticky substance.

ANALYSIS: Many types of scales infest trees and shrubs. They lay their eggs on leaves or bark, and in spring to midsummer the young scales, called crawlers, settle on the leaves, branches, or trunk. The small ($\frac{1}{10}$ inch), soft-bodied young feed by sucking sap from the plant. The legs usually atrophy, and a hard crusty or waxy shell develops over the body. Female scales lay their eggs underneath their shell. Some species of scales are unable to digest fully all the sugar in the plant sap, and they excrete the excess in a fluid called honeydew. A sooty mold fungus may develop on the honeydew, causing the leaves to appear black and dirty. An uncontrolled infestation of scales may kill a plant after two or three seasons.

SOLUTION: Apply an oil spray during the dormant season (only when temperatures are above 40° F for 24 hours following the treatment). Apply a recommended spray when the young, crawling stage is active in spring.

Solving Tree and Shrub Problems
(continued)

Gypsy moth

Gypsy moth larva.

Gypsy moth and egg masses (2× life size).

PROBLEM: Leaves are chewed; the entire tree is often defoliated by late spring or early summer. Large (up to 2½ inches long), hairy, blackish caterpillars with rows of red and blue spots on their backs are feeding on the leaves, hiding under leaves or bark, or crawling on buildings, cars, or other objects outdoors. Some people are allergic to the hairs. Insect droppings accumulate underneath the infested tree.

ANALYSIS: The gypsy moth *(Lymantria dispar)* is a general feeder, devouring more than 450 species of plants. Gypsy moth populations fluctuate from year to year. When moths are low in number, they prefer oaks as their host. When their numbers increase, moths defoliate entire forests and spread to other trees and shrubs. Repeated, severe defoliation weakens trees and reduces plant growth. Defoliated deciduous trees are rarely killed unless already in a weakened condition. They are more susceptible, however, to attack by other insects and plant diseases, which may kill them. Gypsy moths are also an extreme nuisance in urban areas and in parks and campgrounds. Overwintering masses of eggs, covered with beige or yellow hairs, are attached to almost any object outdoors. Eggs hatch from mid- to late spring. Tiny larvae crawl to trees to feed. They drop on silken threads to be carried by the wind to other plants. As caterpillars mature, they feed at night and rest during the day. The larvae may completely cover sides of houses or other objects during these resting periods. When population levels are high, the insects feed continually on the tree, and large amounts of excrement accumulate beneath it. The larval hairs may cause allergies. The larvae pupate in sheltered places, and dark brown male or white female moths emerge in midsummer.

SOLUTION: If the insects are bothersome or if trees are weak or unhealthy either from the previous year's gypsy moth feeding or from drought, mechanical damage, other insects, or plant diseases, treatment with an insecticide is required. Apply the insecticide from the beginning of hatching until the larvae are 1 inch long, about the blooming period of spirea. Contact a professional arborist for large trees.

Spray smaller trees with the bacterial insecticide Bt or other recommended spray when tiny larvae are first noticed. Repeat the spray at weekly intervals if damage continues. Reduce infestations by destroying egg masses during winter. In spring, when larvae are feeding, place burlap bands on trees, leaving the bottom edge unattached. Larvae will crawl under these flaps to hide during the day. Collect and destroy them daily. Keep trees healthy: Fertilize regularly, and water during periods of drought. When planting trees, choose species that are less appealing to the gypsy moth (check with your local extension office). When trees less favored by the insects are interplanted with more favored hosts, they may reduce damage by preventing a large buildup of insects in the area. It is a federal offense to transport items that have eggs or larvae attached to them.

Japanese beetle

Japanese beetle (2× life size).

PROBLEM: Leaf tissue is chewed between the veins, giving the leaves a lacy appearance. The entire plant may be defoliated. Metallic green-and-bronze-winged beetles, ½ inch long, feed in clusters on the plant.

ANALYSIS: The Japanese beetle *(Popillia japonica)* is native to Japan. It was first seen in New Jersey in 1916 and has since become a major pest in the eastern United States. It feeds on hundreds of different plants. Adult beetles are present from June to October. They feed only in the daytime and are most active on warm, sunny days. The female beetles live for 30 to 40 days. Before they die, they lay their eggs under the soil surface in lawns. Grayish-white grubs soon hatch and feed on grass roots. As the weather turns cold in late fall, the grubs move 8 to 10 inches down into the soil, where they remain dormant for the winter. When the soil warms up in spring, the grubs move back up nearer the surface and resume feeding on roots. They soon pupate, and in late May or June they reemerge as adult Japanese beetles.

SOLUTION: Because beetles are slow and lethargic, handpicking is highly effective. A strong jet of water will knock beetles off larger plants. If these simple measures are ineffective, check with your extension service for a recommended spray. Also consider hiring a licensed pest control applicator to apply it. The best time to spray is in late May or June, but repeat sprays are often needed. The following year, begin spraying as the adults emerge.

Leaf-feeding caterpillars

Looper (2× life size).

PROBLEM: Caterpillars are clustered or feeding singly on the leaves. The surface of the leaf is eaten, giving the remaining tissue a lacy appearance, or the whole leaf is chewed. Sometimes the leaves are covered with webs. The tree may be completely defoliated. Damage appears anytime between spring and fall.

ANALYSIS: Many different species of caterpillars, such as loopers, feed on the leaves of trees and shrubs. Depending on the species, the moths lay their eggs from early spring to midsummer. The larvae that hatch from these eggs feed singly or in groups on buds, on one leaf surface (these are called skeletonizers), or on the entire leaf. Certain caterpillars web leaves together as they feed. In some years, damage is minimal because of unfavorable environmental conditions or control by predators or parasites. When conditions are favorable, however, entire plants may be defoliated. Defoliation weakens the plants because no leaves are left to produce food. When heavy infestations occur several years in a row, branches or entire plants may be killed.

SOLUTION: Spray with the bacterial insecticide Bt when damage is first noticed. The best time to spray is late afternoon or early evening. Repeat the spray if the plant becomes reinfested.

Tent caterpillars

Western tent caterpillars (¼ life size).

PROBLEM: In spring or summer, silk nests appear in the branch crotches or on the ends of branches. Leaves are chewed; branches or the entire tree may be defoliated. Groups of caterpillars are feeding in or around the nests.

ANALYSIS: Tent caterpillars and fall webworms (*Malacosoma* spp. and *Hyphantria cunea*) feed on many ornamental trees. In summer, tent caterpillars lay masses of eggs in a cementing substance around twigs. They hatch in early spring as the leaves unfold, and the young caterpillars construct their nests. On warm, sunny days, they emerge from the nests to devour the surrounding foliage. In mid- to late summer, brownish or reddish moths appear. The fall webworm lays many eggs on the undersides of leaves in spring. In early summer, the young caterpillars make nests over the ends of branches and feed inside them. As the leaves are devoured, the caterpillars extend the nests over more foliage. Eventually, the entire branch may be enclosed with this unsightly webbing. The caterpillars drop to the soil to pupate. Up to four generations occur between June and September. Damage is most severe in late summer.

SOLUTION: Spray with the bacterial insecticide Bt. Remove egg masses found in winter.

Bagworms

Bagworm case on honeylocust (life size).

PROBLEM: Leaves are chewed; branches or the entire tree may be defoliated. Hanging from the branches are carrot-shaped cases, or "bags," from 1 to 3 inches long. The bags are constructed from interwoven bits of dead foliage, twigs, and silk. When a bag is cut open, a tan or blackish caterpillar or a yellowish grublike insect may be found inside. A heavy attack by bagworms may stunt deciduous trees or kill evergreens.

ANALYSIS: Bagworms (*Thyridopteryx ephemeraeformis*) eat leaves of many trees and shrubs. Larvae hatch in late May or early June and immediately begin feeding. Each larva constructs a bag that covers its entire body; as the larva develops, it adds to the bag. The worm partially emerges from its bag to feed. When all leaves are eaten off a branch, the bagworm moves to the next one, dragging its bag along. By late August, the larva spins silken bands around a twig, attaches a bag permanently, and pupates. In fall, the winged male moth emerges from his case, flies to a bag containing a female, mates, and dies. The female bagworm spends her entire life inside her bag. After mating, she lays 500 to 1,000 eggs and dies. Eggs spend the winter in the mother's bag.

SOLUTION: Spray with Bt between late May and mid-July to kill the young worms. Handpick and destroy bags in winter to reduce the number of eggs.

Solving Tree and Shrub Problems
(continued)

Powdery mildew

Powdery mildew on lilac.

PROBLEM: Leaves, flowers, and young stems are covered with a thin layer or irregular patches of a powdery, grayish-white material. Infected leaves may turn yellowish or reddish and drop. Some leaves or branches may be distorted. In late fall, tiny black dots (spore-producing bodies) are scattered over the white patches like grains of pepper.

ANALYSIS: Powdery mildew is caused by any of several fungi that thrive in both humid and dry weather. Some fungi attack only older leaves and plant parts; others attack only young tissue. Plants growing in shady areas are often severely infected. The powdery patches consist of fungal strands and spores. The spores are spread by the wind to healthy plants. The fungus saps plant nutrients, causing discoloration and sometimes the death of the leaf. Certain powdery mildews also cause leaf or branch distortion. Because these powdery mildews often attack many different kinds of plants, the fungus from a diseased plant may infect other plants in the garden.

SOLUTION: When planting new trees and shrubs, use resistant varieties. Some groups of highly susceptible plants—such as crape myrtles, lilacs, and roses—have cultivars selected for resistance to powdery mildew. Several fungicides are available that will control this mildew.

Wilting

Wilting mockorange.

PROBLEM: The plant wilts often, and the soil is frequently or always dry. The leaves or leaf edges may turn brown and shrivel.

ANALYSIS: Water in the soil is taken up by plant roots. It moves up into the stems and leaves and evaporates into the air through microscopic breathing pores in the surfaces of the leaves. Water pressure within plant cells keeps the cell walls rigid and prevents the leaves and stems from collapsing. When the soil is dry, the roots are unable to furnish the leaves and stems with water, the water pressure in the cells drops, and the plant wilts. Most plants will recover if they have not wilted severely. Frequent or severe wilting, however, will curb a plant's growth and may eventually kill it.

SOLUTION: Water the plant immediately, wetting the leaves to increase humidity. Apply water to the soil slowly, and confirm that it is soaking in to root depth. Apply a 1- to 2-inch-thick mulch over the root area to slow water evaporation from the soil.

Extreme heat or wind

Wilting dogwood.

PROBLEM: The plant is wilting, but the foliage usually looks healthy. No signs of insects or disease are present, and the soil is moist. Wilting is most common on shrubs or plants with limited root systems.

ANALYSIS: During hot, windy periods, small or young plants may wilt, even though the soil is wet. Wind and heat cause water to evaporate quickly from the leaves. If the roots can't absorb and convey water fast enough to replenish this loss, the leaves wilt.

SOLUTION: Keep the plant well-watered during hot spells, and sprinkle it with water to cool off the foliage. The plant will usually recover when the temperature drops or the wind dies down. Provide shade during hot weather, and use temporary windbreaks to protect the plant from wind. Plant shrubs adapted to your area.

Salt burn

Salt burn on azalea.

PROBLEM: The tips and edges of older leaves turn dark brown or black and die. The rest of the leaf may be lighter green than normal. The browning or blackening can develop in both dry and wet soils, but it is more severe in dry soil. In the worst cases, leaves drop from the plant.

ANALYSIS: Salt burn is common along the seashore and in areas of low rainfall. It also occurs in soils with poor drainage, in areas where salt has been used to melt snow and ice, and in areas where too much fertilizer has been applied. Excess salts dissolved in the soil water accumulate in the leaf tips and edges, where they kill the tissue. These salts also interfere with water uptake by the plant. This problem is rare in areas of high rainfall, where the soluble salts are leached from most soils. Poorly drained soils accumulate salts because they do not leach well; much of the applied water runs off instead of washing through the soil. Fertilizers, most of which are soluble salts, also cause salt burn if too much is applied or if they are not diluted with water after application.

SOLUTION: In areas with low rainfall, leach accumulated salts from the soil with an occasional heavy watering (about once a month). If possible, improve drainage around the plants. Follow package directions when using fertilizers; several light applications are better than one heavy application. Water after fertilizing. Avoid the use of bagged steer manure, which may contain large amounts of salts.

Leaf rust

Cedar-apple rust on hawthorn.

PROBLEM: Leaves are discolored or mottled yellow to brown. Yellow, orange, red, or blackish powdery pustules appear on the leaves. The powdery material can be scraped off. Leaves may become twisted and distorted and may dry and drop off. Twigs may also be infected. Plants are often stunted.

ANALYSIS: Many species of leaf rust fungi infect trees and shrubs. Some rusts require two plant species to complete their life cycle. Part of the life cycle is spent on the tree or shrub and part on various weeds, flowers, or other trees or shrubs. Rust fungi survive the winter as spores on or in living plant tissue or in plant debris. Wind and splashing water spread the spores to healthy plants. When conditions are favorable (with moisture on the leaf and with moderate temperatures, 54° to 74° F), the spores germinate and infect the tissue. Leaf discoloration and mottling develop as the fungus saps nutrients from the plant. Some rust fungi produce spores in spots or patches; other rust fungi develop into hornlike structures.

SOLUTION: Some rust fungi are fairly harmless to the plant and do not require control measures. Where practical, remove and destroy infected leaves as they appear. Rake up and destroy leaves in fall. Several fungicides are available that can control rust fungi. Check with your extension service for current recommendations.

Lack of nitrogen

Nitrogen-deficient fuchsia.

PROBLEM: Leaves turn yellow and may drop, beginning with the older, lower leaves. New leaves are small, and growth is slow.

ANALYSIS: Nitrogen, one of the most important nutrients for plant growth, is deficient in most soils. Nitrogen is essential in the formation of green leaf pigment and many other compounds necessary for plant growth. When short on the nutrient, plants take nitrogen from their older leaves for new growth. Poorly drained, overwatered, compacted, and cold soils are often infertile. Plants growing in these soils often show symptoms of nitrogen deficiency. Various environmental soil problems and other nutrient deficiencies may also cause discolored leaves.

SOLUTION: For a quick response, spray the leaves and the soil beneath the plant with liquid or water-soluble fertilizer. Add organic amendments to compacted soils and those low in organic matter, and improve drainage in poorly drained soils. Do not keep the soil constantly wet.

Solving Tree and Shrub Problems
(continued)

Iron deficiency

Iron deficiency in rhododendron.

Apple scab

Scab on crabapple.

Aphids

Aphids on hawthorn (life size).

PROBLEM: New leaves are pale green or yellow. The veins may remain green, forming a Christmas-tree pattern on the leaf. Old leaves remain green. In extreme cases, new leaves are all-yellow and stunted.

ANALYSIS: Plants frequently suffer from deficiencies in iron and other minor nutrients, such as manganese and zinc, elements essential to normal plant growth and development. Deficiencies can occur when one or more of these elements is depleted in the soil or otherwise not available to roots. An alkaline pH (greater than 7) or wet soils cause these nutrients to be less available to plant roots. Alkalinity can result from overliming or from lime leached from concrete or mortar. Regions where soil is derived from limestone or where rainfall is low usually have alkaline soils.

SOLUTION: To correct the iron deficiency, spray the foliage with a chelated iron fertilizer, and apply the fertilizer to the soil around the plant. Apply soil sulfur or ferrous sulfate to lower the pH. When planting in an area with alkaline soil, add a handful of soil sulfur, or add enough peat moss to make up 50 percent of the amended soil, and mix well.

PROBLEM: Velvety, olive-green spots, ¼ inch or more in diameter, appear on the leaves. The tissue around the spots may be puckered. The leaves often turn yellow and drop. In a wet year, the tree may lose all of its leaves by midsummer. The fruit and twigs develop circular, rough-surfaced, olive-green spots that eventually turn corky and black. The fruit is usually deformed.

ANALYSIS: Apple scab is caused by a fungus (*Venturia inaequalis*). It is a serious problem on crabapples and apples in areas where spring weather is cool and humid. The fungus spends the winter in infected fallen leaves. In spring, spore-producing structures in the dead leaves discharge spores into the air.

The spores are blown by the wind to new leaves and flower buds. If water is on the tissue surface, the fungus infects the tissue and a spot develops. More spores are produced from these spots and from twig infections from the previous year. The spores are splashed by the rain to infect new leaf and fruit surfaces. As temperatures increase during the summer, the fungus becomes less active.

SOLUTION: If scab is prevalent in your area, plant varieties of trees and shrubs that are naturally resistant to it. Rake up and destroy infected leaves and fruit in the fall to reduce the number of spores that survive winter. Various sprays and fungicides are available that can control scab, but check with your extension service first for the latest information.

PROBLEM: Tiny (⅛ inch), soft-bodied, green, yellow, black, brownish, or gray insects cluster on the bark, leaves, or buds. Some species are covered with fluffy white wax. The insects may have wings. Leaves are discolored and may be curled and distorted. They sometimes drop off. A shiny or sticky substance may coat the leaves. Plants may lack vigor, and branches sometimes die.

ANALYSIS: Many types of aphids infest ornamental trees and shrubs. They do little damage in small numbers. They are extremely prolific, however, during a cool growing season. Damage occurs when the aphid sucks the juices from the plant. Sap removal often results in scorched, discolored, or curled leaves and reduced plant growth. A severe infestation of bark aphids may cause branches to die. Aphids are unable to digest fully all the sugar in the plant sap, and they excrete the excess in a fluid called honeydew, which often drops to cover anything beneath the tree or shrub in a sticky film.

A sooty mold may develop on the honeydew, causing the leaves to appear black and dirty. Ants feed on this sticky substance and are often present where there is an aphid infestation.

SOLUTION: Wash off the infested plant with a strong spray of water or, better, water with insecticidal soap. Repeat as needed. Aphid infestations are usually worst in early spring, then diminish with the onset of hot weather.

Spider mites

Spider mite damage and webbing.

PROBLEM: Leaves are stippled yellow, white, or bronze and are dirty. A silken webbing is sometimes found on the leaves or stems. New growth may be distorted, and the plant may be weak and stunted. To determine whether a plant is infested with spider mites, examine the bottoms of the leaves with a magnifying glass, or hold a sheet of white paper underneath an affected leaf or branch and tap it sharply. Green, red, or yellow specks the size of pepper grains will drop to the paper and begin to crawl around.

ANALYSIS: Spider mites, related to spiders, are pests of many plants. They cause damage by sucking sap from leaves and buds. As a result of their feeding, the plant's green leaf pigment vanishes, producing the stippled appearance. While they feed, many mites produce a fine webbing over the foliage that collects dust and dirt. Some mites are active throughout the growing season, but they thrive especially in dry weather when temperatures are 70° F and above. Other mites, especially those infesting conifers, are most prolific in cooler weather. They are most active in spring and sometimes fall and during warm periods in winter in mild climates. By the onset of hot weather, these mites have usually caused their maximum damage.

SOLUTION: Spray horticultural oil when damage is first noticed. If the problem is persistent, release predatory mites.

Fire blight

Fire blight on crabapple.

PROBLEM: Blossoms and leaves of some twigs suddenly wilt and turn brown as if scorched by fire. Leaves curl and hang downward. Tips of infected branches may hang down in a "shepherd's crook." The bark at the base of the blighted twig becomes water-soaked, then dark, sunken, and dry; cracks may develop at the edge of the sunken area. In warm, moist spring weather, drops of brown ooze appear on the sunken bark.

ANALYSIS: Fire blight is caused by a bacterium (*Erwinia amylovora*). The bacteria spend the winter in the sunken areas (cankers) on the branches. In spring, the bacteria ooze out of the cankers onto the branches and trunk and are carried by insects to the plant blossoms. The bacteria spread rapidly through the plant in warm, humid weather. Bees, rain, and tools spread the disease.

SOLUTION: During spring and summer, prune out infected branches about 12 inches beyond any visible discoloration and destroy them. Disinfect pruning tools by dipping after each cut in a solution of 1 part chlorine bleach and 9 parts water. Avoid excess nitrogen fertilizer in spring and early summer. It forces succulent growth, which is more susceptible. In summer or fall, prune out any remaining infected branches. A spray of a bactericide containing basic copper sulfate or streptomycin applied before bud-break in spring helps prevent infection.

Verticillium wilt

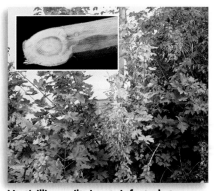

Verticillium wilt. Inset: Infected stem.

PROBLEM: The leaves turn yellow at the margins, then brown and dry. During hot weather, the leaves may wilt. New leaves may be stunted and yellowish. The infected tree may die slowly, branch by branch, over several seasons—or the whole tree may wilt and die within a few months. Some trees may recover. The tissue under the bark on the dying side shows dark streaks, which may be very apparent or barely visible when exposed. To examine for streaks, peel back the bark at the bottom of the dying branch.

ANALYSIS: Verticillium wilt affects many trees and shrubs. It is caused by a soil-inhabiting fungus (*Verticillium* spp.) that persists indefinitely on plant debris or in the soil. The disease is spread by contaminated seeds, plants, soil, tools, and water. The fungus enters the tree through the roots and spreads up into the branches through the trunk. The vessels become plugged, which cuts off the flow of water and nutrients to the branches, causing leaf discoloration and wilting.

SOLUTION: Fertilize to stimulate vigorous growth. Remove deadwood, and disinfect pruning tools after each cut by dipping in a solution of 1 part chlorine bleach and 9 parts water. Don't remove wilted branches immediately. They may produce new leaves in three to four weeks or the following spring. Remove dead trees. If replanting in the same area, plant trees and shrubs that are resistant to Verticillium wilt.

Solving Tree and Shrub Problems
(continued)

Oozing sap

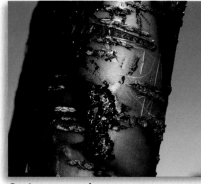

Oozing sap on cherry.

Oozing sap on Coulter pine.

PROBLEM: Beads of sticky, amber-colored or whitish sap appear on healthy bark, or sap oozes from patches of bark, cankers, wounds, or pruning cuts.

ANALYSIS: Oozing sap, also called gummosis, occurs in all trees and shrubs to some degree. One or a combination of the following factors causes it.

SOLUTION: The numbered solutions below refer to the numbered items in the analysis.

1. Natural tendency: Certain species of plants have a tendency to ooze sap. Frequently, small beads of sap form on the healthy bark of these plants.

1. As long as the bark appears healthy, there is nothing to worry about.

2. Environmental stress: Plants that are stressed because they are growing in wet soil may produce large quantities of sap, even though they are not diseased. Many plants respond to changes in weather conditions or soil moisture by oozing profusely.

2. If your plant is growing in poorly drained soil, allow the soil to dry out between waterings. Provide for drainage away from trunks and roots. Reduce the effects of stress on the plant by keeping it healthy. Maintain health and vigor of the plant by fertilizing and watering regularly.

3. Mechanical injury: Most plants ooze sap when their bark is wounded. This is especially noticeable on maple and birch. If these trees are injured during the fall, they ooze a large amount of sap the following spring.

3. Avoid mechanical injuries to the plant. Stake, tie, and prune properly.

4. Disease: Plants respond to certain fungal and bacterial infections by forming cankers—dark, sunken areas that ooze profusely. Gummosis, or oozing sap, is one of the initial signs of infection.

4. Remove badly infected branches, and cut out cankers. Keep the plant vigorous by fertilizing and watering regularly.

5. Borer damage: Many different insects bore holes into bark. Sap oozes from these holes. The tunnels these insects bore in the wood often become infected by decay-causing organisms.

5. Borers are difficult to control once they have burrowed into the wood.

Galls or growths on leaves, branches, or trunks

Galls on common witch hazel.

PROBLEM: Swellings and growths develop on the leaves, shoots, or trunk. Plants with numerous galls may be weak, and leaves may yellow. Branches may die.

ANALYSIS: These growths can be caused by one of three factors.

1. Fungal leaf or stem gall: Several fungi cause enlargement and thickening of leaves and shoots. Affected plant parts are usually many times larger than normal and are often discolored and succulent. Some leaf or stem galls turn brown and hard with age. The galls are unsightly but rarely harmful to the plant. Fungal galls are most severe when spring weather is wet.

2. Bacterial crown gall: This plant disease is caused by a soil-inhabiting bacterium (*Agrobacterium tumefaciens*) that enters plants through wounds in the roots or the base of the trunk (the crown). The galls disrupt the flow of water and nutrients up the roots, stems, and trunk, weakening and stunting the growth but usually not killing the plant.

3. Insect galls: Many insects cause galls by feeding on plant tissue or by injecting a toxin into the tissue. As a result of this irritation, blisters or growths of various shapes form on leaves, swellings develop on roots or stems, and buds and flowers grow abnormally. Most gall-forming insects cause only minor damage to the plant, but the galls may be unsightly.

Holes or cracks in bark

Leaf galls on willow.

Sunscald on tree trunk.

Sunscald on dogwood.

SOLUTION: The numbered solutions below refer to the numbered items in the analysis.

1. Pick off and destroy affected parts as soon as they appear. If galls are a problem this year, spray next spring with a fungicide just before the buds open. Add a spreader-sticker to the spray. Repeat the spray 2 weeks later.

2. Infected plants cannot be cured. They often survive for many years, however. To improve the appearance of shrubs with stem galls, prune out and destroy affected stems below the galled area. Disinfect pruning shears after each cut by dipping in a solution of 1 part chlorine bleach and 9 parts water. Destroy severely infected shrubs. Consult a professional horticulturist to remove galls from valued trees. The bacteria will remain in the soil for at least 2 to 3 years.

3. Many gall-forming insects require no controls. If you feel that the galls are unsightly, however, or if the galls cause dieback, control measures may be necessary.

PROBLEM: Patches of bark die, crack, and later develop into cankers. The dead bark eventually sloughs off, exposing undamaged wood. The affected bark area is usually on the southwest side of the tree. Trees with naturally dark bark are likely to be more severely affected. The cracks and cankers develop in either summer or winter.

ANALYSIS: When a tree growing in a deeply shaded location is suddenly exposed to intense sunlight, or when a tree is heavily pruned, the southwest side of newly exposed bark is injured by the rapid change in temperature. This may develop when a forested area is excessively thinned or when a tree is moved from a shaded nursery to a more exposed area, such as a lawn.

Summer sunscald: With intense summer heat, exposed bark is killed, and a canker develops, usually revealing the undamaged wood beneath the bark. Within several seasons, the tree may break at the cankered area and topple. Summer sunscald is most severe when the soil is dry.

Winter sunscald: Bark injury develops with rapid changes in bark temperature from cold nights to sunny winter days. Exposed bark becomes much warmer than the air during the day but cools rapidly after sunset. This rapid temperature change often results in bark cracking and, later, cankering. Trees with thin, dark bark are most severely affected.

SOLUTION: Once the bark is injured, you cannot do anything about sunscald. Wrap the trunks of recently exposed or newly transplanted trees with tree-wrapping paper, available in nurseries. White interior latex paint or whitewash is also effective. The wrap or paint should be left on for at least two winters. Remove the wrap for the spring and summer months to prevent it from harboring plant diseases and insects. Reapply the paint the second season if it has washed off. Trees will eventually adapt to increased exposure by producing thicker bark. Give trees, especially recently transplanted ones, adequate water in summer and, if necessary, in fall. Water transplants when the top 2 inches of the root ball are dry. Remove badly infected branches, and cut out cankers. Avoid wounding the plant. Keep the plant vigorous by fertilizing and watering regularly.

THE ART AND
Science of Pruning

Prune bougainvillea in early spring to promote maximum summer bloom.

Properly pruned trees and shrubs show naturalistic shape and plentiful bloom.

At first, pruning may seem a bit intimidating. But it really isn't. Like many other gardening techniques, pruning combines art and science. The science involves learning the simple rules of how plants grow, why they might need pruning, the best time to do it, and the proper techniques for each type of plant. Think of these as the principles of pruning. Once you've learned them, you will know exactly what to do, how to do it, and when. That's what this chapter is all about—answering the questions you might have, giving you step-by-step directions, and making you feel confident when you pick up a pruning saw or loppers.

The artistic side of pruning is an outgrowth of the scientific side. If you follow specific pruning techniques, your plants are going to look better and produce more flowers and fruit. But you have some leeway to express your artistic temperament and imagination. In common with all art, pruning first calls for envisioning what the final result will be, then shaping the plant to what was visualized, keeping in mind your style of landscaping and the natural look of each plant.

The main thing is to prune with a purpose. To do that, you need to know when to prune and why and how proper pruning will help your plants rather than hurt them.

Prune Japanese stewartia to reveal mottled colors of flaking bark.

Limber stems of Chateau de Reux rose are attached to a wall and pruned to stay flat.

Why Prune?

Many people think of pruning only in connection with a shrub or tree that has grown too big for the spot where it's planted. But there are equally important reasons to prune that have nothing to do with size. Proper pruning also improves the condition and the appearance of your plants in numerous ways.

Timely pruning repairs damage before further problems can occur. It also encourages greater quantity and quality of fruit and flowers. Pruning can shape a plant so that it's more attractive and better able to withstand heavy snow and storms. It stimulates new growth and directs that growth where you want it to go. You can even use pruning to create living works of art in your landscape—a whimsical topiary elephant, for instance, or a candelabra espalier.

Rather than picking up your hand pruners only when a shrub has grown out of bounds, look at the numerous benefits that regular pruning provides all your plants.

To increase flowers and fruit

What's the purpose of growing roses, raspberries, apples, or camellias? To produce plenty of flowers or fruit. How do you do that? One way is by pruning correctly. For instance, hybrid tea roses are borne only on what's called new wood, the current season's growth. Cutting back the stems of a rosebush early each spring stimulates new growth and therefore new flowers. If you want larger flowers and don't mind if there are fewer of

Frequent pruning maintains plant size and requires little time or effort.

them, disbud the rose. To do that, remove all of the buds on a stem except the terminal one. Then the plant's energy is directed to that one bud, which grows large.

In a similar technique to ensure a larger fruit crop on apple trees, pick off some of the apples on each branch while they are still small, and the ones remaining will grow bigger than if all were left to ripen. Another way is to thin a fruit tree to remove unproductive branches and open the center of the tree to sunlight.

Of course, you need to be careful about timing because pruning in the wrong season can decrease flowers or fruit. Cut back a forsythia during winter, and it won't bloom much in spring because pruning has removed most of the flower buds, which grow on old wood.

For specific advice on when, how, and whether to prune specific plants, check the gallery entries in the following chapters.

Renew summer flowering shrubs, such as this butterfly bush, by removing the oldest stems to the base in spring.

How to Prune

For the closest cuts, position the shears so that the sharp cutting blade is nearest the main stem.

Practically every homeowner has sheared a few inches from the stems of an overgrown shrub, hoping to make it smaller. Usually, the result is a shrub that is just as large, if not bigger and bushier, the next year. How you prune is as important as when or why you prune.

Pruning cuts

Each cut has its own specific results, and it's to your advantage to know them well. In fact, it would be almost impossible to realize your goals in pruning without knowing the effect of each type of cut.

THINNING: To thin a plant, you cut a lateral stem or limb all the way back to a main branch, the trunk, or the ground. Thinning encourages the growth of the branches that remain while it maintains the natural habit of the plant. It also opens up the interior of the plant to sunlight, which helps to keep the internal branches healthy.

You can keep a plant at the same height and width for many years through selective thinning. If an overgrown shrub is thinned instead of sheared, it won't be too large six months later. This is because the terminal buds are not removed so they continue to control growth.

HEADING: Removing the terminal bud by cutting in no particular spot on a stem is a heading cut. In this type of cut, buds breaking and growth begins below the cut. Heading results in new stems or branches clustered together, which creates such crowded conditions that the interior of the plant dies from lack of light penetration.

LATERAL PRUNING: This is a type of heading cut that's made to a shoot not less than one-third the diameter of the cut shoot. This type of cut will usually behave like a thinning cut, and not cause growth to begin below it. Arborists and others often use the term "heading back" when talking about pruning. Heading back means to shorten the branch using a lateral pruning type of cut.

SHEARING: This involves shortening all stems by a certain amount, as in pruning a hedge with shears or an electric trimmer. Robust new growth occurs just below the pruning cut.

Shearing provides a formal appearance and must be repeated often and regularly to be effective. It is useful for hedges and topiary but not for most shrubs or trees. The

Heading cuts remove the terminal bud by cutting anywhere on the main stem.

Another form of heading is called lateral pruning. By cutting back the main stem to a lateral branch, the plant becomes dense but not twiggy.

Thinning cuts remove a stem completely back to its origin on a larger branch.

Thinning opens plants up and encourages them to develop their natural shape.

Shearing shortens stems arbitrarily. It encourages vigorous growth in a thin, outer layer.

dense outer shell of leaves and stems blocks light to the inside of the plant, killing off leaves and stems in the interior. If the outer shell is injured, the damage may lead to more serious problems. Many plants do not sprout in this "dead zone," and an injury may prove fatal, or more likely, leave an open hole in the plant.

PINCHING: No equipment is involved, making this the easiest method. With your thumb and forefinger, gently remove the tip of a plant's soft new growth. Gardeners often pinch the pine candles (young shoots before the needles expand) to ensure denser growth.

How much to prune

Heavy pruning removes one-half or more of a plant's growth. In the case of shrubs, it includes cutting all shoots to within a few inches of the ground. Use heavy pruning to renovate plants and on plants that grow vigorously.

Light pruning removes one-fourth or less of the plant's stems. Use it on slow-growing plants and those that don't tolerate heavy pruning.

Cutting correctly

HOW TO HOLD PRUNERS: There's a right and a wrong way to hold pruning shears and loppers. Place the thin blade on the bottom, and as close to the trunk as practical. This avoids leaving stubs.

HOW TO CUT: For plants with alternate branches, make a slightly slanted cut about ¼ inch above a bud pointing in the direction you want new growth to go. The slant should angle away from the bud so rain doesn't stand at its base and rot it.

With an opposite branching pattern, buds are in pairs, so make a flat cut that is equidistant from both. Or make a slanting cut to remove one of the two buds. When cutting back to main branches or to the trunk, prune just outside the collar (a raised or swollen area at the base of the branch).

Examples of pruning cuts: When cutting a small branch, make the cut slant away from the bud and ¼ inch above it. The correct cut is at the far left.

When to Prune

Prune plants that bloom in early spring after flowers fade.

Regardless of time of year, make pruning cuts on limbs just outside the branch collar.

There isn't one time of year that's right for pruning every tree or shrub. Timing depends less on species than on your goal—whether you want flowers, fruit, or growth suppression. Plants as diverse as spring-flowering shrubs, roses, junipers, and deciduous trees are pruned during different seasons because timing affects their response.

What time of year?

WINTER: Pruning deciduous plants in winter, when most plants are dormant, promotes fast regrowth in spring. It's also easier to prune at this time of year because with foliage out of the way, you can see the shape of the plant. Schedule pruning for the end of winter because wound closure begins in spring.

EARLY SPRING: Pruning just before new growth begins allows plants to recover quickly and stimulates growth.
SUMMER: Pruning in summer when plants are actively growing can damage a plant by exposing previously shaded tissue to full sun. The exposure may scorch the tissue. It may also dwarf a plant because it has to use energy to close the wounds left by pruning. This isn't all bad, however. With fast-growing hedges, summer pruning can subdue their growth. And hot-weather pruning minimizes the formation of suckers.
FALL: This is the worst time to shear plants because it encourages new growth that may not have time to harden off before winter. Consequently, the new growth may be killed by the cold. However, it's okay to thin plants in fall, especially after plants are dormant.

Exceptions to the rules

Naturally, there are plants that don't fit the guidelines. Exceptions include needled evergreens, flowering trees and shrubs, and deciduous trees that ooze sap. Also, there are pruning chores you can do any time of the year: cutting off dead, diseased, or broken branches and removing suckers and water sprouts (vigorous shoots arising from stem tissue).

Most larger deciduous and evergreen trees can be safely pruned year-round as long as you avoid pruning elms during the flight times of elm bark beetles and avoid pruning oaks in April through June in areas where oak wilt is a problem.

In late spring or early summer, pinch the tips of stems to encourage bushiness. This includes candles of pines and other needled evergreens. However, don't remove flower buds of summer-flowering plants.

Flowering trees and shrubs

SPRING BLOOMERS: If you prune an evergreen azalea, forsythia, or other spring bloomer in late winter, it won't bloom the following spring because you've removed the flower buds. Spring-flowering shrubs or trees should be pruned within a month after blooming. That's when plants begin forming the buds that will produce the next year's blossoms. Most spring bloomers flower on what's called year-old or previous season's growth.

SUMMER BLOOMERS: Shrubs and trees that flower in summer produce blooms on new growth, so prune in early spring. This encourages lots of vigorous growth and bud formation. Examples include butterfly bush, crape myrtle, and hibiscus.

Some plants produce blooms on both year-old branches and on new growth; others produce their flowers on branches that are two years old.

Trees that ooze

Although many people are horrified to see a tree ooze sap, it only looks harmful. To avoid sap oozing, don't prune birches, elms, maples, dogwoods, walnuts, and yellowwood in late winter or early spring when their sap is rising. Prune them in summer, after temperatures are warmer.

How often to prune

How frequently a plant requires pruning depends on its growth, shape, site, weather, and your reason for pruning. Plants in warm-winter climates and plants that grow quickly generally need more frequent pruning than slow-growing plants in cold regions. Some trees never need pruning except to remove occasional storm damage.

At the other extreme are formal hedges or shrubs that block a window. Once a month during the growing season, prune these plants to help keep them in bounds. (Or replace them with shrubs that fit the space.)

Most trees need more attention when they're young than they do after they've matured. Once you've trained them correctly, you will find that their maintenance time greatly diminishes.

Sheared azaleas look unnatural, and produce flowers only at stem tips.

Prune trees with attractive branching patterns by removing crowded or dead branches.

PRUNING CALENDAR

EARLY SPRING
Prune summer-flowering trees and shrubs, which bloom on new growth, nonblooming broadleaf evergreens, and evergreen or deciduous hedges. Also prune hybrid tea, floribunda, grandiflora, and miniature roses. Remove winter-killed growth from climbing and rambling roses.

LATE SPRING OR EARLY SUMMER
Prune spring-flowering shrubs immediately after their blossoms fade. Pinch or trim one-half of candles (new elongating shoots) on pines and other needled evergreens.

SUMMER
Shear deciduous or evergreen hedges. Prune mature climbing roses (more than two or three years old) and rambling roses after they bloom. Prune dogwoods, maples, walnuts, and yellowwood, if needed. Prune summer-flowering shrubs and trees as blossoms fade.

FALL
Trim long rose canes. (If they remain, the winter wind will damage them and surrounding objects as wind whips them.)

WINTER
Prune berried shrubs or trees by harvesting for holiday decorations. In late winter or spring, prune deciduous trees, fruit trees, and deciduous shrubs that are not spring bloomers, but make sure the temperature is above 20° F.

Tools of the Trade

Having the right tool for each job makes pruning easier and faster. Because high-quality tools can last a lifetime, take time to try them out before you buy. The tool should be balanced and feel comfortable in your hand. Today's tools are lighter and more comfortable than in the past. Look for ergonomic designs and lightweight materials that produce stronger action with less effort: slip-resistant handles, strong construction, contoured handles, cushioned grips, and gear or ratchet mechanisms. These can make pruning a pleasure even for those with little hand strength.

Taking care of your tools will keep them in good shape and make them last longer. Clean them after each use and rub them with a few drops of oil to prevent rust. Occasionally oil the moving parts so they'll operate smoothly. Always store them in a dry place.

Pruners

A high-quality pair of hand pruners is the most important pruning tool because you will use them the most. They come in two main types: bypass and anvil. Use them to cut stems up to ¾ inch in diameter.

Straight anvil types have a sharp blade that cuts against a flat anvil. They rarely need adjusting, and the blade is easily replaced, but often

Bypass pruner

Anvil pruner

they crush a stem rather than cut it, especially if the blade is dull. For this reason, their use is often discouraged.

Bypass pruners have one sharp blade and one hooked anvil. They make clean cuts close to the stem but can't be used on branches greater than ½ inch in diameter. A third type of pruner works like scissors but is appropriate only for small twigs.

Pole pruners have either anvil or bypass pruners attached to a long wooden or fiberglass shaft. They're operated by a rope or handle on the pole. They are safer than standing on a ladder to cut high in a tree.

Geared lopper for added leverage

Loppers

For stems up to 1¾ inches in diameter, long-handled loppers (sometimes called lopping shears) are best. They give good leverage and allow

Pruner with rotating handle

you to reach into the base of an overgrown shrub. Loppers come in anvil and bypass styles. Ratcheted or geared models provide more power with less effort. When buying loppers, make sure that there is enough space between the handles so your fingers don't get pinched as the handles close.

Folding saw

Saws

When a limb is too large for loppers, turn to a pruning saw, which can cut branches up to 4 or 5 inches in diameter. Large-toothed saws produce a rough edge. The smaller teeth of Japanese-type saws cut quickly and neatly. Carpenter's saws aren't suitable for pruning because they're made to cut dry, not green, wood. Also, pruning

Lopper

saws cut on the pull stroke, as opposed to the push stroke of a carpenter's saw.

A folding saw is handy because it can be carried in a pocket. Use it for cutting smaller branches. Be certain the locking mechanism works well, or the saw can collapse while you're cutting. Most

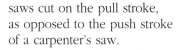

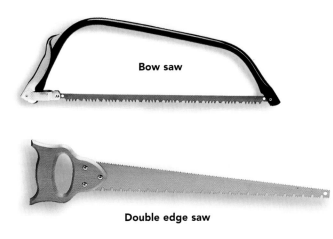

Bow saw

Double edge saw

Chain saws

A 12- to 16-inch chain saw is the most convenient size for homeowners. It can handle the largest pruning jobs that an amateur should tackle, while being lightweight and easy to maneuver. Chain saws can be dangerous. Observe safety rules by wearing safety glasses, a hard hat, and gloves, and keep both hands on the saw's handle.

Pole saw

folding saws have a curved blade, which is convenient when branches are crowded.

A bow saw is inexpensive, cuts quickly, and has a replaceable blade. Because of the bowed side, it can't always cut as close as other saws.

A saw with a wide blade is ideal for cutting larger limbs, but beware if it has two cutting edges. It's very easy to cut something you didn't mean to when there are sharp teeth on both sides of the saw blade.

For cutting overhead limbs up to 2 inches in diameter, use a pole saw or an extension saw.

Hedge shears

Manual hedge shears are best for pruning hedges. Look for notched or wavy blades, which do a good job of keeping the foliage from slipping out of your grasp. A lightweight handle and some kind of shock absorption are important if you do large quantities of hedge trimming.

Electric trimmers, which have a blade that oscillates, make fast work of shearing the top of a hedge evenly, but you have to be careful to not cut the cord. Gas-powered models are also available, as are battery-powered shears. Always hold power shears with both hands.

Chain saw

SHARPENING YOUR PRUNING TOOLS

To sharpen pruners, loppers, or manual hedge shears, you'll need a whetstone or grindstone. If possible, take the pruner apart for better access to the edges. Wet the stone with water or light oil, and hold the blade against the stone. Move the stone against the sharp edge, as you would when sharpening a kitchen knife. With bypass pruners, hone only the outside edge of the cutting blade. Sharpen both sides of the curved blade of anvil pruners so the blade will hit the flat edge evenly.

Leave saw sharpening to a professional because it's a specialized technique. You can find a saw sharpener by asking at a hardware store or lawn-mower repair shop.

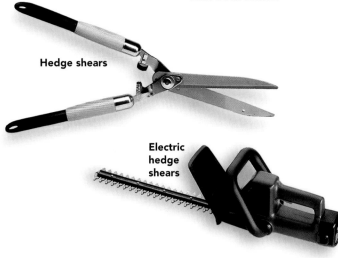

Hedge shears

Electric hedge shears

Pruning Safety

Because pruning involves using sharp blades and power equipment, and puts you near limbs that can fall in unexpected directions and stems that can snap back, it's potentially one of the most hazardous gardening activities. Follow a few commonsense rules to avoid being harmed.

PROTECTIVE GEAR: Wear protective clothing and equipment every time you prune. This includes goggles, long pants and a long-sleeved shirt, thick gloves, and sturdy shoes with good traction. For overhead branches, add a hard hat. Use hearing protectors or earplugs with power equipment.

Pruning large trees is a job for trained and well-equipped professionals.

Commonsense safety includes not standing directly below a branch that you're removing. It may fall before you expect.

LADDERS: Never prune while standing on a ladder when working alone, or use a chair instead of a ladder. If you do use a ladder, position the ladder's feet so that they don't wobble. The top of the ladder should rest firmly against a sturdy branch or crotch. Don't operate power equipment while on a ladder, or stand on either of the top two steps. Take care when stepping off a ladder. You should hire a professional to do pruning that requires a ladder if you're uncomfortable climbing a ladder or not accustomed to working on one.

LOOK AROUND: Stay away from power lines. If there are wires in the tree, hire an arborist (tree care professional). If you are using a pole pruner or saw, stand to the side of where you expect branches to fall. Always be aware of the location of your power cords so you don't accidentally cut through them.

WEATHER: Quickly stop pruning and go indoors at the first sign of lightning. Even after the storm has passed, it's still not safe to operate electric hedge trimmers or a chain saw. You can slip and fall or be electrocuted when the ground and plants are wet.

CHAIN SAW TIPS: Chain saws are the most hazardous tool used in pruning. To reduce the dangers, read the owner's manual, and follow its instructions closely. Also, wear the recommended safety gear, especially eye and ear protection. Don't use a chain saw if you have to reach above your shoulders to cut, and never climb onto a ladder or into a tree with a chain saw. Always hold the saw firmly and correctly. Turn off the saw before walking anywhere with it. Be alert for kickback, where the chain saw guidebar suddenly kicks back toward the operator.

Know when to hire an arborist

Hire a professional when you feel the least bit

Pruning safety includes not pruning from the top rungs of a ladder, and never working around electrical lines.

uncomfortable about doing a pruning job yourself. Also, let a pro evaluate your tree for insects and diseases and do any cabling, bracing, working near power lines, pruning high in mature trees, or any job that requires tools you don't have.

Contact the International Society of Arboriculture (ISA), 217-355-9411, or write ISA at P.O. Box 3129, Champaign, IL 61826-3129 for a list of certified arborists in your area (www2.champaign.isa-arbor.com). Its members have passed an examination and have at least three years of experience.

The Tree Care Industry Association is a trade association of tree-care professionals. For a list of members, call 800-733-2622, or visit the website at www.natlarb.com.

Ask a tree service company to show proof of adequate liability insurance and workers' compensation for any accidents that might occur on your property. Also ask for and check out the company's local references.

Talk to previous customers. Get an estimate and contract, and request that the bid include removal of all debris.

Don't hire someone who goes door-to-door looking for tree work, who climbs into live trees wearing spikes, or who offers to "top" your trees. These are not good practices for trees.

Keep plants safe, too

You can avoid ragged or torn bark by keeping your tools sharp and using the right-size tool. A jagged cut results when a 2-inch limb is cut with hand pruners. The same is true of cutting off a large branch in one step rather than in three (see page 69).

SAFETY CHECKLIST FOR PRUNING

■ Always use common sense when working with a sharp pruning saw, electric shears, or chain saws.
■ Check for electrical lines and dead or hanging branches before beginning.
■ Consider where the branch will fall when it is cut or dropped from the tree. Make sure no one will be hit or that it will not knock over the ladder.
■ Use a stepladder or tie an extension ladder securely to the tree. Keep one hand on the ladder and one on the saw.

■ Station a helper on the ground as a lookout and safety checker. Wear nonskid rubber-soled shoes, snug-fitting clothing, and leather gloves.
■ If you use a chain saw, wear leather boots.
■ It is advisable to wear a hard hat and protective glasses because you can easily bump into a branch and scratch an eye or lose a contact lens.
■ Call a professional if you lack proper equipment or if the branches to be removed are heavy or too high to reach safely.

Pruning Deciduous Trees

Because this dogwood was trained with care when young, it is now attractive and requires minimal pruning.

The adage to "train up a child in the way he should go and when he is old, he will not depart from it" applies to young trees as readily as it does to children. A tree doesn't develop into a handsome, mature specimen by accident. Its well-spaced branches and broad crown result from careful selection, correct planting, and regular, early pruning.

Young trees

A modest investment of time and effort over a tree's first four or five years will pay big dividends later on. Pruning to correct a large tree is expensive and creates slow-closing wounds. Most young trees, on the other hand, quickly recover from pruning. Some of the tasks for the early years:

■ Cut off broken branches so they won't become magnets for insects or pathogens.
■ Dig up suckers (vigorous upright growth from roots). Also, remove water sprouts (fast-growing shoots that are weakly attached to limbs).
■ For certain species, train the tree to a central leader, or one main stem. Remove competing leaders to give the tree a better form and make it more structurally sound.
■ Prune branches that join the trunk at a narrow angle, leaving branches with wide, and therefore strong, evenly spaced angles. (Exceptions are trees with upright forms.)
■ Remove any branch that crosses over or rubs against another stem.

In this section, learn how and why to train young trees. We'll follow the principles outlined earlier: use thinning or lateral cuts, do the work at the recommended time of year for the particular tree, and practice safety.

Training young trees

When training a young tree, imagine what it will look like

TREE SHAPES

Columnar

Open head irregular

Weeping

Broad cone

when it is older. As the illustrations show, trees have a variety of shapes. Part of your early pruning will be to form the tree's shape and to help the tree grow up strong.

With a new tree, prune only limbs broken or damaged in transit. Make cuts close to the trunk but outside the collar. Nothing else is needed the first year except to prune diseased growth and damaged or dead branches.

The time to actually begin guiding the young tree is during the second year after planting. The most common goal is to develop a natural-looking tree. However, in confined spaces or in a formal garden, a more controlled appearance may be the goal.

For that reason, the first step in training trees is to select a goal: Do you want a natural-looking tree, one with a small size, or perhaps one with a formal shape? Each goal requires a different pruning strategy. Some trees won't need much training. Others, such as Bradford pear, must be trained and pruned to avoid weak narrow crotches. If this isn't done, its limbs will eventually split apart.

DEVELOP A CENTRAL LEADER:
Starting the second year after planting, develop a strong central leader in the tree. (Central leader refers to the main trunk of the tree from which the branches grow.) To develop a central leader, use thinning cuts, as illustrated on page 56, to remove all but the strongest, most vigorous, or most central of the upright-growing branches in the tree's crown.

Training a tree to one central leader gives the tree the sturdiest branching structure possible, even in trees that develop multiple leaders with age.

SELECT SCAFFOLD BRANCHES:
The second task is to develop the scaffolds. These are the large branches that are the framework of the tree. Begin this task in the tree's third or fourth year. It will take two to three years to complete the process.

The spacing of scaffolds is important. The rule of thumb for vertical spacing is 3 percent of the tree's mature height. Therefore, on a tree that will eventually grow 50 feet tall, keep the scaffolds about 18 inches apart. Choose limbs that are evenly distributed around the trunk and not too close to another or directly above one another. Also, the permanent scaffolds should be at least 6 feet off the ground to allow traffic underneath the tree.

Another important quality is the angle at which the limb joins the trunk. Avoid angles that are less than 45 degrees. The wider the angle at which the trunk and branches join, the stronger their attachment. Ideally, the branches should approximate a clock, growing at 10 or 2 o'clock (with the trunk being 12 o'clock).

A third quality to look for is the diameter of the limb. A scaffold that is smaller in diameter than the trunk to which it is attached will be stronger and less likely to split from the trunk than one that's the same size as the trunk.

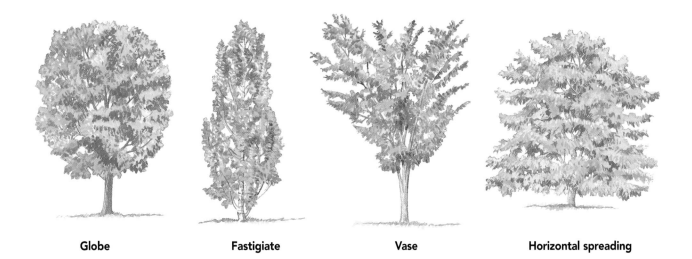

Globe   Fastigiate   Vase   Horizontal spreading

Pruning Deciduous Trees
(continued)

If a tree is growing into power lines or against your house, it may become necessary to reduce its height or its spread by lateral pruning. For mature trees, this large-scale pruning is best left to professional tree trimmers.

CROWN THINNING AND REDUCING: Thinning the crown, or upper portion of the branches, is the process of removing some limbs for the good of the tree. Thinning lets more light and air into the tree, which discourages fungal diseases and promotes good health. When fast-growing trees are thinned, their resistance to wind is reduced, and they aren't as likely to lose limbs in storms.

If a rapidly growing tree is producing lots of spindly new growth, the top may become larger than the roots can support. When the crown of such a tree is thinned, the demand on the roots is lessened and, therefore, balance is restored.

However, thinning is one of the most misused arboricultural practices. Few mature trees need it. If overdone, it leads to the "10-year takedown syndrome"; thin the tree now, and in 10 years you'll have to remove it because pruning off too much leaf area from a mature tree will kill it slowly.

Thinning is typically done only on rapidly growing trees of intermediate size. Mature trees should be thinned only if they are overly dense or likely to fail if not thinned.

To thin a tree, first clean the crown; remove any dead, dying, or crossing limbs. Then remove live branches evenly along the limb. Because there usually are more branches near the ends of limbs, take more off the ends than from the center. Removing only interior limbs (sometimes called "lion's tailing") is a damaging and improper pruning practice.

Before thinning a tree's crown, reread page 56, which explains and illustrates this pruning technique, and pages 64 and 65, which show the natural shapes of trees. Also, check out the photo above to ensure you recognize the collar on a tree branch.

CROWN RAISING: If the lower branches of a mature tree create a hazard or obstruct traffic—perhaps getting broken by the tops of passing trucks—you can raise the tree's crown to eliminate the problem. Another common reason to raise the crown is to allow more sunlight directly under a shade tree for growing lawn or flowers.

Raise the crown of a mature tree just as you would a younger one—gradually, over a number of years. Be sure to cut carefully, so as not

Compressed rings of bark at the junction of branch and trunk are the branch's collar.

to introduce disease, and to incorporate these cuts into your normal maintenance. That is, as you inspect your tree for weak branches, take off those that fit into your crown-raising plan first.

If for some reason you need to speed up this process, thinning back to upright-growing laterals can be done.

MAKING THE CUT: A tree's response to pruning depends greatly on where and how the cut is made. Tree pruning cuts should almost always be thinning cuts, which remove the branch back to where it is attached to the parent limb or to the trunk. Cuts that remove only portions of branches may result in decay and growth of excessive sprouts.

Make all cuts just outside the swollen branch collar (see photos above and at right), not flush with the trunk. The collar stores a compound that is toxic to decay-causing organisms. Removing or cutting into the collar causes the tree to lose this protective barrier. It also causes the wound to close more slowly.

Remove strong vertical branches that compete with the central leader in stages, one-third per year over three years.

Trees seal bark exposed by pruning or breakage by enclosing it with callus.

When it becomes necessary to remove a large, heavy limb, use three cuts. Don't try to do it with one cut, which can rip the bark from the tree. For the first cut, make an undercut one-third of the way through the branch at a point between 6 and 12 inches from the trunk. Make the second cut from the top of the branch about 1 to 3 inches farther from the trunk than the first cut, removing the branch. With the last cut, remove the short stub that's left, cutting at the outer edge of the branch collar. If working in a tight area, you may need to make the cut from the bottom to achieve the correct angle.

CLOSING WOUNDS:

To encourage wounds made by tree pruning to close quickly, cut cleanly and smoothly with a sharp saw or loppers, taking care to leave no ragged edges.

A cut on a tree doesn't heal the way a cut on your finger does. A tree closes the wound and isolates or compartmentalizes the injured area to form a barrier to decay. Callus tissue (an unorganized mass of cells) forms around the wound, appearing first as a circle and later as more doughnut-shaped. If the cut develops more callus on the sides than on the top or bottom, it was probably made too close to the trunk.

WOUND DRESSINGS:

Research has shown that wound dressings rarely help and can, in fact, harm a tree. Exceptions to this involve oaks in areas where oak wilt is a problem and, for aesthetic reasons, when large cuts have been made. Some wound treatments may help suppress suckers and water sprouts.

CORRECTING BAD PRUNING:

If there are many vertical branches, reduce the number of them to just a few on each main limb, then thin these back to a lateral branch. This opens the interior of the tree to more light and air. At first, these branches will be only weakly attached, but they will strengthen over time.

Remove crossed branches, even if this leads to a gap in the canopy. The opening will eventually fill in. If you find decay, prune the branches back to healthy wood.

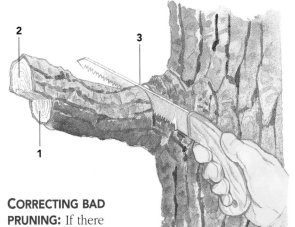

Prune large, heavy branches by making three cuts, beginning with a cut from the bottom up, as shown. This will prevent tearing bark on the trunk.

AVOID TOPPING TREES

Neither thinning nor reducing the crown destroys the natural shape of a tree; topping does. Topping involves heading branches to random stubs or small lateral branches rather than to a main branch or to the trunk of the tree.

The problems topping causes are numerous: decaying stubs, sunburn from lack of leaves, water sprouts instead of healthy new growth, and stress from the loss of so much tissue.

As explained in "Pruning Cuts" on page 56, heading cuts activate numerous latent buds. This results in multiple weak shoots growing below each cut. Because these shoots grow quickly, the tree soon needs pruning again. You can improve topped trees by removing some of the water sprouts, but it will never be the same.

An alternative to topping is pollarding, where the shoots are cut to the main branch every year. Pollarding creates a thick tuft of small branches and keeps the tree at the same height.

Pruning Deciduous Shrubs

Although mature deciduous trees can get by with infrequent pruning, established shrubs may need pruning at least once a year to either control size or maintain vigor. Also, unlike trees, where only thinning cuts are recommended, shrubs might also require lateral pruning and shearing, depending upon your goal for the shrub. You may want to review these pruning techniques, which are described earlier (page 56).

Before picking up your pruners, always have a goal in mind, and know which type of pruning cut produces the effect you want. You may want to maintain a shrub's natural form or create a hedge, a topiary, or an espalier.

Red Prince weigela produces flowers in spring on stems that are one year old, and a smaller crop of blooms in summer on new shoots. To maximize flowering, prune the shrubs right after spring bloom.

Shrub shapes

Spreading

Weeping

Prostrate

Upright

Rounded

Oval

Other typical goals

CONTROLLING SIZE: When shrubs grow too large, use thinning cuts to reduce size without changing the natural branching habit. First, remove excessive twiggy growth and crowded, weak, and misshapen stems, as well as suckers and water sprouts. Then use loppers to cut the longest stems back to where they join a lateral branch. This opens the plant to sunlight, which encourages new growth and gives it a graceful shape. If you shear or head a shrub to control size, you'll get a fast flush of growth that requires more pruning—exactly the opposite of what you want.

Two other methods of reducing the size of a shrub are explained on page 72.

ENCOURAGING THICKER GROWTH: A shrub that is grown to screen an unsightly view needs to be dense, not loose and open. In this situation, greater branching and thicker growth are what you want, so shearing or lateral pruning is appropriate.

PROMOTING FLOWERS: When a shrub isn't blooming as well as it has in the past, the first thing to check is whether it's still receiving enough sunshine. As surrounding trees grow, they gradually shade an area. If the light hasn't become too dim to support healthy plant growth, thinning the shrub's older branches can help. Thinning lets light into the interior of the shrub to help stimulate growth and improve flowering.

If light is not the problem, make sure you're pruning the

shrubs at the correct time. For example, trimming a weigela or other spring bloomer in September removes most of the buds that would flower the next spring. Wait to prune shrubs that bloom on old or previous season's wood until after flowering is over. Prune shrubs that bloom on new or current-season wood before they bloom, in late winter or early spring, to stimulate new growth on which flowers develop. If you're hoping for berries, remember, flowers produce the berries.

REMOVING REVERTING FOLIAGE: On variegated shrubs—the ones with mottled or bicolor foliage—cut out any branches with solid green leaves. If you don't, the entire shrub may revert to green as the stronger green branches shade out the variegated branches. If uncharacteristic fast-growing sprouts appear on dwarf varieties, cut them out, too.

Age makes a difference

Before deciding to prune a shrub, consider its age and vigor. Older, less vigorous shrubs should be pruned more lightly than younger ones, unless you are pruning to rejuvenate. Then you can prune the older shrub's branches back to the ground.

Don't wait until a shrub has outgrown its site to begin pruning or training. Start when it is young so it will develop a compact branching system. Lightly head limbs of small shrubs to encourage branching at the base of the plant. Then thin the shrub to make sure the basal branches are evenly spaced.

SPRING-FLOWERING SHRUBS

Late winter: Leaf and flower buds are ready to grow.

Early spring: Flowers open, and leaves begin to grow.

Late spring: Prune once flowers are faded.

Summer: Next year's flowers develop on new stems.

SUMMER-FLOWERING SHRUBS

Late winter: Leaf buds are ready to grow, but flower buds are not yet developed.

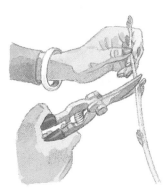

Early spring: Prune just before peak growth begins.

Late spring: Each cut yields at least two new stems, each of which produces flower buds.

Summer: Flower clusters develop on new branches.

Rejuvenating Shrubs

Rejuvenate shrubs over three years, removing one-third of the oldest stems to the ground each year.

When faced with neglected or overgrown shrubs, homeowners often feel helpless. They wonder whether the only solution is digging them out and replacing them with new plants. But such shrubs can be given a new lease on life through one of three renovation techniques. Within three years, they will be back in shape, flowering better than before. A little patience pays off in the end.

Gradual renewal

This method takes a bit longer to see results, but it's easy on the shrubs, and it doesn't create a temporary eyesore. Each year for three years, cut approximately one-third of the oldest stems off at ground level, using loppers or a folding saw. The result is a "new" shrub with a pleasing, natural shape and a size that fits the spot where it's planted. Some gardeners like to perform renewal pruning over five years instead of three, taking out one-fifth of the stems each year. After the plant has been through this process, keep its size under control with yearly thinning.

Severe pruning

Another good way to renovate shrubs is to cut all of the stems back to within 1 to 2 inches of the ground. On a shrub with heavy branches, you may want to make two cuts: First remove the top growth with loppers, then cut the thick stem base with a pruning saw.

When a shrub has been cut back hard, it won't look attractive for a year, but generally it will regrow quickly. This is often the best way to treat a shrub, such as viburnum, that was sheared by a previous owner rather than allowed to grow into a natural shape.

A CAUTION: Not all shrubs respond well to this treatment. It works best for vigorous growers, such as forsythia, glossy abelia, and spirea.

Transforming a shrub into a tree

Another solution to the problem of overgrown deciduous shrubs is to turn the shrub into a single- or multiple-trunk tree. This technique—often used on crape myrtles—produces a shrub that has a light, airy look to it and open areas at the base for planting ground covers or flowers. See the box at left for how-to directions.

When to renovate a shrub

The best time to prune is in early spring before new growth begins because the plants recover quickly then. You can wait until after flowering to rejuvenate a shrub, but regrowth will be more vigorous in early spring.

HOW TO TURN A LARGE SHRUB INTO A SMALL TREE

Start by selecting one to three stems to be the main trunk or trunks and remove all other stems. Expose the trunks by cutting off the side limbs up to where you'd like the tree canopy to begin— usually about 4 to 6 feet, although it can be shorter on some shrubs. Continue to remove side shoots as they appear. Sprouting will lessen over time. You can also treat the shrub with a growth regulator.

Pruning Roses

More so than with other shrubs, it's easy to see quick results from pruning roses. Not only do correctly pruned roses produce more abundant flowers, they're healthier and have a more pleasing shape.

Pruning at planting

It is rarely necessary to prune bare-root rosebushes when planting them. Ordinarily, the grower has already done this. But if stems or roots were damaged in transit, clip those off with a pair of sharp pruning shears.

Established roses

How and when a rose is pruned depends upon its type—hybrid tea, floribunda, climber, grandiflora, rambler, miniature, shrub, or old garden rose. See the step-by-step illustrations on pages 74 and 75 for specifics.

PRUNE ANYTIME: Some tasks apply to all roses: removing dead, diseased, weak, crossing, or damaged stems, and cutting off suckers from below the bud union (swollen grafting site).

PRUNE AS YOU CUT FLOWERS: Some pruning is done throughout the summer as you deadhead or snip off blooms to enjoy indoors. Cut ¼ inch above the next five-leaflet cluster below the blossom. Choose a cluster that's facing the outside of the plant. Don't leave faded flowers on the bush because they slow the formation of new blooms.

PRUNE IN LATE WINTER OR SPRING: When's the best time to do major pruning of hybrid tea, floribunda, polyantha, grandiflora, miniature, and tree roses? It depends upon where you live.

Prune roses in early spring, occasionally removing the oldest stems to their base.

A properly pruned rose has a natural shape and heavy flower production.

In cold climates, prune in early spring, as soon as the buds have begun to swell but before new growth has started. Be careful though: Late frosts can kill new growth.

In mild climates, late winter is an ideal time to prune. But in areas where spring temperatures waver between 30 and 70° F, wait to prune until 30 days before the average last frost to avoid exposing new growth to a killing cold spell.

With an old garden rose, shrub rose, rambler, or climber, pruning time depends upon whether it blooms on this year's or last year's canes.

If the flowers are on the tips of the stems, your plant blooms on new canes. If the roses are a bit farther down the stem, it probably blooms on last year's canes.

Prune Lady Banks rose in late spring, after flowers fade. A vigorous plant, it can withstand heavy pruning.

Pruning Roses
(continued)

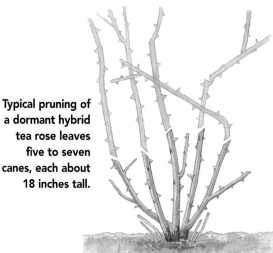

Typical pruning of a dormant hybrid tea rose leaves five to seven canes, each about 18 inches tall.

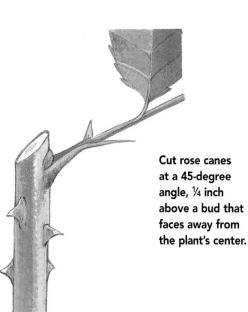

Cut rose canes at a 45-degree angle, ¼ inch above a bud that faces away from the plant's center.

Pruning to an outward-facing bud directs the new stem to the outside and maintains the plant's shape.

In early spring, prune roses that bloom on this year's canes, such as hybrid teas, grandifloras, and floribundas. Wait until after flowering to prune roses that bloom on older wood (many species of roses). However, don't prune climbers or ramblers until they're at least three years old, except to remove diseased or damaged canes.

Old garden roses frequently need only minimal pruning. Remove one-third of the oldest canes—they'll be brown or black—of alba, centifolia, and moss roses after they finish flowering. Prune China, Bourbon, Portland, and modern shrub roses in the same manner in late winter or early spring.

Miniature roses need only minimal pruning. If it's necessary, prune them as you would hybrid teas. You can also shear them with hedge pruners to increase bushiness.

Light and heavy pruning

Roses that bloom on current-year wood respond well to heavy and light pruning. With heavy—or hard—pruning, you remove all but three to five of the plant's canes and head remaining canes to three buds. This method produces larger flowers but fewer of them. It also stimulates new growth on weak bushes.

Light pruning has the opposite result: more and smaller flowers. With light pruning, you remove all but five to seven canes, cutting remaining canes to 18 to 36 inches tall.

Gardeners in cold climates are more likely than those in warm climates to have to prune back hard because of winter damage. But if there's a choice, inexperienced rose growers should choose light to moderate pruning rather than cutting back hard. A general rule for hybrid teas, grandifloras, polyanthas, and miniature roses is to remove only one-third to one-half of the plant's growth.

The bud union

The knob at the base of the canes is the bud union. This is where one variety of rose was grafted to the root system of another. Usually, the rootstock is a strong grower; however, because of its vigor, canes may develop from below the bud union. These canes grow robustly and will take over if not removed. They also produce inferior flowers that may not be the same color as the desired variety. If, for example, a red rose appears among the yellow ones, trace that cane back to its origin and remove it at the lowest point possible.

Tips

WHEN TO STOP: In areas with cold winters, quit pruning four to six weeks before the average first fall frost date. Pruning later may promote late growth and winter injury.
TECHNIQUE: Cut at a 45-degree angle ¼ inch above an outward-facing bud. Wear a pair of long, thorn-proof gloves as you work.
SEALING: Many gardeners seal the tips of the canes to prevent borers from damaging them. In warm climates, cover all cuts—even those from deadheading—with white glue, shellac, fingernail polish, or special rose-pruning sealants. In cold climates, seal ½-inch-diameter or larger cuts.

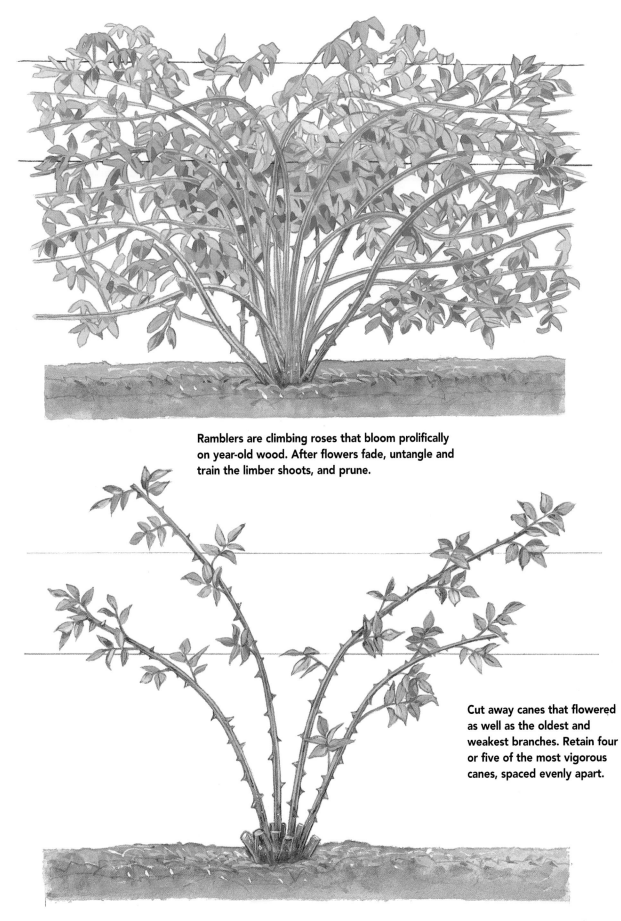

Ramblers are climbing roses that bloom prolifically on year-old wood. After flowers fade, untangle and train the limber shoots, and prune.

Cut away canes that flowered as well as the oldest and weakest branches. Retain four or five of the most vigorous canes, spaced evenly apart.

Pruning Hedges

To keep a photinia hedge neat, shear it after its spring growth surge.

Maintain informal hedges by removing the oldest branches and stems annually. Use lateral pruning cuts to promote dense growth.

How you prune your hedge depends upon whether it's formal or informal. A formal hedge has straight sides and a flat top or other geometrical shapes. To keep it looking good requires frequent light shearing. An informal hedge, which grows to its natural form, needs less maintenance. Informal hedges that flower are given their main pruning of the year right after they bloom.

Training a young hedge

The treatment you give your hedge the first few years after planting makes a big difference in how it looks and grows in the long run. Within a month after planting, head the young nursery stock by one-third to one-half.

Gardeners are often reluctant to prune these small, young shrubs that have so recently been planted. True, early pruning will make the young plants smaller temporarily, but more importantly, it encourages the development of many new stems from the existing stems, resulting in a thicker hedge, especially at its base. If young hedge plants are allowed to grow unpruned until they reach their intended height, the inner growth will be weak, and branching will occur only at the tips of the stems. The hedge won't be dense enough to support any weight, and snow or strong winds can break the weak branches, which will leave holes in the hedge.

Shearing and shaping

FORMAL HEDGES: In the spring of a formal hedge's second and third years, use hedge trimmers to level its top

and sides. Each time there's 2 to 3 inches of new growth, clip it back just above the previous trimming.

Part of the training of young formal hedges is to shape them so the bottom is wider than the top. If you prune the opposite way, the top shades the base, which eventually grows bare. One way to maintain a base that's wider than the top is to begin shearing at the bottom, then work up, tapering the sides.

Shearing long formal hedges is easier with gas, electric, or battery-powered hedge trimmers. Manual hedge shears work fine for shorter hedges. Hand pruners are best for hedges made up of broad-leaved shrubs because, unlike trimmers, they allow you to avoid clipping the wide leaves in half, which detracts from the appearance of the hedge.

It isn't easy to shear a formal hedge to an exactly straight edge by eye. To get the angles correct, set up stakes at each end of the hedge, and stretch string between them as a guide.

Once the plant is established, shear before growth begins in spring so that the new leaves cover the pruning cuts. You can also shear during or after the first growth spurt. Stop trimming in late summer—late July through early September— or early enough that the new growth isn't damaged by early cold spells.

INFORMAL HEDGES: Informal hedges offer more leeway with your schedule: Most can be thinned any time of the year. Let them grow without pruning through their second season, except to remove broken or diseased branches.

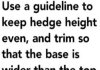

Use a guideline to keep hedge height even, and trim so that the base is wider than the top.

Hand pruners or loppers are recommended for pruning informal hedges because you use thinning and lateral cuts to remove branches and allow sunlight into the center of each shrub.

Renovating a hedge

When a hedge becomes overgrown or bare at the bottom, it needs rejuvenating. Some hedges rebound quickly if cut back to within 2 to 3 inches of the ground. This works well with vigorous hedge plants such as privet, bayberry, and spirea, but may be too extreme, especially for a privacy hedge. In most situations, cutting back to the hedge's minimum useful height, 5 feet for example, is the best course.

Cutting a hedge back to a few inches high temporarily destroys its screening ability. For that reason, you may prefer to rejuvenate a hedge over three years, cutting one-third of the stems to the ground each year.

While a hedge is being renovated, it won't look very good. But within a few years of severe pruning and three to four years of gradual rejuvenation, its appearance will be better than before you started the process.

Make a hedge guide of 1×1s, joined by wing nuts to make angle adjustment easy.

Pruning Evergreen Trees and Shrubs

How evergreens grow

Pyramidal

Columnar

Irregular

Rounded

Weeping

Spreading or Prostrate

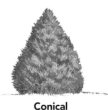

Conical

Most evergreens develop a characteristic shape without being pruned.

Just as deciduous trees and shrubs grow in various shapes dictated by their branching patterns, so do evergreens. They may be rounded, spreading or prostrate, conical, or irregular. One of the main goals in pruning evergreen shrubs and trees is to preserve the plants' natural form while limiting their size.

Evergreens are divided into two distinct groups: needled and broadleaf. The way you prune depends on which group the plant belongs to.

Needled evergreens

Also called conifers, needled evergreens have narrow, needlelike leaves. With these minimized leaves, the plants are able to resist low temperatures and drying winds. Needled evergreens can be further divided into two more groups: those that grow from terminal buds and those with random buds on their stems. (There are also deciduous needled conifers: dawn redwood, larch, golden larch, and bald cypress.)

TERMINAL BUDS: Most evergreens send out one flush of growth each spring that matures by midsummer. New buds then develop but remain dormant until the next year. Many needled evergreens, including pines, firs, cedars, and spruces, grow only from terminal buds (on the end of the branches). Usually, several buds are at the terminals, producing a whorled branching pattern.

The resulting new growth is called a candle because it starts out pressed into a narrow, cylindrical shape. Conifer candles are lighter green than older growth and are more flexible.

Needled evergreens have few if any latent buds, and the ones they do have remain active for only a few years. Also, these evergreens rarely form adventitious buds. So if cuts are made into older, leafless areas, these terminal-bud evergreens don't regrow. Some, such as pine, won't regrow unless buds are actually visible, even if the stem has foliage.

Because the main reason for pruning candled trees or

Prune camellia, a broadleaf evergreen, lightly after flowers fade. Prune them to shape anytime.

To maintain their screening value, the lowest branches of these Black Hills spruce trees are not pruned.

shrubs is to keep the plants bushy, the best way to prune is to pinch half of the candle before it expands completely. **RANDOM BUDS:** Evergreens with random buds are often called narrowleaf because they have scalelike needles compressed against their stem, such as arborvitae, juniper, cypress, and cedar. In the random branching pattern, new branches grow anywhere along the trunk and old stems, and plants grow in spurts throughout spring and summer. That's why these tolerate severe pruning. However, arborvitae will not regrow if pruned into wood without visible buds. Yews and junipers resprout from old wood only if it has foliage.

Prune random-bud evergreens by thinning wayward growth. To keep them from growing too large, slightly shorten their branches in late winter.

Broadleaf evergreens

Broadleaf evergreens have wide, often leathery, leaves like those of deciduous plants. Popular broadleaf evergreens include some azaleas, boxwood, camellia, holly, mahonia, mountain laurel, southern magnolia, rhododendron, and Japanese pieris. In cold climates, broadleaf evergreens may be semievergreen or even deciduous.

Some broadleaf evergreens, such as rhododendrons, grow just from the terminal, with leaf buds sprouting below the flower buds. Dormant buds develop at the stem tips in midsummer for the next spring's growth. Many other broadleaf evergreens, such as azaleas, pyracantha, and holly, develop latent or adventitious buds. Rejuvenate these by cutting into old wood.

Tips

For most evergreens, pruning at a precise time of year is not important. But if you want to keep plants growing slowly and within bounds, prune them just after new growth stops, usually late spring or early summer.

If pruned while new growth is still soft, some evergreens develop new buds. No new buds will form after the new growth has hardened. The pruned tips may then become dead twigs.

Junipers, arborvitae, cypress, and false cypress can be pruned safely at any time, but it is best to prune them before or during new growth. Avoid pruning in late summer.

Pines pruned during a dry summer or in any kind of summer in southern areas are prone to attack by bark beetles. In extreme cases, they attack in such numbers as to kill the tree.

Pruning Evergreen Trees

Pruning a broadleaf evergreen tree, such as southern magnolia, is much the same as pruning a deciduous tree. Thin dense growth to let light into the tree's center, cut off competing leaders, and remove wayward branches that spoil the natural form. It's best to prune most broadleaf evergreens when they are young because large wounds close slowly.

Remove limbs from Colorado blue spruce in winter; pinch new tips in spring to promote dense growth.

Training young evergreen trees

Broadleaf evergreens, needled evergreens, and many deciduous trees are similar in that a central leader is important to all. Pine, fir, hemlock, spruce, and other conifers usually develop a central leader naturally. If a leader is broken, a new one may develop from a bud nearest the damaged leader. Immediately cut off competing leaders if more than one develops. If a new leader doesn't develop, bend a side shoot near the broken leader upward, and tie it to a wooden splint. Leave this in place until the leader can stay upright on its own, which may take as long as two growing seasons.

Some needled evergreen trees are sheared at the nursery to keep them neat. When they outgrow this shape in a year or two, don't shear them again. Let the tree grow for a year, then use selective thinning cuts to let in light. Selective pruning produces a less rigid plant form and controls size better than shearing.

Pinching candles

In many respects, needled evergreen trees are pruned like needled evergreen shrubs. To maintain compact size, pinch the top and side candles. Cut the candles with hand pruners at a 45-degree angle to minimize the possibility that a second leader will develop. It's important to pinch before the new candles harden. Some candles, such as those of white pines (*Pinus strobus),* harden quite early and must be pruned by early summer.

Pinching off half the new growth results in a bushier tree. If you want to reduce the size of the tree, cut below the year-old growth into two-year-old wood.

Lower limbs sweeping the ground and a strong pyramidal shape define the beauty of many evergreens. Removing their lower branches makes the trees look top-heavy. The limbs won't grow back, and rarely will new branches grow to replace them, so think long and hard before cutting them off. Pines are an exception. Their lower limbs often die from being shaded by upper limbs. Because of their irregular habit, pines look OK after losing their lower limbs.

Thinning branches

Clear away dead needles and other debris in the center of the tree so you can see what you're doing. Then, cleanly cut crowded shoots and branches growing in the wrong direction at their base. Avoid pruning into bare inner branches because these usually won't regrow.

Most conifers have a prominent branch collar, so be sure to cut only to the collar and not into it. If you do, the wound might not close correctly.

Shearing needled evergreens

Have you ever noticed that when you shear a needled evergreen, the ends of the stems turn pinkish brown? One way to avoid this is by shearing the tree when it's wet from dew or immediately after a rain. (Do this only with manual, gas-, or battery-powered hedge shears; never use electric trimmers when the ground or plant is wet.)

When you shear, keep in mind the tree's natural shape. Although shearing "smooths the edges" of an evergreen tree, it shouldn't change its basic form. Let the top come to a point, which helps to prevent a heavy snowfall from weighing down the tree, and make sure to prune the lower branches so they stretch farther out than the upper ones and can intercept plenty of sunlight.

Rejuvenating evergreen trees

Overgrown evergreen trees, especially needled evergreens, are difficult to renovate because they cannot be cut back to old branches. They are best thinned while young to avoid becoming overgrown.

Broadleaf evergreen trees can be rejuvenated much the same as a deciduous tree; however, spread the renovation over three or four years rather than doing it all at once.

Patches of dead needles

If you notice a section of brown needles in the tree or shrub, identify its cause so you can correct the situation. If the cause is a canker, gall rust, or other disease, prune the limb to the trunk. If it is needlecast disease or an insect such as sawfly, treat the problem with the appropriate fungicide or insecticide. Identifying the problem may require the help of a extension agent or professional arborist. Either can give you advice for treating the problem.

Cutting out the brown patch may reveal a gap or opening. Although new growth will eventually fill in the opening, in the meantime it can look unsightly if the tree is in a prominent location. You can improve the tree's appearance by tying a short wooden stake to the

If the growing tip of an evergreen is damaged or broken, select a replacement from the nearest branch, and tie it in place.

main branch near the gap. Then tie nearby shoots to the stake to fill in. Soon, new growth will take over, and you can remove the stake.

Prune an overgrown holly by cutting branches back to short stubs, increasing their length as you work down the shrub. Sometimes called "hat racking," don't take off foliage beyond that on the branches being removed.

Pruning Broadleaf Evergreen Shrubs

Broadleaf evergreen shrubs such as pyracantha, holly, and boxwood are pruned like deciduous shrubs rather than needled evergreens. They rarely need as frequent pruning as deciduous shrubs, though. In fact, slow-growing broadleaf evergreens may never need to be pruned.

Because many broadleaf evergreen shrubs flower or produce berries, the time that they bloom or form fruit is a consideration when pruning them. The best time to prune blooming broadleaf evergreen shrubs is immediately after flowering; late winter or early spring is ideal for berried bushes. However, pruning while the shrub is flowering lets you see how much you are removing so you can have both: berries in fall and flowers the next year. Shrubs without flowers or berries should be pruned in late winter or early spring.

Prune overgrown broadleaf evergreen shrubs by removing major limbs to side branches.

Pruning pieris, a broadleaf evergreen shrub, requires little more than removing faded flowers.

Many of the basic duties for pruning broadleaf evergreen shrubs are the same as for other shrub pruning. First remove all diseased, dead, or damaged areas, cutting back to healthy buds on the branch or to the main trunk. Thin selected branches to control size and reduce height, keeping in mind the natural form of the shrub.

Using hedge shears on broadleaf evergreen shrubs is not recommended because their leaves are so large. Shearing mutilates the foliage, and the shrubs are left looking unattractive. The best tools for pruning broadleaf evergreen shrubs are hand pruners and loppers (and a pruning saw for old specimens). However, you may shear small-leaved evergreens, such as boxwood, inkberry, or Japanese holly, particularly when they are used in a hedge.

Rejuvenating broadleaf evergreens

If you've inherited a broadleaf evergreen shrub that hasn't previously been thinned to control height and width, you may have to resort to a three- or four-year renovation. Cut one-third to one-fourth of the oldest stems to the ground each year in early spring. This encourages new growth and helps side shoots develop.

An easy way to rejuvenate hollies and other vigorous growers in mild-winter climates is to cut them back to 3 to 4 inches tall in early spring and let them grow back. Not all will, but if the shrub was so overgrown that it would have had to be replaced anyway, this method is certainly worth trying.

Another method that works well on a large, neglected holly is called "hat-racking." Cut back the top branches to short stubs. Then, working downward, increase the length of the pruned branches to shape the plant into a pyramid. The plant will look unsightly after pruning, but, because new growth readily sprouts from latent buds, the holly will regain its natural shape in a couple of years.

Tips for rhododendrons

After flowers have faded, remove them so they don't sap the energy the plant normally devotes to growing leaves and buds. (See the illustration below at right for the best way to deadhead rhododendrons.) Deadheading also prevents the shrubs from blooming heavily in alternate years. If you can't reach all the brown blossoms because the rhododendron is too tall, knock them off with a strong blast of water from a hose.

Don't let dead branches accumulate inside the plant. Trim them off to the first live rosette of leaves, or remove the whole branch. Remove suckers on older, grafted rhododendrons. These divert energy from the main plant and have different flowers.

If a rhododendron becomes leggy, with most of its leaves at the ends of the branches, prune it in early spring by cutting back to 4 to 5 inches above a fork in the main stem. A dormant bud in that area will begin growing. When the interior of a rhododendron becomes crowded, thin the shrub over several years to let light penetrate inside.

Tips for evergreen azaleas

After azaleas bloom, pinch the tips to encourage bushier growth. Shearing an azalea during summer interferes with bud formation as well as reduces the crop of flowers. It also disturbs the natural shape of the shrub.

To renovate an evergreen azalea, cut one-third of the

older branches back to 6 to 12 inches high each year for three years. Some species will tolerate even harder pruning.

Tips for camellias

You can do minor shaping and maintenance on camellias at any time, but wait until after blooms fade to do major pruning. Avoid heading back camellias because that often results in lanky new growth.

Prune a camellia by cutting just above the slightly thickened bud scale scar, which signals where one year's growth ends and another begins. This forces three or four dormant buds into growth, helping to ensure a bushier shrub. All camellias except *Camellia reticulata* can tolerate heavy pruning when necessary.

To avoid dropped buds and ensure larger flowers on Japanese camellia, disbud or remove some of the excess buds. Note that camellia flower buds are plump; leaf buds are slender.

Prune most broadleaf evergreen shrubs by selectively removing wayward growth, keeping the natural shape of the plant in mind.

To encourage rhododendrons to branch, pinch tips of new growth (left). To remove faded flowers, gently bend the stalk until it cleanly snaps off.

Pruning Needled Evergreen Shrubs

Needled evergreen shrubs are popular because they make attractive foundation plants. Available in a wide variety of shapes, colors, and sizes, needled evergreen shrubs are a dependable element in your landscape's design, year in and year out.

To keep them looking their best, they must be pruned correctly. Many of these plants—especially arborvitae, false cypress, juniper, and yew—can quickly get out of hand if not trained correctly. And they require annual pruning to stay in check.

Alternatives to consider when selecting needled evergreen shrubs are dwarf or slow-growing varieties. Although they cost more initially because they are slow to grow to a marketable size, planting them instead of standard-size shrubs will greatly reduce your pruning maintenance time over the lifetime of the shrub.

Prune slow-growing evergreen hedges, such as this yew, just prior to spring growth.

Techniques

SHEARING: To create a formal appearance for evergreen shrubs, shearing with hedge shears or trimmers is the easiest technique. Evergreen shrubs with random buds respond the best to shearing.

As with deciduous plants, shearing induces denser growth on the outside edge of the shrub and causes the plant to grow larger. For that reason, shearing is a high-maintenance task, which you may want to limit to use on hedges. Once you begin shearing a needled evergreen shrub, it will continue to need regular trimming forever after.

The time to shear is in winter or early spring so that the new growth will hide the cuts. Then, lightly shear once again in early to midsummer if new growth warrants it. Don't wait too long to shear. Shearing an evergreen shrub in late summer or fall leads to soft, new growth that may be killed by cold weather. The snipped leaves will be unsightly all winter as well.

THINNING: This is the best method to use with needled evergreen shrubs. If done regularly, it effectively controls their size. Unlike shearing, it doesn't stimulate excessive growth.

Use loppers or hand pruners to thin evergreen shrubs in late winter or early spring, when plants are dormant, or perform touch-up pruning in late spring just after a spurt of growth. Selectively remove branches to maintain the natural shape while opening the shrub to more light. Cut back to a main branch or to the trunk, leaving no stubs. Remember to avoid cutting into old growth, which, on most needled evergreen shrubs, won't resprout. You can remove up to one-quarter of the branches by thinning each year.

If quite a bit of thinning is needed, start at the top of the shrub and work downward, pruning on alternate sides of the shrub as you go. Prune more lightly as you progress down. This will help preserve the shrub's natural shape.

Thin needled evergreens for an informal look by reaching into the interior and cutting branches back to their parent branch.

Because upper branches receive the most sun, they grow the fastest and need more aggressive pruning than lower branches.

PINCHING: You can encourage denser growth on needled evergreen shrubs that develop candles by pinching the new growth in half during late spring to early summer as the candle begins to expand. It's important to get the timing right because pines, such as mugho, won't form new buds near cuts unless they're pruned while candles are actively growing.

Shearing a needled evergreen for a formal look removes many growing points at once. Dormant buds begin to grow, resulting in denser growth on the exterior (right).

Pruning symmetrical, needled evergreen shrubs

Sometimes, owners must give Mother Nature a hand in maintaining needled evergreen shrubs that grow in symmetrical pyramidal forms. Prune wayward branches by thinning them back to an inward-growing side branch, which will form a new stem that should grow upward and outward toward the light.

SHINGLE CUTS: The illustration at right shows you how to taper an upright shrub so that it remains narrow at the top and wider at the bottom. Use thinning cuts, not shearing. Trimming the upper branches so they are the shortest exposes the lower branches to the sun and helps keep them full and healthy.

With one hand, lift up the branch to be pruned. Holding the pruning shears in the other hand, reach beneath the branch into the shrub. Cut the branch at the point where it meets a side branch or the parent stem. With this "shingle cut" method, overhanging

branches camouflage the cut ends so the shrub maintains its natural appearance.

You can use a similar technique to maintain the natural shingled shape of a spreading needled evergreen. Thinning in this manner maintains shapeliness and promotes dense, compact growth, keeping the plant handsome and in bounds for years to come.

Pruning prostrate junipers

When junipers grown as ground covers reach the edge of the sidewalk or curb, they must be cut back. What often happens is that gardeners whack off the branches that are too long, leaving ugly, bare stems.

Instead of shearing or lopping off the ends of the stems, use hand pruners to thin stems from underneath much like the shingle cut (illustration, lower right). Doing this will give the shrubs a more attractive, natural appearance, and it doesn't promote excessive growth that will soon need trimming again.

Pruning new shrubs

At many nurseries, young needled evergreens are sheared to encourage bushiness or fullness. This increases fullness

on the outside of the plant; however, it doesn't encourage growth of interior branches.

For the first two years after bringing home and planting needled evergreen shrubs, thin them to loosen the tight growth and allow light and air into the interior. By the third year, the shrub should have a normal appearance.

Top: Prune upright yews with thinning cuts hidden beneath overhanging foliage. Taper the shape of the plant from top to bottom.

Bottom: Prune spreading yews with thinning cuts to emphasize the shingled look of the branches.

The Right Tree for the Right Effect

The first chapter explored the permanent structural value of trees in the landscape. But many trees also offer short-term yet spectacular seasonal effects that provide a constantly

Apple serviceberry in brilliant fall color.

changing drama around your home. Some trees drape themselves with beautiful flowers in spring or summer. Others provide attractive fruit in late summer and autumn or burst into flaming foliage colors in fall. Still, others come into their greatest glory after their leaves drop to reveal startling sculptural form and beautiful bark.

Of course, a number of trees offer a colorful show over a long season. Many cultivars selected for brightly colored leaves, such as red-leaved Japanese maple or white-and-pink-variegated dogwood, provide summer-long color as effective as any flowering tree. And a wide

range of evergreens offers colorful foliage all year long.

All-star trees

Selecting trees that provide a showy, changing effect in not just one but two or more seasons is an excellent way to pack the most colorful punch into your landscape and get the most for your money. Such hardworking, multiple-season trees are relatively rare in the horticultural world; we call them "all-stars."

Billows of apple-like white blooms on Allegheny serviceberry announce the early spring, giving way to red-orange autumn foliage and striped gray bark in

MULTISEASON ALL-STARS

Plant Name	Spring	Summer	Fall
Japanese maple (*Acer palmatum*)	Attractive new foliage	Green summer foliage	Strong fall color
Red maple (*Acer rubrum*)	Haze of red flowers	Good shade tree	Strong fall color
Apple serviceberry (*Amelanchier ×grandiflora*)	White flowers	Attractive fruit	Strong fall color
Allegheny serviceberry (*Amelanchier laevis*)	Bronze foliage, white flowers	Attractive fruit	Strong fall color
American yellowwood (*Cladrastis lutea*)	Attractive bark and foliage	Attractive white flowers	Strong fall color
Flowering dogwood (*Cornus florida*)	Spectacular flowers	Good foliage, red berries	Fall color
Kousa dogwood (*Cornus kousa*)	Spectacular flowers	Good foliage, red berries	Fall color
Washington hawthorn (*Crataegus phaenopyrum*)	White flowers	Lustrous green leaves	Fall color
Winter King green hawthorn (*Crataegus viridis* 'Winter King')	White flowers	Lustrous green leaves	Fall color
Crape myrtle (*Lagerstroemia indica*)		Spectacular flowers	Strong fall color
Flowering crabapples (*Malus*)	Covered with flowers	Good foliage	Colorful fruit
Sourwood (*Oxydendrum arboreum*)		White tassel-like flowers	Strong fall color, white fruits
Sargent cherry (*Prunus sargentii*)	Pink flowers	Good foliage	Strong fall color
Japanese flowering cherry (*Prunus serrulata,* Sato-zakura Group)	Attractive flowers	Good foliage	Occasional fall color
Chinese quince (*Pseudocydonia sinensis*)	Pink flowers	Attractive fruit	Strong fall color
Callery pear (*Pyrus calleryana* 'Autumn Blaze', 'Redspire', or 'Chanticleer')	Brilliant white flowers	Good foliage and form	Fall color
Sassafras (*Sassafras albidum*)	Yellow flowers before foliage	Good foliage	Neon fall color
European mountain ash (*Sorbus aucuparia*)		White flowers	Bright, dramatic berries
Korean stewartia (*Stewartia pseudocamellia* 'Korean Beauty')	Camellia-like flowers	Fall color	Outstanding bark

winter. Flowering dogwood is truly a tree for four seasons, with showy spring flowers, shiny red summer fruit, crimson autumn foliage, and fissured, blocky winter bark. Korean stewartia bears flowers like single camellias in midsummer; its foliage turns gold to yellow-orange in autumn, and its multicolored bark peels off in large, spectacular, rounded flakes for interest all winter long.

Use the charts below to develop a landscape with seasonal drama throughout all the seasons of the year.

Apple serviceberry with spring flowers.

Winter

Sculptural winter form	
Good winter structure	
Silvery bark	
Good winter form	
Attractive structure	
Horizontal winter structure	
Good winter structure, bark	
Showy fruit	
Showy fruit and bark	
Showy bark and structure	
Attractive structure	
Good winter structure	
Very attractive bark	
Attractive bark, structure	
Attractive bark	
Distinctive structure	
Good structure	

FLOWERING TIMES OF TREES

Tree	Spr. E	Spr. M	Spr. L	Sum. E	Sum. M	Sum. L	Fall
Red maple (*Acer rubrum*)	■						
Serviceberries (*Amelanchier* spp.)	■						
Bottlebrush (*Callistemon*)		███	███	███	███	███	
Eastern redbud (*Cercis canadensis*)	■						
Sassafras (*Sassafras albidum*)	■						
Empress tree (*Paulownia tomentosa*)		■					
Cherry plum (*Prunus cerasifera*)		■					
Sargent cherry (*Prunus sargentii*)		■					
Japanese flowering cherries (*Prunus serrulata*)			■				
Callery pear (*Pyrus calleryana*)		■					
Flowering dogwood (*Cornus florida*)			■				
Saucer magnolia (*Magnolia ×soulangiana*)			■				
Flowering crabapples (*Malus* spp.)			■				
Carolina silverbell (*Halesia tetraptera*)			■				
Bigleaf magnolia (*Magnolia macrophylla*)			■				
Red horsechestnut (*Aesculus ×carnea* 'Briotii')				■			
Horsechestnut (*Aesculus hippocastanum*)				■			
American yellowwood (*Cladrastis lutea*)				■			
Southern magnolia (*Magnolia grandiflora*)				███	███		
White fringe tree (*Chionanthus virginicus*)				■			
Dove tree (*Davidia involucrata*)				■			
European mountain ash (*Sorbus aucuparia*)				■			
Hawthorns (*Crataegus* spp.)					■		
Goldenchain tree (*Laburnum ×watereri*)				■			
Black locust (*Robinia pseudoacacia*)					■		
Japanese snowbell (*Styrax japonicus*)					■		
Kousa dogwood (*Cornus kousa*)					■		
Japanese tree lilac (*Syringa reticulata*)					■		
Southern catalpa (*Catalpa bignonioides*)						■	
Silk tree or mimosa (*Albizia julibrissin*)						■	
Red-flowering gum (*Eucalyptus ficifolia*)						██	
Japanese stewartia (*Stewartia pseudocamellia*)						██	
Golden rain tree (*Koelreuteria paniculata*)						██	
Crape myrtle (*Lagerstroemia indica*)						██	
Five-stamen tamarisk (*Tamarix ramosissima*)						██	
Sourwood (*Oxydendrum arboreum*)						■	
Chaste tree (*Vitex agnus-castus*)						██	
Japanese pagoda tree (*Sophora japonica*)							■
Franklin tree (*Franklinia alatamaha*)							██

E = Early   M = Midseason   L = Late

Showy Flowers

The flowers of Franklin tree open in late summer.

Flowering dogwood is a woodland tree.

Bell-shaped flowers of Japanese snowbell come in early summer.

Everyone has a special place in his or her heart for flowering trees because of their spectacular blooms. For many trees, peak flowering is late spring and early summer, but some bloom from early spring until autumn. Yoshino cherries, for example, flower briefly; watch quickly, or you'll miss them. Stewartia, on the other hand, remains in bloom for more than a month. A few trees, such as bottlebrush, flower most of the year in mild climates. Choose a tree for its size and shape in addition to its flowers. Plant medium-height trees with wide canopies in front of taller, denser trees or next to buildings. If there is room, plant several to increase the effect of the floral display.

Blooming Makamic crabapple is a traffic stopper in spring.

Showy Fall Foliage

Brilliant autumn foliage lets even those trees that have gone unnoticed in the other seasons claim the spotlight. Some have one characteristic fall color; others display different colors all at once. Try to show them off against a good, dark green background of evergreens. Fall color varies: with the climate and soil, from season to season, and from tree to tree. To keep this variability to a minimum, buy your tree from the nursery in fall when you can see its color. The accompanying list of trees with showy fall color includes a number of trees that are well-known, but you'll find others that may surprise you. Use the list and the gallery section to help you select your own planting of fall show-offs.

Japanese flowering cherries bloom in early April in Washington, D.C.

The flowers of this redbud come in early spring.

OUTSTANDING AUTUMN FOLIAGE

Amur maple (*Acer tataricum ginnala*)
Japanese maple (*Acer palmatum*)
Red maple (*Acer rubrum*)
Sugar maple (*Acer saccharum*)
Apple serviceberry (*Amelanchier ×grandiflora*)
Allegheny serviceberry (*Amelanchier laevis*)
Pawpaw (*Asimina triloba*)
Paper birch (*Betula papyrifera*)
Katsura tree (*Cercidiphyllum japonicum*)
Flowering dogwood (*Cornus florida*)
Kousa dogwood (*Cornus kousa*)
Cockspur hawthorn (*Crataegus crus-galli*)
Persimmon (*Diospyros* spp.)
American beech (*Fagus grandifolia*)
Franklin tree (*Franklinia alatamaha*)
White ash (*Fraxinus americana*)
Green ash (*Fraxinus pennsylvanica*)
Ginkgo (*Ginkgo biloba*)
Crape myrtle (*Lagerstroemia indica*)
Sweet gum (*Liquidambar styraciflua*)
Tulip tree (*Liriodendron tulipifera*)

Black gum or tupelo (*Nyssa sylvatica*)
Sourwood (*Oxydendrum arboreum*)
Chinese pistachio (*Pistacia chinensis*)
Quaking aspen (*Populus tremuloides*)
Sargent cherry (*Prunus sargentii*)
Flowering cherry (*Prunus serrulata*)
Chinese quince (*Pseudocydonia sinensis*)
Golden larch (*Pseudolarix amabilis*)
Callery pear (*Pyrus calleryana*)
White oak (*Quercus alba*)
Scarlet oak (*Quercus coccinea*)
Chinese tallow tree (*Sapium sebiferum*)
Sassafras (*Sassafras albidum*)
Japanese stewartia (*Stewartia pseudocamellia*)
Bald cypress (*Taxodium distichum*)
Littleleaf linden (*Tilia cordata*)
Elms (*Ulmus* spp.)
Japanese zelkova (*Zelkova serrata*)

The Goldenchain tree enchants.

Late-Season Display

Colorful fruit

Fruit-bearing trees often keep their fruit longer than their flowers. Some are also "for the birds" and will help animate your garden with these feathered friends seeking a source of food. Some fruit trees, such as serviceberry and cherry, ripen by early or midsummer and become food for early birds. Others ripen in late summer, such as the flowering dogwood. The fruit of American holly and Washington hawthorn is not palatable until late winter (and waits for the birds of spring). Meanwhile, the fruit adds a touch of color to the fall and winter landscape.

Dolgo crabapple makes excellent preserves.

European mountain ash berries are showy.

English holly enlivens the winter landscape.

TREES WITH SHOWY FRUIT

Amur maple *(Acer tataricum ginnala)*
Japanese persimmon *(Diospyros kaki)*
Flowering dogwood *(Cornus florida)*
Kousa dogwood *(Cornus kousa)*
Washington hawthorn *(Crataegus phaenopyrum)*
Winter King green hawthorn *(Crataegus viridis* 'Winter King')
American holly *(Ilex opaca)*
Golden rain tree *(Koelreuteria paniculata)*
Magnolias *(Magnolia* spp.)
Flowering crabapples *(Malus* spp.)
Black gum *(Nyssa sylvatica)*
Sourwood *(Oxydendrum arboreum)*
Chinese quince *(Pseudocydonia sinensis)*
Pepper tree *(Schinus molle)*
European mountain ash *(Sorbus aucuparia)*

WINTER STRUCTURE

Winter is the time when the structure of trees comes into its own. No longer shrouded in a mantle of foliage or adorned with berries and flowers, the arching or upright limbs and branches are now what we see first. For certain trees, it's this framework that is their most outstanding feature, and it shows only after the leaves have fallen. Then sculptural trees truly dominate the winter garden. Highlight, for example, the intricate weeping habit of a cutleaf Japanese maple or the twisting branches of a contorted Hankow willow by planting one near the front walk. Visitors will never fail to comment, winter or summer, about this unusual and unique tree.

Many other weeping trees are sculptural, but those with spreading branches are also outstanding in winter. They may take a while to reach their peak but are well worth the wait.

The bark of Paperbark cherry has a copper hue.

Mottled bark of London plane tree.

Distinctive bark

When was the last time you thought of a tree in terms of its bark? It's the most often-overlooked feature of a tree, but in some it's an outstanding asset. And it can add to the look of the tree year-round. Bark character, in fact, is the most interesting aspect of the paperbark maple, paper birch, and Amur chokecherry. It's an interest that is present all the time but more noticeable when the tree is without its leaves. There are evergreens, too, such as false cypress and coast redwood, with striking bark. In these trees, the bark adds to the appeal of the tree and year-round interest.

Lacebark pine is named for its colorful flaking bark.

Himalayan birch has attractive white bark.

Evergreens

BROADLEAF EVERGREEN TREES

Lemon bottlebrush *(Callistemon citrinus)*
Camphor tree *(Cinnamomum camphora)*
Loquat *(Eriobotrya japonica)*
Eucalyptus or gum *(Eucalyptus spp.)*
American holly *(Ilex opaca)*
Southern magnolia *(Magnolia grandiflora)*
Olive *(Olea europaea)*
Cherry laurel *(Prunus laurocerasus)*
Coast live oak *(Quercus agrifolia)*
Pepper tree *(Schinus molle)*

Looking for a permanent fixture in your landscape? Consider evergreen trees; their year-round interest can unify your garden through the seasons. Also, in winter they contrast with the stark outlines of deciduous trees and thus take on a whole different look. Within this class of plants are needled and broadleaf evergreens; they vary both in the conditions they prefer and in their landscape uses.

NEEDLED EVERGREENS: Needled evergreens are called conifers because they bear cones. Most are pyramidal or conical, at least while young, and prefer full sun. Some, however, benefit from light shade, and a few, such as hemlocks and yews, tolerate considerable shade. Most need little or no pruning if you give them growing space.

DECIDUOUS CONIFERS

European larch *(Larix decidua)*
Japanese larch *(Larix kaempferi)*
Dawn redwood *(Metasequoia glyptostroboides)*
Golden larch *(Pseudolarix amabilis)*
Bald cypress *(Taxodium distichum)*

This American arborvitae planting makes an effective year-round screen.

Slower-growing conifers will save you time and effort (and space in small places).

BROADLEAF EVERGREENS: Broadleaf evergreens have leaves that overwinter. They lose their leaves but, unlike deciduous trees, only after a new set has appeared. Most prefer mild climates, and few will survive northern winters. Some offer bright red berries in winter, such as American and English hollies; others have huge, waxy white flowers in spring and summer, such as southern magnolia.

DECIDUOUS CONIFERS: Not all conifers hold their leaves in winter. A few, such as bald cypress and larch, lose their leaves in fall. They offer an interesting combination of leaves, cones, and tree shapes, similar to needled evergreens, with fall foliage color before they drop their leaves. And because they do lose their leaves, in winter they bring unique silhouettes and trunk and branch shapes to the garden. They usually don't color as dramatically as deciduous trees but instead offer a more muted color palette with which to experiment.

Evergreen pine trees are matched here with flowering dogwoods and azaleas.

ODD-SHAPED EVERGREENS: Evergreens may be constant in their color, but they are not so in their shape. They come as tall pyramids and dwarf cones, and in conical, weeping, columnar, and open forms. One columnar Skyrocket juniper will punctuate a flower bed; two can bring formality to an entryway. The Tanyosho pine, wide and spreading over its trunks, almost qualifies as a sculpture in the garden.

EVERGREENS WITH COLORFUL FOLIAGE

Colorful evergreen foliage brightens your garden. Blue-toned conifers, such as blue Atlas cedar or Hoops blue spruce, mix well with other evergreens or bright flower colors. Yellow-tinged trees, such as golden false cypress, work well as a focal point, or as a contrast with duller colors, such as gray or maroon red.

NEEDLED EVERGREEN TREES

Firs *(Abies* spp.)
False cypresses *(Chamaecyparis* spp.)
Japanese cedar *(Cryptomeria japonica)*
Leyland cypress *(×Cupressocyparis leylandii)*
Monterey cypress *(Cupressus macrocarpa)*
Italian cypress *(Cupressus sempervirens)*
Spruces *(Picea* spp.)
Pines *(Pinus* spp.)
Yew pine *(Podocarpus macrophyllus)*
Japanese umbrella pine *(Sciadopitys verticillata)*
Coast redwood *(Sequoia sempervirens)*
Giant sequoia *(Sequoiadendron giganteum)*
American arborvitae *(Thuja occidentalis)*
Canadian hemlock *(Tsuga canadensis)*

Abies concolor
AY-bees CON-kah-lar

- Graceful evergreen, silver-blue needles
- Pyramidal growth habit
- Dense, fine-textured foliage
- Growth rate: slow to medium, 6 to 9 inches per year
- Zones 4 to 8

Blue noble fir (*Abies procera* 'Glauca').

Nordmann fir is one of best firs for warmer climates.

WHITE FIR

15'

10'

Few trees exhibit the style, grace, and striking foliage of the white fir. Native to the western mountain states, it also grows well in the midwest and east. It can grow up to 100 feet tall with age.

USES: Use it as a screening plant, as the tallest step in a layered design, or in groups. Its foliage, color, and texture create a pleasing contrast with the greens of deciduous trees and shrubs.

SITING AND CARE: Plant in full sun on well-drained or sloping terrain; it does not tolerate wet soils. At the south edge of its range, keep the soil evenly moist. Inspect periodically for spider mites. Prune only diseased or broken branches.

RECOMMENDED VARIETIES: 'Candicans' is a narrow, upright tree with large, bright silver-blue needles. 'Compacta' is a dwarf tree with bright blue needles.

RELATED SPECIES: Balsam fir (*Abies balsamea*, Zones 3 to 6). Native to Canada and the Great Lakes states, balsam fir is a valuable specimen tree, dark green with a silver overtone. Its narrow, upright form offers a strong vertical element and is ideal as a living Christmas tree (although it does not hold its needles as long as other firs). Balsam fir is adapted to cold climates, tolerates light shade, and prefers well-drained, moist, acidic soils. It is susceptible to several pests, including canker diseases, spruce budworm, and spruce wooly aphid.

A. lasiocarpa (Rocky Mountain fir, Zones 3 to 7). Native from Alaska to New Mexico. The subspecies *A. l.* ssp. *arizonica* is slow growing, with silvery blue-green foliage. The cultivar 'Compacta' is dwarf, making a striking specimen in the midwest and east, but the northern species type does not do as well in the east.

Verkade's Prostrata dwarf balsam fir.

Nordmann fir (*A. nordmanniana*, Zones 5 to 8). Native to Asia Minor and the Mediterranean region, this fir is handsome and stately, with shiny, dark green needles with silvery undersides. Useful as a screen or windbreak, it is relatively heat-tolerant.

Noble fir (*Abies procera*, Zones 5 and 6). Native to the Pacific Northwest. Its pyramidal shape and narrow form produce a striking accent in the landscape. Noble fir grows best in cool, moist areas and in well-drained soil; it grows at a slow-to-medium rate. Its growth rate is a bit slower outside its native area. 'Glauca' has interesting light blue foliage with a silvery cast.

White fir is noted for its silvery-blue foliage and conical shape.

AMUR MAPLE

Acer tataricum ginnala
AY-sir ta-TARE--ee-come ginn-ALL-uh

- Brilliant red fall color
- Bright red summer samaras (fruit)
- Graceful, small habit
- Growth rate: medium, 10 to 12 inches per year
- Zones 3 to 8

10'
8'

A sturdy tree for the small front yard, Amur maple is native to China and Japan. It will eventually grow to 20 feet tall and wide.

USES: Ideal for patio gardens, courtyards, and containers, Amur maple adds texture and year-round interest to any small landscape.

SITING AND CARE: Tolerant of dry and alkaline soils. Allow clump to grow naturally; remove only aberrant growth.

RECOMMENDED VARIETIES: 'Flame' grows as a dense, small tree or large shrub and has red fruits and red fall color.

Amur maple in summer (above) and fall.

PAPERBARK MAPLE

Acer griseum
AY-sir GRIH-zee-um

- Naturally peeling, reddish-brown bark
- Spectacular red fall color, especially in the east
- Rounded, open habit
- Growth rate: slow, 4 to 6 inches per year
- Zones 5 to 7

10'
5'

A good-looking specimen tree. Its slow growth, rounded shape, and moderate size make it ideal for small landscapes. Native to western and

central China. Will reach 20 to 30 feet tall and wide.

USES: A fine front-yard tree for the residential landscape, paperbark maple offers year-round interest: dark green leaves turning an impressive red (in most areas) in fall, and a distinctive curling, exfoliating cinnamon-brown bark. It has enough impact to be used in island plantings or as a centerpiece surrounded by large shrubs.

SITING AND CARE: Grows best in full sun but tolerates light shade. Mulch under tree to help reduce grass competition.

RELATED SPECIES: The closely related three flower maple (*A. triflorum*) also has interesting curling bark but is less spectacular than paperback maple. It is somewhat faster growing and gaining in popularity in Zones 5 to 7.

Peeling bark of paperbark maple.

BOX ELDER

Acer negundo
AY-sir neb-GUN-do

- Horizontal oval shape
- A tough tree for rough climates
- Growth rate: fast, up to 2 feet per year
- Zones 2 to 9

25'
25'

Although it can be messy, weedy, and short-lived, box elder thrives in the Canadian plains, the Dakotas, western Nebraska, and eastern Colorado, where other choices can

be limited. And it is a fast grower as well. Native to Canada and the eastern United States. It can reach 65 feet tall.

USES: Useful as a temporary tree until more slow-growing trees are established. It is also a good choice for a windbreak in cold climates.

SITING AND CARE: Adaptable to light or medium shade; often found near creek banks. Box elder requires no special care and will grow on most sites.

RECOMMENDED VARIETIES: 'Flamingo' has showy, variegated

pink-and-green leaves with white borders. 'Variegatum' has variegated green-and-white leaves.

Box elder (*Acer negundo* 'Flamingo').

Acer palmatum
AY-sir pall-MAY-tum

Japanese maple in fall leaf color.

Deeply dissected foliage of the cutleaf form of Japanese maple.

JAPANESE MAPLE

- Blazing fall foliage
- Elegant, sculptural, spreading form
- Medium-fine texture
- Growth rate: slow, averaging 4 to 6 inches per year
- Zones 5 to 8, depending on cultivar

10'
10'

Although a must for the Japanese-style garden, this gorgeous tree adds appeal to any landscape. Native to Japan, China, and Korea. Can grow to 25 feet tall and as wide with age.

USES: Japanese maple offers striking color, form, and texture and is ideal as an accent or in groupings and shrub borders.

SITING AND CARE: Grows best in morning sun, filtered shade in the afternoon, and cool, moist, mulched soil. Prune only to retain natural shape.

RECOMMENDED VARIETIES: Cultivars are numerous. 'Atropurpureum' and 'Bloodgood' have deep reddish-purple leaves, red flowers, and fruit. 'Sango Kaku' has coral-colored stems and yellow leaves in fall. The dissectum types (cutleaf Japanese maples) have many threadlike leaves.

Bark and foliage of Japanese maple (*Acer palmatum* 'Sango Kaku').

Acer platanoides
AY-sir plat-uh-NOY-deez

Norway maple (*Acer platanoides* 'Crimson King').

NORWAY MAPLE

- Yellow fall color
- Large, thick leaves cast dense shade
- Grows fast, spreads via plentiful seeds
- Attractive ridged bark
- Growth rate: medium, 10 to 15 inches per year
- Zones 3 to 7

20'

15'

This maple offers deep green foliage and is native to Europe, from Norway to Switzerland. Can grow to 40 feet tall and 65 feet wide.

USES: Produces a beautiful upright, oval shape and dense shade. Good street tree. Fast-growing, aggressive, and potentially invasive.

SITING AND CARE: Spreads out to 30 feet or more, so give it plenty of room. Protect the bark from sunscald, and prune only to retain its natural shape.

RECOMMENDED VARIETIES: 'Emerald Queen' has upright branches, dark green leaves, and an oval-to-round growth habit. 'Cleveland' has deep green leaves in summer, yellow in fall, and an upright, oval habit. 'Summershade' is a rapid grower with an upright habit. 'Crimson King' and 'Royal Red' have very dark red foliage all summer. 'Crimson Sentry' is similar to 'Crimson King' but much narrower. 'Deborah' and 'Fairview' have dark red foliage in early summer, fading to green by fall.

Norway maple in brilliant fall color.

Acer rubrum
AY-sir ROO-brum

- Outstanding red color in fall
- Upright, rounded growth habit
- Growth rate: medium to fast, 12 to 15 inches per year
- Zones 3 to 9

20'
12'

A good shade tree with excellent fall color, red maple is native to the East Coast, from the Deep South north to New England. Grows to 50 feet tall and 40 feet wide.

RED MAPLE

USES: Red maple is a fine shade tree. Locate it near the southwest corner of a home for shade or in the back for framing views from indoors. **SITING AND CARE:** Plant in sun in rich, well-drained soil. Prune only to retain its natural shape. **RECOMMENDED VARIETIES AND RELATED SPECIES:** Freeman maple (*Acer ×fremanii*), a hybrid of silver and red maples, grows faster than red maple, slower than silver maple, and has gray bark and red fall color. 'Jeffersred' (trademarked as Autumn Blaze) has a broad, oval crown and orange-red fall color. 'Indian Summer' has an oval-to-rounded crown with red fall color; it is a vigorous grower but is not heat-resistant.

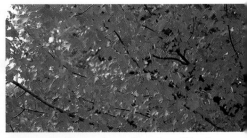

Red maple (*Acer rubrum* 'October Glory').

Acer saccharinum
AY-sir sack-uh-RYE-num

- Good for rapid effect
- Beware of greedy surface roots and weak wood
- Prolific seed producer
- Growth rate: fast, 12 to 20 inches per year
- Zones 3 to 9

30'
15'

A tree for wide open spaces, such as parks and acreages. Native to the eastern half of the United States. Grows to 100 feet tall and 70 feet wide.

SILVER MAPLE

USES: Silver maple offers fast growth and shade for home lawn landscapes. It is best used in open areas but not close to power lines, drainage or septic lines, and sidewalks. **SITING AND CARE:** Grows best in cool, moist, well-drained soils but will tolerate a wide variety of soil conditions. **RECOMMENDED VARIETIES:** 'Silver Queen' has an upright, oval form and bears few seeds. 'Blarii' grows with stronger branch angles than the species type. 'Skinneri' (Skinner's cutleaf) has deeply cut leaves and a stronger framework than most silver maples.

Silver maple becomes a large tree.

Acer saccharum
AY-sir sah-KAIR-um

- Brilliant yellow, orange, or red fall color
- Superb shade tree
- Upright-to-oval growth habit
- Growth rate: medium, 10 to 15 inches per year
- Zones 4 to 7

80'
60'

A stately, elegant tree, sugar maple is native from eastern Canada to the Great Lakes and south to Georgia.

SUGAR MAPLE

USES: Fiery fall color and shade make it an outstanding choice for large backyards and open areas. **SITING AND CARE:** Not tolerant of compacted soils or of small or restricted root zones. Mulch young trees to help keep the roots cool and moist. **RECOMMENDED VARIETIES:** 'Green Mountain' has thick, deep green leaves. 'Bonfire' is vigorous with an oval habit. 'Green Column' has an upright, columnar shape and yellow-orange fall color. 'Legacy' is drought-resistant and has thick, heavy leaves.

Red maple is noted for its fall color and for maple syrup.

RED HORSECHESTNUT

Aesculus ×carnea
ESS-kuh-luss car-NEE-uh

Red horsechestnut (**Aesculus × carnea** 'Briotii') blooms in spring.

- Bright red flowers in early summer
- Stately, rounded growth habit
- Deep green foliage
- Growth rate: medium, 10 to 12 inches per year
- Zones 4 to 8

20'
15'

This is a hybrid between Common horsechestnut (*Aesculus hippocastanum*) and the red buckeye (*A. pavia);* a small tree from the south-central United States. Grows to 40 feet tall and 30 feet wide.

USES: Good for large yards, red horsechestnut is an excellent accent in open areas. Its deep green foliage contrasts nicely with lighter shrubs and dwarf evergreens.

SITING AND CARE: Grows best in deep, rich, moist soils.

RECOMMENDED VARIETIES AND RELATED SPECIES: 'Briotii' has 10-inch red flowers and dark green leaves; tolerates urban conditions. This is the most widely available cultivar of red horsechestnut. Red buckeye (*A. pavia*) grows to only 20 to 25 feet tall, with tubular deep red flowers in early summer.

OHIO BUCKEYE

Aesculus glabra
ESS-kuh-luss GLAY-bra

Ohio buckeye foliage and fruit.

- Yellowish-white flowers in early summer
- Medium-sized, spreading growth habit
- Growth rate: medium, 10 to 12 inches per year
- Zones 3 to 7

20'
15'

Its 2-inch, warty, beige fruit adds color, texture, and interest. Native to the Ohio River valley. It can reach 40 feet tall by 30 feet wide.

USES: This buckeye offers an attractive rounded growth habit and shade but is not a tree for limited spaces. Give it a large, open area for proper root development.

SITING AND CARE: Does not tolerate extreme drought. Keep roots cool and moist with mulch. Inspect for spider mites and leaf scorch on dry sites.

RELATED SPECIES: Yellow or sweet buckeye (*A. flava*) is a larger version of Ohio buckeye, about the same size as common horsechestnut. It is used mostly from the Central Plains to Georgia, where it makes a fine large shade tree more trouble-free than common horsechestnut.

COMMON HORSECHESTNUT

Aesculus hippocastanum
ESS-kuh-luss hih-poh-CASS-tuh-num

Common horsechestnut is a large shade tree with showy blooms.

- Pyramidal, rounded growth habit and great size at maturity
- Leaves compound and 5 to 9 inches long
- Growth rate: medium, 7 to 10 inches per year
- Zones 4 to 7

20'
15'

This sizable tree has large leaves and white flowers in early summer and is native to the mountains of Greece and Albania. Grows 55 to 70 feet tall, with a similar spread.

USES: Common horsechestnut is a good tree for large areas and adds color, texture, and interest to acreages, estates, and larger backyards. It is not for the small residential landscape.

SITING AND CARE: Locate it in full sun or light shade. Avoid dry conditions. Horsechestnut is often badly disfigured by a leaf-blotch disease in addition to leaf scorch from drought.

RECOMMENDED VARIETIES: 'Baumannii' has long-lasting, showy flowers but does not bear fruit.

SILK TREE OR MIMOSA

Albizia julibrissin
awl-BIH-zee-uh ju-lib-BRISS-in

- Brushlike pink flowers in summer
- Wide-spreading, umbrella-like canopy
- Ferny, fine-textured foliage lends tropical effect
- Growth rate: medium to fast, 8 to 12 inches per year
- Zones 6 to 9

25'
35'

With exotic flowers and ferny foliage, silk tree offers a distinct tropical feel. Native to Asia, from Iran to China. Can grow to 40 feet tall.

USES: In mass plantings or on hillsides away from residential settings. Its fairly fast growth produces a rapid tropical effect. Susceptibility to vascular wilt limits its usefulness.

SITING AND CARE: Best looking if allowed to develop natural multitrunked form. When disease or winterkill strikes, prune severely to produce regrowth. Keep it away from sidewalks or patios, where it might cause a serious litter problem.

Feathery foliage and flowers of Silk tree.

EUROPEAN BLACK ALDER

Alnus glutinosa
AWL-nuss gloo-tih-NOH-suh

- Glossy dark green leaves in summer
- Upright-to-slightly-pyramidal habit
- Tolerant of wet soils
- Growth rate: fast when young, slows to a moderate 12 to 15 inches per year
- Zones 4 to 8

30'
15'

Alder is an ideal medium-to-large tree for low wet spots in the landscape (where most other trees fail) and is native to most areas of Europe. Reaches 40 to 60 feet tall and 20 to 40 feet wide.

USES: A good choice for landscapes with streams, alder can also be grown as an understory tree. It is frequently found naturalized along waterways and does quite well in residential lawns if properly sited. It is considered one of the best trees for a wet site.

SITING AND CARE: Avoid planting near sidewalks and sewer lines. Grow in full sun to full shade. Mildew and leaf rust can be problems in rainy seasons.

RECOMMENDED VARIETIES: 'Aurea' has golden yellow leaves. 'Imperialis' has deeply cut lobes on light green leaves; 'Pyramidalis' displays a pyramidal-to-upright form. Cultivars can be hard to find; usually sold only as the species.

European black alder.

APPLE SERVICEBERRY

Amelanchier ×grandiflora
ah-mih-LAN-kee-er grand-i-FLOR-a

- White flowers emerge in spring before leaves
- Red to purple fruit, attractive to birds
- Elegant, small tree or large shrub
- Growth rate: medium, 10 to 15 inches per year
- Zones 3 to 8

35'
30'

Growing well in most of the east or midwest, apple serviceberry is a versatile tree for the landscape and is loved by birds.

USES: Incorporate apple serviceberry into front-yard landscape beds or islands, courtyards, and patios or in windbreaks for wildlife. Its flowers, fruit, and silvery gray bark contrast well with nearby perennials and ground covers.

SITING AND CARE: Prefers well-drained, moist soils.

RECOMMENDED VARIETIES AND RELATED SPECIES: Of many named varieties, 'Autumn Brilliance' has orange to red fall leaf color and abundant fruit. Allegheny serviceberry (*Amelanchier laevis*) is a large shrub with bronze emerging foliage; its fruit is sweet, purple, and favored by birds.

Apple serviceberry produces edible fruits in early summer.

PAWPAW

Asimina triloba
ay-SIM-ih-nuh trye-LOH-buh

Flower of Pawpaw (*Asimina triloba*).

- Good yellow fall foliage
- Large, tropical-looking leaves
- Small, multitrunked tree or large shrub
- Produces delicious fruit with the flavor of banana custard
- Tolerant of shade
- Growth rate: medium, 8 to 12 inches per year
- Zones 5 to 8

15' / 8'

Pawpaw is loved by gardeners and wildlife alike. It is native to the east, from New York to Florida, but will grow west to Missouri. Older trees can reach 30 feet tall and 20 feet wide.

USES: Allow it to grow in masses for wildlife and conservation value and to promote diversity in the landscape. This tree favors moist woodland sites but is also adaptable to semishade, woodland, or understory conditions.

SITING AND CARE: Locate it in loose, fertile, woodland soil and grow it without shaping to allow it to form large thickets, or prune it carefully to train it as a pyramidal tree with a single trunk.

RIVER BIRCH

Betula nigra
BET-yoo-luh NYE-gruh

Heritage river birch (*Betula nigra* 'Cully').

- Peeling, cinnamon-brown bark
- Pyramidal-to-oval growth habit
- Growth rate: medium to fast, 15 to 20 inches per year
- Zones 4 to 9

30' / 20'

A versatile, large tree, this birch fits in most landscapes. It is a midwest native, growing from Minnesota and Kansas east to New England. It can reach 50 to 70 feet tall.

USES: Its uses are multitudinous: as a shade tree, in large landscape beds, or massed alongside stream banks. Resistance to bronze birch borer is a real plus.

SITING AND CARE: Grows best in acid, moist soils and adapts to full sun or partial shade. Keep roots cool with a ground cover. Prune only low-hanging branches.

RECOMMENDED VARIETIES AND RELATED SPECIES: 'Cully' (trademarked as Heritage) bark ages pink and brown. Cherry birch (*Betula lenta,* Zones 4 to 7) is native to Appalachia. It has beautiful yellow fall foliage color and lustrous reddish-brown bark similar to cherry.

EUROPEAN WHITE BIRCH

Betula pendula
BET-yoo-luh PEN-dyoo-luh

Weeping European white birch makes a graceful tree.

- Outstanding white bark, dashes of black
- Yellow fall foliage
- Upright, pyramidal form

- Growth rate: medium to fast, 12 to 15 inches per year
- Zones 3 to 6

25' / 12'

Superb for rapid-effect groves in cool-summer areas. Native to Europe and northern Asia. Occasionally reaches 60 feet tall.

USES: Soften a corner of the yard, or use it as a screen or background. Bark color and branch texture make it an excellent medium-sized tree.

SITING AND CARE: Needs moist but well-drained soil. Grow ground cover to keep roots cool. Tolerates light shade. Drought and heat stress invite birch borer.

RECOMMENDED VARIETIES AND RELATED SPECIES: Cutleaved, columnar, and weeping cultivars are available. Paper birch (*Betula papyrifera*) exhibits delightful stark white bark, and its dark green leaves turn yellow in fall. Subject to heat stress and borers in hot climates but slightly less than European white birch (*B. platyphylla* 'Whitespire', Zones 4 and 5), it is resistant to borers; good for the midwest.

LEMON BOTTLEBRUSH

Callistemon citrinus
kal-ih-STEE-mon sih-TRY-nuss

- Bright red bottlebrush flowers nearly all year in mild climates
- Upright in habit; rounded crown shape
- Stems and leaves produce citrus odor when bruised
- Growth rate: fast, 10 to 15 inches per year
- Zones 9 and 10

Tolerant of southern heat and drought, and a favorite in California. With age, it reaches 20 to 25 feet.

USES: Excellent as a specimen, hedge, or screen. Makes an interesting espalier. In northern climates, grow it in large containers, and bring it indoors for the winter.
SITING AND CARE: Best in moist, well-drained soils in full sun. Tolerant of many soil types and extreme temperatures.
RECOMMENDED VARIETIES: 'Splendens' has glossy, bright red flowers that are larger than those of the species.

Flowers of Lemon bottlebrush resemble brush bristles.

EUROPEAN HORNBEAM

Carpinus betulus
car-PYE-nuss BET-yoo-luss

- Regular, oval habit good for formal effects
- Growth rate: slow to medium, 10 to 12 inches per year
- Zones 5 to 7

This medium-sized tree does well in a wide range of conditions. Native to Europe and Asia Minor. Reaches 40 feet at maturity.
USES: European hornbeam is suitable in urban landscapes, for screens, for street plantings, and in residential lawns.
SITING AND CARE: Grows best in full sun but tolerates light shade.
RECOMMENDED VARIETIES AND RELATED SPECIES: 'Fastigiata' grows in an upright form, 35 to 45 feet tall. 'Globosa' is rounded and has dense foliage. American hornbeam (*Carpinus caroliniana,* Zones 3 to 9) is a small-to-medium upright tree with dark green foliage that turns yellow to orange and scarlet in fall, and twisted, muscular trunks and branches effective in winter. Its size lends itself to smaller landscapes.

European hornbeam (*Carpinus betulus* 'Fastigiata').

SHAGBARK HICKORY

Carya ovata
CARE-ee-uh oh-VAY-tah

- Large, stately tree with wide, spreading habit
- Grown for edible nuts or as a shade tree in parklike settings
- Growth rate: slow to moderate, usually 10 to 12 inches per year
- Zones 4 to 9

Grown mainly for its exfoliating gray bark and striking golden fall color, shagbark hickory can be used in the landscape or other open areas. Its open, upright habit allows turf growth underneath the wide-spreading branches, but it drops much nut, leaf, and twig litter creating a hazard when mowing the lawn. Will grow to 80 feet tall and 30-40 feet wide.
USES: Hickory is a good tree for parks and large residential lots, not for smaller lots. Expect squirrels.
SITING AND CARE: Requires a large, open space. Prune to maintain central leader. Insects and diseases are seldom serious problems except for inhibiting nut production.

Peeling bark of Shagbark Hickory.

SOUTHERN CATALPA

Catalpa bignonioides
kuh-TALL-puh big-noh-nee-OY-deez

Southern catalpa (*Catalpa bignonioides* 'Aurea').

- White flowers cover the tree canopy in early summer
- Fast-growing tree with bold texture
- Long, narrow seedpods are a litter problem
- Growth rate: fast, 12 to 15 inches per year
- Zones 5 to 9

15'

15'

Southern catalpa is a medium-sized tree often associated with old-fashioned landscapes. It is native to the south-central United States. With age, it can reach 40 feet tall and wide.

USES: Can be used for fast shade in open spaces. Not well suited to the front-yard residential landscape; best in background settings.

SITING AND CARE: This tough tree requires little care and adapts well to a wide range of sites.

RECOMMENDED VARIETIES AND RELATED SPECIES: 'Aurea' has rich yellow leaves. 'Nana' has a dwarf, bushy form that is usually grafted on a standard rootstock. These can be hard to find. Northern catalpa (*C. speciosa*, Zones 4 to 8) flowers two weeks earlier than *C. bignonioides*.

ATLAS CEDAR

Cedrus libani atlantica
SEE-druss at-LAN-tee-ca

Weeping Atlas cedar (*Cedrus libani atlantica* 'Glauca Pendula').

- Blue-green needles
- Conical when young; large, flat-topped, and picturesque with age
- Growth rate: moderately slow, 10 to 12 inches a year, slowing with age
- Zones 6 to 9

20'

10'

Resistant to drought and requiring little maintenance, Atlas cedar is native to the Atlas Mountains of Morocco and Algeria. With age, a mature specimen can reach 60 feet tall and 40 feet wide.

USES: Place this specimen tree in the landscape where it can shine, with complementary-colored shrubs planted nearby, keeping in mind the ultimate size of the tree.

SITING AND CARE: Prefers full sun but can grow in partial shade.

RECOMMENDED VARIETIES AND RELATED SPECIES: 'Glauca' has bright blue needles, similar to those of Colorado blue spruce clones. This is the cultivar usually seen in landscapes. Cedar of Lebanon (*C. libani*) with dark green foliage is also a fine accent tree. Hardiest cultivars are useful in warmer areas of Zone 5.

COMMON HACKBERRY

Celtis occidentalis
SELL-tiss ock-sih-den-TAL-iss

Rough bark protects the trunk of Common hackberry.

- Rough, tough tree for difficult places
- Upright, round shape
- Branches tend to droop with an arching habit
- Growth rate: medium to fast, 12 to 15 inches per year
- Zones 4 to 8

25'

20'

Although it is a bit coarse and rough-looking, hackberry will grow in dry and windy sites in the plains and prairie states and is a substitute for American elm in those areas. Grows to 80 to 100 feet on a good site with fertile soil.

USES: Makes a good shade or street tree in residential settings if not sited too close to the house.

SITING AND CARE: Grows in moderately wet or dry soils and requires little care. Hackberry nipplegall is a harmless insect that inhabits the leaves.

RECOMMENDED VARIETIES: 'Prairie Pride' has leathery foliage and is upright and fast-growing.

Cercidiphyllum japonicum
sir-sih-dih-FYE-lum juh-PAW-nih-kum

- Emerging reddish foliage changes to soft blue-green
- Some trees develop pinkish to red autumn foliage
- Graceful, spreading growth habit; single or multiple trunks
- Growth rate: medium, 12 to 14 inches per year
- Zones 5 to 8

With many fine attributes if properly sited, this tree has interesting, heart-shaped leaves and a moderate

KATSURA TREE

growth rate. Graceful and stately, Katsura tree is native to Japan and China. Grows to 60 feet tall and sometimes wider.

USES: This is a medium-to-large tree, full and dense even when young, and a good choice for creating dappled shade.

SITING AND CARE: Best in full sun to part shade and moist, well-drained soil. Provide additional moisture during periods of drought.

RECOMMENDED VARIETIES: *C. magnificum* 'Pendulum' is a weeping form whose height can vary from 20 to 50 feet.

Bluish-green leaves of Katsura tree turn red and yellow in fall.

Cercis canadensis
SIR-siss can-uh-DEN-siss

- Pink-purple flowers open in spring before the heart-shaped leaves emerge
- Zigzag branch pattern in winter
- Growth rate: medium, 6 to 10 inches per year
- Zones 5 to 9

This is a versatile, small tree that provides interest throughout most of the year. It is native to the eastern and central United States. It can grow 25 to 35 feet tall and wide.

EASTERN REDBUD

USES: This is an excellent front-yard tree to accent shrub borders, soften harsh corners, or use as an understory tree near larger, established shade trees.

SITING AND CARE: Tolerates shade, but best with some sun. Protect trunk and bark from damage, which can lead to cankers.

RECOMMENDED VARIETIES: 'Forest Pansy' is a purple-leaved cultivar that needs shade in warmer climates. 'Alba' and 'Royal White' have white flowers. 'Flame' has semidouble purple-pink flowers. 'Pinkbud' and 'Wither's Pink Charm' have clear pink flowers.

Flowers of Eastern redbud emerge along branches.

Chamaecyparis lawsoniana
kam-uh-SIP-uh-ris law-so-nee-AY-nuh

- Pyramidal shape, graceful appearance
- Evergreen screen
- Growth rate: slow, 6 to 10 inches a year
- Zones 6 to 8

An outstanding tree in the Pacific Northwest. Native to southern Oregon and northern California. Matures to 50 feet tall.

USES: Excellent as a specimen or for

LAWSON FALSE CYPRESS

screening, it has lacy foliage and fibrous red-brown bark.

SITING AND CARE: Best in well-drained, moist soils with wind protection, in light shade or in sun.

RECOMMENDED VARIETIES: Cultivars are numerous. 'Alumii' has blue-green foliage and grows more rapidly than the species. 'Ellwoodii', a dwarf plant, grows slowly to 8 feet. 'Garden King' is columnar, 40 to 50 feet tall, with pendulous branch tips and golden foliage that turns bronze in winter. 'Oregon Blue' has blue foliage and grows to 50 feet

tall. 'Silver Queen' is conical, to 30 feet tall, with variegated foliage.

Flowers at leaf tips of Lawson false cypress make striking color contrast.

Chionanthus virginicus
kee-oh-NAN-thuss ver-JIN-uh-kuss

Flowers of White fringe tree are fragrant.

WHITE FRINGE TREE

- Clouds of threadlike fragrant white flowers in late spring
- Light green foliage
- Large, multistemmed shrub or small tree
- Growth rate: slow, 6 to 10 inches per year
- Zones 5 to 9

An excellent plant for use near buildings and in masses, white fringe tree is native to the southeast. It reaches 20 to 30 feet tall and as wide or wider. Female plants bear blue-black fruit in late summer and fall. Foliage turns clear yellow in autumn in some years.

USES: Ideal for a patio garden, courtyard, shrub border, and in a variety of locations in the landscape. The flowers can be quite attractive and refreshing to the passerby. Tolerant of many urban and street conditions.

SITING AND CARE: Plant in full sun. Grows well in moist, well-drained soils. Prune only to control aberrant growth.

RECOMMENDED VARIETIES: Chinese fringe tree *(C. retusus)* is larger and less hardy, Zones 6 to 9.

Cinnamomum camphora
sih-nah-MOH-mum KAM-foh-rah

Leaves of Camphor tree contain camphor oil.

CAMPHOR TREE

- Bronze-red spring foliage turns shiny yellow-green in winter
- Rounded growth habit and clean, fissured bark
- Growth rate: slow, 6 to 8 inches per year
- Zones 9 and 10

This attractive, evergreen shade tree grows to 50 feet tall and wide. With its handsome, changing foliage and pleasing, rounded shape, it has something to offer in all seasons. Native to Japan and China.

USES: Camphor tree is a good street tree if given enough room, and it provides shade in all seasons. Its evergreen foliage is an effective background and contrasts well with lighter-colored plants, but the dense shade and surface-rooting tendency of this tree limit planting other specimens in close proximity; also, because of the rooting problem, avoid planting near sidewalks.

SITING AND CARE: Locate in full sun, allowing room on all sides. Mulch under drip line to limit evaporation and to keep area attractive. Not bothered by pests.

Cladrastis lutea
kluh-DRASS-tiss LOO-tee-uh

Zigzag branches are characteristic of American yellowwood.

AMERICAN YELLOWWOOD

- Showy, heavily fragrant white flowers borne in hanging chains in late spring
- Zigzag branching pattern evident in winter, accompanied by seedpods
- Lovely, smooth bark
- Growth rate: slow to medium, 10 to 12 inches per year
- Zones 5 to 8

American yellowwood is a refined, medium-sized tree for restricted spaces. It is native to streamsides and riverbanks of the southeastern United States. Clear yellow autumn foliage. Grows 30 to 50 feet tall and almost as wide.

USES: This is a good tree for the rear corner of the residential backyard landscape bed. Use it as a shade tree on smaller properties; place it in larger areas alongside small trees or larger shrubs such as arrowwood viburnum or blackhaw viburnum.

SITING AND CARE: Best in sun to part shade and moist, well-drained soil. Prune in summer to avoid excessive sap bleeding. Pruning is usually necessary only to prevent poor or weak branch angles.

FLOWERING DOGWOOD

Cornus florida
KORE-nuss FLO-rih-duh

- Graceful, horizontal branching; good fall color; and red fruit
- Showy flower bracts emerge before the leaves in late spring
- Growth rate: slow to medium, 10 to 12 inches per year, slower with age
- Zones 6 to 9 (Zone 5 if northern seed sources are used)

Native to the eastern United States. Reaches 20 to 30 feet tall. It is most useful within its native range.

USES: Particularly effective in masses and in partial shade as an understory tree. Excellent for all-season appeal: spring flowers, summer foliage, fall color and fruit, and winter bark and branches.

SITING AND CARE: Keep roots cool to avoid leaf and trunk scorch. Use an acidifying fertilizer if in a high-pH area. Lawn-mower damage to trunks provides almost certain entry for this disease.

RECOMMENDED VARIETIES: 'Barton White', 'Cherokee Princess', 'Cloud Nine', and 'Fragrant Cloud' are good selections for form and early white flowers (technically "bracts"). 'Cherokee Chief' and 'Rubra' are pink-flowering forms, 'Welchii Junior Miss' has bicolored pink-and-white flowers and is one of the few that perform well on the Gulf Coast (Zone 9). In Zones 6 to 8, anthracnose disease is serious enough to preclude planting, but 'Barton White' is reported to be resistant (also see *C. rutgersensis* hybrids, below).

Flowering dogwoods:
***C. florida* 'Rubra' (above) and
C. florida, white form.**

KOUSA DOGWOOD

Cornus kousa
KORE-nuss KOO-suh

- White-bracted flowers bloom 2 to 3 weeks later than flowering dogwood
- Beautiful flaking bark, fleshy red fruits, outstanding fall foliage color
- Open, horizontal branching habit
- Resistant to pests that trouble flowering dogwood
- Growth rate: slow when young, 8 to 10 inches per year with age
- Zones 5 (southern half) to 8

A tree with tremendous impact and appeal in all seasons. Native to Japan and Korea. Grows to 20 feet tall.

USES: A natural for courtyards or for softening harsh corners of buildings. Grows robustly without impeding surrounding plants.

SITING AND CARE: Best in well-drained soils. Can grow in full sun but does better in partial shade, growing into its natural, open shape. Thrives with some protection from sun and wind.

RECOMMENDED VARIETIES AND RELATED SPECIES: 'Chanticleer' has white flowers and strongly horizontal branching. 'Lustgarten Weeping' has a graceful, weeping form. *C. rutgersensis* represents hybrids between flowering dogwood and kousa dogwood, developed at Rutgers University. Faster-growing than kousa dogwood, the cultivars in this group are known to be resistant to anthracnose and dogwood borer; they are safe alternatives to flowering dogwood in Zones 6 to 8 and perhaps other zones as well. Their flowering season is about midway between flowering dogwood and kousa dogwood. 'Rutban' (Aurora), 'Rutdan' (Galaxy), 'Rutcan' (Constellation), and 'Rutlan' (Ruth Ellen) are white-bracted clones in the *C. rutgersensis* group; 'Rutgan' (trademark Stellar Pink) is a clone with pink bracts.

Bracts of Kousa dogwood and variety 'Gold Star' (inset).

Crataegus crus-galli
kruh-TEE-guss krooz-GALL-eye

Berries of Cockspur hawthorn provide food, and thorny branches provide protection for birds.

COCKSPUR HAWTHORN

- White flowers in early spring
- Shiny, dark leaves turn orange in fall
- Abundant bright red fruit from fall to winter; formidable thorns
- Small graceful tee, broad shape
- Growth rate: medium, 6 to 10 inches per year
- Zones 4 to 7

A versatile, small tree with relatively few serious problems. Its native range is from eastern Canada to Kansas and the Carolinas. Reaches 30 feet tall and wide.

USES: It can be trained into a tall hedge but is best as a single specimen in borders and at corners of buildings. Provides excellent definition and height in the shrub border. Tolerates urban conditions. Its ornamental fruit remains effective in late summer and fall and into winter.

SITING AND CARE: Full sun but can tolerate light shade. Leaf miner and aphids are minor pests. Fruit may be disfigured by cedar-apple rust if eastern red cedar (*Juniperus virginiana*) trees are nearby.
RECOMMENDED VARIETIES: 'Inermis' is thornless (important for homeowners with small children).

Cockspur hawthorn at peak of spring bloom.

Crataegus phaenopyrum
kruh-TEE-guss feh-NAW-puh-rum

Berries of Washington hawthorn persist into winter.

WASHINGTON HAWTHORN

- Abundant white flowers in late spring and early summer; large clusters of scarlet fruit
- Attractive fall foliage
- Tough constitution
- Good for border and screens; numerous thorns
- Small with elegant, spreading habit
- Growth rate: medium, 10 to 12 inches per year
- Zones 4 to 8

Native from Virginia to Alabama and Missouri, this is one of the best hawthorns for fall fruiting and color—a hardy, versatile, small tree for almost any landscape. Will grow to about 20 feet tall.

USES: Use as a single specimen, a background for hedges, or in shrub borders. Parents of small children should be aware of the thorns.

SITING AND CARE: Locate in full sun or partial shade, accompanied by shrubs or other small trees. Very resistant to cedar-apple rust.
RECOMMENDED VARIETIES AND RELATED SPECIES: 'Vaughn', a *C. crus-galli* and *C. phaenopyrum* hybrid, produces abundant fruit, which remain through winter, but its numerous thorns limit its use. 'Toba' *C. ×mordenensis*, from Canada, has white flowers that gradually turn rose; they produce few fruits. Almost thornless, 'Toba' is hardy to Zone 3 but is susceptible to cedar-hawthorn rust. 'Winter King' green hawthorn *Crataegus viridis* is a broad, vase-shaped tree, slightly larger than Washington hawthorn and faster-growing. It has spring clusters of applelike flowers, followed by lustrous green leaves that change to purplish red in fall, and distinctive silvery branches. It holds its fruit as long as Washington hawthorn.

Cryptomeria japonica
krip-toh-MARE-ee-uh ja-PON-ih-kuh

- Formal, with textured evergreen foliage
- Upright, pyramidal growth habit
- Growth rate: medium to fast, 10 to 15 inches per year
- Zones 6 to 8

15'
8'

Japanese cedar is a good evergreen specimen tree for larger residential landscapes. Native to China and Japan, it eventually grows 50 to 60 feet tall.

JAPANESE CEDAR

USES: A good specimen tree for the corner of a large lot. Locate it in semiprotected sites, near other plant groupings.

SITING AND CARE: This tree does not tolerate drought well; water during dry periods.

RECOMMENDED VARIETIES: 'Yoshino' is relatively fast-growing, and its bright green summer foliage bronzes slightly in winter. 'Lobbii' refers to a clone of mature form and foliage and probably differs little from the species. There are also many dwarf, shrubby forms.

Japanese cedar showing fresh spring candle growth.

×Cupressocyparis leylandii
koo-press-oh-SIP-uh-riss lay-LAWN-dee-eye

- Stately, graceful, horizontal branches; columnar form
- Dense evergreen
- Growth rate: fast, 1 to 3 feet per year
- Zones 7 to 10

20'
5'

This century-old hybrid between *Chamaecyparis nootkatensis* and *Cupressus macrocarpa* is vigorous in the extreme, screening quickly, then dominating landscapes until cut down. In time, it will reach 70 feet tall.

LEYLAND CYPRESS

USES: Useful as a specimen tree, for tall hedges, and for screening where there is ample space.

SITING AND CARE: Plant it in full sun. Tolerates many soil types and conditions. Protect the trunk from bruising to reduce the chances of canker disease.

RECOMMENDED VARIETIES: 'Naylor's Blue' is the bluest cultivar available and has a more open form than the species. 'Castlewellan Gold' is slower-growing, with yellow foliage that bronzes in winter. 'Leighton Green' is narrowly columnar with bright green foliage.

A hedge of Leyland cypress makes a good screen.

Cupressus sempervirens
koo-PRESS-us sem-per-VYE-renz

- Upright, very narrow, columnar form
- Dense, thick growth
- Growth rate: medium to fast, 1 to 2 feet per year
- Zones 7 to 9

20'
4'

A strong, vertical line to balance horizontal architecture, and a must for formal gardens in mild climates. Native to southern Europe, it grows 30 to 40

ITALIAN CYPRESS

feet tall and 3 to 6 feet wide.

USES: The ideal sentinel. A good screen if planted close together.

SITING AND CARE: Tolerates drought and a wide range of soils but is not tolerant of heavy, wet, or poorly drained soils.

RECOMMENDED VARIETIES AND RELATED SPECIES: 'Swane's Golden' is slow growing and columnar with golden green foliage. 'Glauca' has blue-green foliage. Monterey cypress (*Cupressus macrocarpa*) is a large tree that is upright when young, broad and spreading with age. Grows best on southern California's coast (to 40 feet). Humid areas in Zones 7 to 9 are stressing and often result in disease. Most often used as a windbreak.

Italian cypress soar skyward.

Davidia involucrata
dah-VIH-dee-uh in-voh-LOO-cra-tuh

Winglike white bracts surround the flowers of Dove tree.

DOVE TREE

- Unusual flowers are effective in late spring
- Distinctly pyramidal
- Golf-ball-shaped fruit and orange-brown bark add winter interest
- Growth rate: slow to medium, 8 to 12 inches per year
- Zones 6 to 8

This unique, broadly pyramidal tree is native to the interior of China. It grows to 30 to 40 feet after about 50 years, and eventually taller. **USES:** Best on medium- to large-sized lots as a handsome flowering specimen. Whereas other flowering trees can look "busy" if planted nearby, dove tree is effective with rhododendrons at its base.

SITING AND CARE: Adapted to full sun or partial shade. Grows well in a landscape bed with shrubs and perennials if mulched to keep the bed cool and moist. Prune as necessary to retain shape.

RECOMMENDED VARIETIES AND RELATED SPECIES: *D. i.* var. *vilmoriniana* has leaves that are more glaucous than the species, and it is slightly more cold-hardy.

Diospyros kaki
dye-OSS-per-us KHA-kee

Fruits of Japanese persimmon (*Diospyros kaki* 'Hachiya').

JAPANESE OR ORIENTAL PERSIMMON

- Yellow to light green spring leaves change to reddish orange in fall
- Edible fruit is showy on bare branches well into winter
- Growth rate: slow, 10 to 12 inches per year
- Zone 9

After changing color, the leaves drop a few weeks later, leaving the fruit clinging to the branches for winter display. Native to Asia. Can reach 30 feet tall and wide.

USES: Use as a specimen or in a grove for multiseason effect.

SITING AND CARE: Best in full sun and well-drained soil. Needs periodic thinning in late winter for maximum fruit production. Keep roots evenly moist to avoid premature fruit drop.

RECOMMENDED VARIETIES AND RELATED SPECIES: 'Chocolate' fruit is flecked brown with very sweet flesh. 'Fuyu' has golden orange fruit with firm flesh and is very popular. 'Hachiya' has good ornamental qualities; it bears large fruit that is sometimes seen in the produce section of markets. The American persimmon (*D. virginiana*) is a beautiful eastern native that has similar ornamental qualities but is hardy in Zones 5 to 9.

Fall color of American persimmon.

GUM TREE

Eucalyptus spp.

yoo-kuh-LIP-tuss

- Tough and adaptable; well-suited to low-maintenance regimes
- Showy bark; some have showy flowers
- Growth rate: fast, 2 to 3 feet per year
- Zones 9 and 10 (in the west)

20'

20'

Strong, vigorous growers, gums are impressive trees that can anchor a landscape. Native to Australia and adapted to California and Arizona. Most of the gums will reach 50 to 70 feet.

USES: Good shade or windbreak tree that can double as a privacy screen or a specimen.

SITING AND CARE: Place it where fast shade is required, where the tree has room to grow, and where fallen leaf and stem debris won't cause a problem. Avoid pruning from spring to fall to discourage eucalyptus longhorn beetle infestation. Even though eucalyptus species are listed as hardy in Zones 9 and 10, this does not apply to those zones in the southeast, where climatic extremes and humidity hamper their success.

RECOMMENDED SPECIES: More than 60 species are in cultivation:

30'

10'

Argyle apple *(E. cinerea)* grows to 50 feet tall, with reddish bark, graying on older trees. Juvenile leaves are silvery blue and disklike and persist on older trees. 'Pendula' is weeping, with silver leaves.

30'

20'

Lemon-scented gum *(E. citriodora)* grows very tall (70 feet) in time, with powdery white, pink, or gray bark. Adult leaves are lemon-scented when crushed.

20'

10'

20 years

Red-flowering gum *(E. ficifolia)* is a small-sized (to 25 feet), rapid-growing tree that does well in coastal regions. When in full flower, its usually bright red blossoms are attractive against its dark green canopy of large, heavy leaves. The foliage hides most of the branches from view.

12'

10'

Blue gum *(E. globulus)* is potentially a very large tree but is excessively fast-growing, weak-wooded, and likely to be seriously damaged by occasional freezes in Zones 8 and 9. 'Compacta' is very dense and more useful than the species. Several subspecies are known.

15'

15'

Cider gum *(E. gunnii)* is a large tree, at least 70 feet tall in time, with bicolored pale green-and-white bark. Juvenile leaves are nearly circular and fused in pairs. Yellow flowers are showy in early autumn.

50'

20'

Snow gum *(E. pauciflora* ssp. *niphophila)* is a small, slow-growing, wide-spreading, open tree that reaches 20 to 25 feet. The trunk often turns and bends, creating an interesting effect. Spear-shaped silvery blue foliage contrasts gracefully with its peeling bark. Wind-tolerant, it is useful in open spaces or on slopes.

15'

10'

Silver dollar gum *(E. polyanthemos)* is a medium-sized (45 to 50 feet), fast-growing tree with a slender, upright growth habit. The trunk can be multi- or single-trunked. Mottled, flaking bark adds to its visual and textural appeal. The younger leaves of this tree are quite novel; rounded and suspended individually on lightweight twigs, they look like silver dollars. A hardy and tolerant tree, it struggles in wet or poorly drained places but thrives in coastal or dry conditions.

Bogong gum.

Tingiringi gum.

Red-flowering gum.

Mindanao gum.

Fagus sylvatica
FAY-guss sill-VAH-tih-kuh

Grove of European beech in fall color.

EUROPEAN BEECH

- Consistent russet fall foliage
- Beautiful, smooth, gray bark reminiscent of elephant legs
- Spectacular specimen and landscape tree
- Growth rate: slow, 8 to 12 inches per year
- Zones 5 to 7

15'
15'

This large and stately tree is highly valued for its smooth gray bark and glossy green leaves, which turn yellow-bronze in autumn. Will reach 70 feet tall and 60 feet wide.

USES: Good specimen or accent for large backyards or open areas and for framing. A tree for posterity.

SITING AND CARE: Best in full sun; will tolerate light shade. Adapts to many soils. Allow it plenty of room, and mulch widely around it; branches tend to flow to the ground.

RECOMMENDED VARIETIES AND

RELATED SPECIES: 'Asplenifolia' has fernlike dark green foliage. 'Pendula' has strongly weeping branches. 'Riversii' has purple foliage from early spring through summer, purple-green in fall. American beech *(Fagus grandifolia)* is also large; use in open spaces. Dark green summer leaves change to golden bronze in fall. The leaves stay on the tree for a long time afterward. Silver-gray bark is enhanced by its rugged structure and wide crown. Zones 4 to 8.

Pink, maroon, and white 'Tricolor' beech.

Franklinia alatamaha
frank-LIN-ee-uh al-ah-TAH-mah-ha

Franklin tree is named for Benjamin Franklin.

FRANKLIN TREE

- Flowers late summer into fall
- Lustrous leaves are bright green, turning mahogany red in fall
- Growth rate: slow to moderate, 6 to 8 inches per year
- Zones 6 to 8

12'
8'

With white flowers resembling single camellias in late summer and fall, Franklin tree can accent a patio or courtyard well. Once native to the lowlands of Georgia, it is now extinct in the wild. Discovered by John Bartram of Philadelphia and named for his friend Benjamin Franklin. With age, it grows 20 to 30 feet tall.

USES: A good choice for the large landscape bed. Place it to show off its attractive white flowers. Use as background, and contrast it with small blooming shrubs, such as viburnums, spirea, and azaleas.

SITING AND CARE: Requires moist, acid soils. Best in full sun but tolerates partial shade. Susceptible to verticillium wilt.

The Franklin tree flower resembles a camellia blossom.

Fraxinus americana
FRAK-sih-nuss uh-mare-ih-CAN-uh

- Outstanding red-purple fall foliage
- Sturdy shade tree; lovely, spreading form
- Growth rate: medium, 12 to 16 inches per year
- Zones 4 to 9

25'
15'

White ash is a bright-looking, prized ornamental shade tree for residential landscapes. Native to southern Canada, south to Florida and Texas. In maturity, it develops a majestic, spreading structure 80 to 100 feet tall and about 40 feet wide.

USES: Locate it at the southwest corner of the house for shade or in the backyard. Makes an excellent street tree.

SITING AND CARE: Plant in full sun, and prune only to retain natural

WHITE ASH

shape. Tolerant of a wide variety of soil and site conditions. Seed-bearing samaras (similar to those of maples) cause a litter and weed problem, so use seedless cultivars.

RECOMMENDED VARIETIES: 'Autumn Applause', 'Autumn Purple', and 'Rose Hill' are all cultivars that were selected for their deep green leaves, which reliably turn reddish purple in fall, as well as for being seedless.

White ash develops maroon to red fall color.

Main trunk of a mature White ash.

Fraxinus pennsylvanica
FRAK-sih-nuss pen-sill-VAN-ih-kuh

- Leaves are bright green in summer, yellow-gold in fall in most years
- Upright, broadly pyramidal, medium-sized tree
- Drought-tolerant
- Growth rate: medium to fast, 12 to 18 inches per year
- Zones 2 to 9

20'
15'

An excellent shade tree, adaptable to many soil types, green ash is native from southern Canada south to Florida and Texas. Will grow to about 60 feet tall and 30 feet wide.

USES: Good for framing, shade, and in backyard corner plantings. It is commonly planted in the front yard of residential landscapes and south and west of houses and patios for shade. It's a good street tree.

GREEN ASH

SITING AND CARE: Grows best in moist, well-drained soils but also tolerates dry, compacted soils. Seed litter can be heavy, so use seedless cultivars.

RECOMMENDED VARIETIES: 'Marshalls Seedless' is the oldest nonfruiting cultivar and still among the best. 'Patmore' is upright with an oval crown; it's a hardy specimen with good summer foliage color. 'Summit' has an upright, pyramidal form with a strong central leader and yellow fall color.

Green ash is a common shade tree.

GINKGO

Ginkgo biloba
GING-koh bye-LOH-buh

Brilliant yellow fall color of Ginkgo.

- Leaves turn bright yellow in fall
- Pyramidal when young; broad and spreading with age
- Growth rate: slow to medium, 8 to 12 inches per year
- Zones 4 to 8

20' 10'

Ginkgo is a large, unique tree native to eastern China. Grows to 75 feet tall and 50 feet wide.

USES: Use as a shade or specimen tree in large yards or estates. Male clones are excellent street trees.

SITING AND CARE: Plant in full sun with plenty of room to grow; it becomes somewhat spreading with age. Be sure to select a male clone to avoid messy, smelly fruit. Free of insects and disease. Prune only to remove broken branches.

RECOMMENDED VARIETIES: 'Autumn Gold' has a handsome and symmetrical form and reaches 50 feet. It is nonfruiting and has excellent fall color. 'Fastigiata' (may be male or female), and Princeton Sentry (a registered name; male) are narrow, upright forms. 'Saratoga' is oval in shape.

THORNLESS HONEYLOCUST

Gleditsia triacanthos inermis
gleh-DIT-see-uh try-uh-CAN-thuss
ee-NER-mus

Thornless honeylocust provides light, filtered shade.

- Leaves and branches provide wonderful fine texture and dappled shade
- Branches and slightly open habit allow turf growth underneath canopy
- Growth rate: medium to fast, 16 to 18 inches per year
- Zones 4 to 9

25' 20'

With its graceful, refined form and distinctive compound leaves, honey locust adds textural diversity. Native to the central United States, east to Pennsylvania, it grows 100 feet tall and 50 feet wide.

USES: Use it for filtered or dappled shade over a deck or patio or near a shady perennial garden.

SITING AND CARE: Adaptable, but mimosa webworm is a problem in some regions and in some years. Seedpods are a litter problem; some varieties are neater.

RECOMMENDED VARIETIES: 'Halka' is vigorous with pendulous branches and few fruits. 'Moraine' is the oldest and has the best resistance to mimosa webworm. Sunburst (a trademark name) has yellow spring foliage.

CAROLINA SILVERBELL

Halesia tetraptera
hah-LEE-zee-uh teh-trup-TARE-uh

Mountain silverbell in bloom.

- Clusters of bell-shaped white flowers in late spring
- Small- to medium-size tree
- Pyramidal in youth, rounded with age
- Growth rate: medium to slow, 8 to 10 inches per year
- Zones 5 to 8

25' 20'

Flowers develop into four-winged fruits that remain attractive in winter. Native to southeastern United States With age, it reaches 20 to 30 feet tall.

USES: Place it near a patio or landscape bed where flowers can be seen easily. Also a good addition to shrub and woodland borders and in groupings with other plants, especially evergreens.

SITING AND CARE: Place in full sun or in partial shade as an understory or woodland tree. Can become chlorotic in high-pH soils.

RELATED SPECIES: Mountain silverbell (*Halesia monticola*) is a larger version of Carolina Silverbell, to 60 feet tall and wide, with larger flowers and fruits. It is slightly more cold-hardy than Carolina Silverbell.

AMERICAN HOLLY

Ilex opaca
EYE-lex oh-PAH-kuh

- Evergreen, short-spined leaves
- Handsome red berries on female plants
- Good for background color and massing
- Growth rate: slow, 5 to 7 inches per year
- Zones 6 to 9

12' / 8'

Native to the east, from New England to north Florida and west to Missouri and Texas,

American holly has dozens of cultivars. Mature trees can reach up to 45 feet tall.

USES: Upright, pyramidal shape and dense foliage texture make a good contrast to light-colored and looser plants. Slow growth makes it suitable for small gardens.

SITING AND CARE: Protect from winter winds. Plant one male to several females to ensure fruit set.

RECOMMENDED VARIETIES: Fast-growing 'Merry Christmas' has dark leaves; 'Croonenburg' is compact and fruitful.

Leaves and berries of American holly make colorful mid-winter decorations.

JACARANDA

Jacaranda mimosifolia
jack-a-RAN-da mi-MOSE-i-FOL-ee-a

- Blue-violet flowers late spring into summer
- Doubly compound leaves
- Rounded, open habit
- Zones 10 and 11, mildest Zone 9

15' / 10'

This showy tree from Brazil, growing 25 to 50 feet tall, has an awkward growth habit, often bending to one side, with sparse branching. Its doubly compound bright green leaves produce a fine, fernlike texture, each leaf comprising more than 200 tiny

leaflets. The leaves are semi-evergreen, gradually falling away to offer more winter light. The tree is spectacular in late spring, when its 2-inch trumpetlike flowers open in loose pyramidal clusters 8 inches high; flowering continues into summer.

USES: Shade or avenue tree, specimen for accent and contrast, or lawn tree for filtered shade in summer. Mulching minimizes turf competition.

CULTURE: Best in well-drained, light, sandy soil. Flowers heavily in full sun but will tolerate shade. It is notoriously intolerant of salt.

Jacaranda is a signature tree of subtropical regions.

EASTERN RED CEDAR

Juniperus virginiana
joo-NIH-per-us ver-jih-nee-AYE-nuh

- Excellent tree for windbreaks
- Provides shelter and food for birds
- Growth rate: medium, 8 to 12 inches per year
- Zones 3 to 9

15' / 4'

Eastern red cedar is a good utility tree and is native to large areas east of the Rocky Mountains. Can grow to 60 feet tall and 15 to 20 feet wide with age.

USES: Holds its dense foliage low to the ground, which is useful for screening. Somewhat coarse for the urban landscape, but the cultivars can be good screening plants.

SITING AND CARE: Susceptible to mites and bagworms.

RECOMMENDED VARIETIES: 'Manhattan Blue' has a compact, pyramidal form and bluish-green foliage. 'Glauca' is narrow and loosely pyramidal, to 25 feet tall, with silver-blue foliage. 'Canaertii' has a compact, pyramidal form, dark green foliage; grows to 25 to 30 feet.

Eastern red cedar (*Juniperus virginiana* 'Nova').

Koelreuteria paniculata
kohl-roo-TEER-ee-uh pan-ick-yoo-LAY-tuh

Summer flowers of Golden rain tree.

GOLDEN RAIN TREE

- Covered with yellow flowers in midsummer
- Attractive, papery capsules in fall
- Rounded small- to medium-sized tree, good for the small landscape
- Growth rate: medium, 8 to 12 inches per year
- Zones 5 (southern half) to 9

Golden rain tree is an outstanding, low-maintenance, high-output tree. Native to China and Korea, it reaches 35 feet tall and wide at maturity.

USES: There are few other good trees with yellow flowers in summer. Locate it for shade on the southwest side of a patio or home. This is an ideal tree for the urban landscape in less-than-perfect soils.

SITING AND CARE: Tolerates cold, heat, drought, and low fertility. Requires no special care other than water during extended periods of drought.

RECOMMENDED VARIETIES: 'September' flowers four to six weeks later than the species.

Laburnum ×watereri
lab-BURR-num WAH-ter-er-eye

Goldenchain tree in its breathtaking spring bloom.

GOLDENCHAIN TREE

- Hanging chains of yellow flowers in spring
- Large shrub or small tree, good for the small landscape
- Growth rate: medium, 8 to 12 inches per year
- Zones 6 to 8

A useful tree for small gardens, goldenchain tree grows best in eastern and western coast areas. Can reach 25 feet tall.

USES: Best incorporated into a landscape bed, in a shrub border or in masses, or for vivid spring color and neutral background the rest of the year.

SITING AND CARE: Needs light shade in the afternoon. Prune to train into a tree by removing basal suckers and low-hanging branches. Twig blight can be a serious problem; sanitation and pruning will minimize it.

RECOMMENDED VARIETIES AND RELATED SPECIES: 'Vossii' has a dense growth habit with large chains of flowers up to 2 feet long. Scotch laburnum (*L. alpinum*), one of the parents of this hybrid, is slightly more cold-hardy but not widely available.

Lagerstroemia indica
lah-ger-STREE-mee-uh IN-dih-kuh

Crape myrtle flowers in summer.

CRAPE MYRTLE

- Profuse late-summer flowers in brilliant colors
- Excellent fall color
- Handsome, multicolored bark
- Slow-growing, multitrunked, small tree
- Growth rate: slow to medium, 6 to 10 inches per year
- Zones 7 to 9

A good, small tree for the south and west, crape myrtle is native to China and Korea.

USES: Crape myrtle makes a handsome specimen with superb trunk and bark interest year-round in hot, sunny southern gardens.

SITING AND CARE: Plant in full sun. Feed occasionally to keep foliage healthy. Prune when dormant to produce larger flowers.

RECOMMENDED VARIETIES: Many cultivars are available. 'Comanche' has deep, hot pink flowers and dark, glossy green foliage, and is mildew-resistant. 'Natchez' has dark, peeling, cinnamon-colored bark, dark green leaves, and white flowers.

JAPANESE LARCH

Larix kaempferi
LARE-icks KAM-fur-eye

- Soft-textured foliage is chartreuse in spring, blue-green in summer, golden yellow in fall
- Evergreen look on a deciduous tree
- Large, stately habit
- Growth rate: medium to fast, 12 to 15 inches per year
- Zones 5 to 7

The delicate blue-green foliage of Japanese larch turns golden yellow in fall. Native to Japan, it can

20'
15'

grow to 75 feet tall and 40 feet wide.

USES: With its massive, horizontal branches, this is a good choice for a specimen tree, for framing, or for the corner of a large residential backyard. It is worth growing for its color and texture alone. It also works well as a background plant along with or behind small- or medium-sized flowering shrubs.

SITING AND CARE: Plant it in a well-drained, open location. Best in cool, moist soils; tolerates wet soils.

Weeping Japanese larch (*Larix kaempferi* 'Pendula').

SWEET GUM

Liquidambar styraciflua
lih-kwih-DAM-bar sty-ruh-SIH-flu-uh

- Glossy, star-shaped, bright green leaves turn crimson to purple in fall
- Golf-ball-size, spiny fruit can be messy
- Growth rate: medium to fast, 12 to 15 inches per year
- Zones 5 (southern half) to 10

20'
12'

Multicolored foliage in fall has made this tree a favorite. Native to the eastern United States, it can grow to 75 feet tall and 50 feet wide.

USES: Urban shade or street tree.

SITING AND CARE: Best in moist, rich soils. Needs room, both to spread and also for root development. Spiky "gum ball" litter over a long season can be annoying underfoot. Not reliable in colder areas of Zone 5.

RECOMMENDED VARIETIES: 'Burgundy' leaves turn wine red to deep purple in fall. Festival™ is narrow and columnar; its foliage turns yellow to peach to orange. 'Moraine' is unusually vigorous and cold-hardy. 'Rotundiloba' has rounded leaf lobes, purple fall color, no fruits.

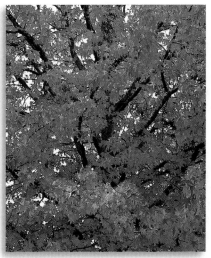

Sweet gum is a native American tree.

TULIP TREE

Liriodendron tulipifera
leer-ee-oh-DEN-dron too-li-PIH-fur-uh

- Unique, tulip-shaped, yellow-orange flowers
- Bright yellow fall foliage
- Tall; broadly oval to round with age
- Growth rate: medium to fast, 15 to 18 inches per year
- Zones 5 to 9

30'
15'

Attractive flowers hidden in a green canopy of unusual leaves are the secret to this tree's

beauty. Popular because of its quick growth, attractive form, and unique flowers. The tallest deciduous tree in North America; native to the eastern United States. Grows 100 feet tall with age.

USES: Use in groupings with other large trees on an estate or in a large landscape for screening or massing.

SITING AND CARE: Inspect regularly for aphids, and control when their numbers are high. Wood is weak: train young trees to develop wide and strong branch angles to avoid losing limbs to splitting later.

The Tulip tree flower is showy.

Magnolia grandiflora
mag-NOH-lee-uh grand-ih-FLOR-uh

SOUTHERN MAGNOLIA

Southern magnolia produces large, showy white blooms.

- Large, glossy, dark, evergreen leaves
- Large (8 to 12 inches), waxy, very fragrant creamy white flowers late spring through summer
- Growth rate: medium, 12 to 15 inches per year depending on culture
- Zones 7 to 9

25'
20'

With its tropical-looking leaves, dramatic flowers, and large size, this is a tree to use as a bold statement. Grows to 65 feet and taller.

USES: Use in massing for color (deep green foliage in winter, white flowers in summer) on large estates or residential lots. Give it room to grow; it's not for the small urban landscape.

SITING AND CARE: Locate in full sun or partial shade; protect from winter winds in the north part of the growing region.

RECOMMENDED VARIETIES: 'Edith Bogue' grows in a tight, pyramidal form with narrow, lustrous dark green leaves and is unusually cold-hardy (reportedly hardy to southern parts of Zone 5). 'Glen St. Mary' has a compact, bushy, pyramidal form, 20 feet by 20 feet, with lustrous dark green leaves. 'Little Gem' is a small, dense, shrubby specimen with small leaves.

Southern magnolia is a large evergreen tree with large, leathery leaves, and large flowers.

Magnolia macrophylla
mag-NOH-lee-uh mack-row-FILL-a

BIGLEAF MAGNOLIA

Leaves and flowers of Bigleaf magnolia.

- Huge leaves, from 24 to 36 inches long
- Fragrant white flowers, 8 to 12 inches across, develop large rose-colored fruits
- Round-headed, medium-sized tree
- Growth rate: slow to medium
- Zones 5 to 9

25'
15'

Bigleaf magnolia gives a luxuriant tropical look to the cold-winter landscape. Its leaves are among the largest on a nontropical tree and are its main distinction. Native to the Deep South and to Kentucky and West Virginia, it will reach 35 to 40 feet.

USES: Best as a specimen or novelty due to its large leaves and fruit. Its striking foliage combines well with other colors and textures in the landscape; could be the centerpiece of a tropically themed garden.

SITING AND CARE: Protect from wind, which will tear the huge leaves apart. Like most magnolias, it takes considerable shade.

Magnolia ×soulangiana
mag-NOH-lee-uh soo-lan-gee-AN-uh

- Pink and purple flowers in spring
- Open, spreading form
- Small- to medium-sized tree
- Growth rate: medium, 10 to 12 inches per year
- Zones 5 to 9

15'
15'

A medium-sized tree with good shape and form; blooms heavily when it's young—often when only 4 feet tall. Native to China. Reaches 20 to 30 feet tall.

SAUCER MAGNOLIA

USES: Form and bold foliage texture all season are appealing, but flowers are the prime attraction.

SITING AND CARE: Adaptable to many locations, but in Zones 5 and 6, plant on the north or east side of the property to slow growth until after spring frosts.

RECOMMENDED VARIETIES: 'Alexandrina' has early-blooming rose-purple and white flowers. 'Brozzonii', a later-flowering cultivar, has white flowers up to 10 inches across. 'Rustica Rubra' has red-purple flowers that are white inside.

Saucer magnolia (*Magnolia ×soulangiana* **'Alexandrina'**).

Magnolia stellata
mag-NOH-lee-uh steh-LAH-tah

- Many-petaled, 4-inch white flowers before leaves in spring
- Broadly oval small tree or large shrub
- Growth rate: slow to medium, 6 to 8 inches per year
- Zones 5 to 9

10'
10'

A small tree with a shrubby form, this magnolia has many uses in the landscape. Native to Japan, it will reach about 20 feet tall and wide.

STAR MAGNOLIA

USES: A good plant for an entryway border, surrounded with perennials and ground cover, or as an accent in the small residential landscape.

SITING AND CARE: Locate it in full sun. Water in dry periods. It naturally retains a tight, dense form without being pruned.

RECOMMENDED VARIETIES AND RELATED SPECIES: 'Royal Star' bears pink buds opening to white flowers. 'Waterlily' is later flowering than the species and highly fragrant. Loebner magnolia (*M. ×loebneri*) is a hybrid between Star magnolia and *M. kobus*. The original selection was 'Merrill', a fine, medium-sized tree.

Star magnolia (*Magnolia stellata* **'Rosea Jane Platt'**).

Magnolia virginiana
mag-NOH-lee-ah ver-jih-nee-AYE-na

- Sweet-scented, 2- to 3-inch flowers, never overpowering
- Branches tossing in the wind expose silvery undersides of deciduous to semievergreen leaves
- Growth rate: medium to fast, 10 to 15 inches per year
- Zones 6 to 9

A good, shrubby tree for wet areas of the landscape, sweet bay magnolia is native to coastal regions

SWEET BAY MAGNOLIA

20'
15'

from Massachusetts to Florida. In the Deep South, it can be evergreen. Size is variable: in the North, 10 to 20 feet; in the South, 30 to 50 feet.

USES: A good smaller version of southern magnolia (deciduous north of Zone 7), it can be grown in the shrub border.

SITING AND CARE: Tolerates semishady conditions and moist to occasionally wet soils. The best magnolia for seashore conditions.

Sweet bay magnolia.

Malus hybrids
MAWL-us

- Spectacular spring flowers
- Small, bright red fruits are favored by birds and remain well into fall
- Growth rate: slow- to medium-growing
- Zones 4 to 8

CRABAPPLE

15'

15'

A good-looking tree with long, slender, branches and small size, it is suitable for the urban landscape. Grows well in temperate regions of the United States.

USES: Its asymmetrical form contrasts well in the perennial garden and is in scale with most spring bulbs, such as late-blooming daffodils and tulips.

Fruits of *Malus* 'David'.

SITING AND CARE: Locate it in full sun for best flowering. Keep the structure of the tree slightly open for good air circulation and disease resistance. Fire blight, apple scab, and powdery mildew are common diseases; choose resistant varieties (noted below).

RECOMMENDED VARIETIES AND RELATED SPECIES: Hundreds of cultivars of several species and hybrids are available. A few are listed below.

Malus 'Hopa' at peak bloom.

Flowers of *Malus* 'Pink Satin'.

CRABAPPLE VARIETIES

Name	Fruit	Flower	Key Features
'Bob White'	Yellow, gold	White	Excellent floral display, may not be consistent from year to year
'David'	Scarlet	Snow white	Attractive round form, sparse flowers
'Donald Wyman'	Red	White	Effective winter fruit display, good rounded form, attractive peeling bark
'Indian Magic'	Red-orange	Pink	Apricot-orange fall foliage, attractive bark, excellent fruit display
'Liset'	Maroon, red	Rose red	Peach-colored fall foliage, attractive fall fruit display
'Mary Potter'	Red	White	Attractive spreading form, attractive bark
'Molten Lava'	Red-orange	White	Spreading, weeping form, good structure in winter; disease resistant
'Prairiefire'	Purple-red	Coral red	Red-tinged foliage, orange fall foliage
'Professor Sprenger'	Orange-red	White	Good persistent fruits; disease resistant
'Red Jade'	Red	White to pink	Spreading, weeping form, very popular
'Ormiston Roy'	Orange-yellow	White	Deep-furrowed, orange-colored bark, attractive fruit in fall
M. sargentii	Red	White	Graceful, horizontal, spreading form to 9 feet tall, 15 feet wide
'Sugar Tyme'	Red	White	Good form and fruit, best for the south
M. ×*zumi calocarpa*	Red	White	Excellent flowers; abundant, tiny red fruit

Metasequoia glyptostroboides
meh-tuh-seh-KWOY-yuh
glip-toh-stroh-BOY-deez

- Bright green foliage turns russet-orange and drops in fall
- Magnificent pyramidal form creates effect of prehistoric forest
- Deep-fluted bark and buttressed trunk
- Growth rate: fast, about 2 feet per year
- Zones 5 to 8

Dawn redwood is a fine-textured, fast-growing tree when sited

DAWN REDWOOD

25'
12'

correctly. Native to central China. Grows to 80 feet tall or more.
USES: A good tree for the corner of an ample residential lot. Combine it with large shrubs or small trees for screening, or wherever there is enough space.
SITING AND CARE: Best in moist or even wet soil, in sun or shade.
RECOMMENDED VARIETIES: 'National' and 'Sheridan Spire' have narrow, upright growth habits.

Dawn redwood foliage is soft and feathery to the touch.

Nyssa sylvatica
NISS-uh sil-VAT-tih-kuh

- Dark, glossy leaves turn crimson in fall
- Pyramidal structure like pin oak when young
- Horizontal, twisting branches
- Medium-sized tree
- Growth rate: slow to medium, 8 to 12 inches per year
- Zones 5 to 9

With strong fall color and a distinctive, pyramidal structure, black gum, also called sour gum or tupelo, can become a dramatic tree. It will

BLACK GUM OR SOUR GUM

20'
15'

reach 40 to 75 feet tall and 20 to 45 feet wide.
USES: This is a good specimen tree, but you can also use it as a background plant.
SITING AND CARE: Can be slow getting started, especially in poor or dry soil. Prefers moist, well-drained, acid soils and some wind protection. Good on elevated pond or streambanks. Juicy purple-black fruit can be messy over paving.

Black gum leaves turn brilliant red in fall.

Olea europaea
OH-lee-uh yoor-roh-PEE-uh

- Attractive, gnarly gray trunk and appealing form
- Willowlike gray-green leaves
- Moderate-sized tree with edible fruit
- Growth rate: slow, 10 to 12 inches per year with irrigation
- Zones 9 and 10

15'
15'

Easy to transplant and relocate even in old age, the olive is native to the Mediterranean region and

OLIVE

grows well in Arizona and California. It reaches 25 to 30 feet tall and wide.
USES: Grow in small landscapes; locate it where fruit droppage is not a problem. Adapts well to hot, dry summers and coastal regions.
SITING AND CARE: Plant in full sun and well-drained soil. Fruit stains paving. Pollen causes serious allergic reactions in some people; before planting it, check to see if it is banned in your area.
RECOMMENDED VARIETIES: 'Manzanillo' is a commercial grove olive with a spreading habit. 'Little

Ollie' is a dense, shrubby tree (to 12 feet), useful as a hedge. 'Wilsoni' has a spreading habit to 25 feet wide and produces few or no fruit.

Harvest and cure ripening fruits of olive.

Pinus densiflora
PYE-nuss den-sih-FLOR-uh

JAPANESE RED PINE

- Decorative orange-red bark
- Densely conical when young, open and picturesque with age
- Growth rate: slow to medium, 8 to 12 inches per year
- Zones 6 and 7 (and milder parts of Zone 5)

This native of Japan and Korea can be used as a subject for bonsai and is a handsome specimen. It can reach 50 feet tall and wide. **USES:** Bark and trunks provide visual appeal.

SITING AND CARE: Prefers well-drained soils and sunny conditions. Needs protection from wind. Allow needles to fall around tree and form a natural mulch.

RECOMMENDED VARIETIES AND RELATED SPECIES: 'Oculus-draconis' (dragon's eye pine) has yellow-banded needles and a picturesque habit; it is slower-growing than the species. 'Pendula' is an attractive, weeping form. 'Umbraculifera' (Tanyosho pine) is multiple-trunked and umbrella-shaped.

Japanese red pine (*Pinus densiflora* 'Umbraculifera').

Pinus nigra
PYE-nuss NYE-gruh

AUSTRIAN PINE

- Dense, dark, evergreen foliage
- Tolerant of heat, drought, poor conditions, and poor soils
- Growth rate: medium, 8 to 12 inches per year
- Zones 4 to 7

Austrian pine is a tough, reliable performer in the garden, tolerating most conditions. It is native to southern Europe, from Austria to Italy and Greece. It can grow 60 feet tall and wide.

USES: Hardy and wind-resistant, it makes a good windbreak or screen. Use it as an anchoring plant in a backyard border or in mass plantings where room allows.

SITING AND CARE: Grows well on many different sites and regions of the country. Subject to tip blight, needle blight, pine moths, and other pests, some of which can do serious damage. Pest inspection is an important part of maintenance for Austrian pine.

Austrian pine.

Pinus pinea
PYE-nuss pye-NEE-uh

ITALIAN STONE PINE

- Dense sphere when young, becoming broad and flat-topped
- Edible fruit (pine nuts)
- Moderate- to large-sized, depending on site
- Growth rate: slow to moderate
- Zones 8 to 10

These trees are handsome when young and bring a striking air of classic Rome with age. They grow well in California valleys and northern Arizona. Native to the Mediterranean region from Turkey through southern Europe. Can reach 40 to 60 feet tall with an equal spread.

USES: Picturesque, open, spreading shape makes this a good specimen tree. It has been used with great effect as a street tree in California. Because of its spreading habit, this is not a tree for the small garden.

SITING AND CARE: Takes heat and drought once established. An excellent choice for sandy soils and coastal gardens.

The trunk of Italian stone pine supports a large, round crown.

EASTERN WHITE PINE

Pinus strobus
PYE-nuss STROH-buss

- Soft, fine-textured needles
- Graceful branches sweep in the wind
- Somewhat open, but gentle to the eye and to the touch
- Growth rate: fast, 12 to 15 inches per year
- Zones 3 to 8

15'
15'

White pine is a fast-growing landscape pine. It is native from southern Canada south to Georgia and west to Iowa. Can grow to more than 100 feet tall.

USES: Where space allows, plant in groves, or use for quick screens. Excellent lawn tree.

SITING AND CARE: Fine for cold sites but needs some protection from constant wind exposure and from road salt. Allow needles to fall and form natural mulch around the tree.

RECOMMENDED VARIETIES: 'Fastigiata' has narrower branching angles than the species and so is not so wide. Good for a limited amount of space. 'Pendula' is a graceful, pendulous form that grows to at least 10 feet in 20 years and is useful as a specimen or accent.

Needles and new growth of Eastern white pine (*Pinus strobus* 'Minima').

SCOTCH PINE

Pinus sylvestris
PYE-nuss sil-VESS-triss

- Classic, gnarled habit and shape with age
- Deeply textured, reddish-brown to orange bark
- Growth rate: medium, 8 to 12 inches per year
- Zones 3 to 8

25'
15'

Commonly acquired as a live Christmas tree, Scotch pine is conducive to shearing. Hardy and wind-resistant, it is native to northern Europe and Siberia and is commonly grown across North America. It will eventually reach 60 to 75 feet tall.

USES: Good for screening on the property lines of most any size landscape, it can also be grown as a specimen tree in large landscapes.

SITING AND CARE: Grows best in full sun. Adapts to a wide range of soil types. Allow needles to fall; collect them under the drip line. Susceptible to needle blights, especially in the midwest.

RECOMMENDED VARIETIES: 'French Blue' has bright blue-green leaves; it's a uniform, compact tree. 'Watereri' has steel blue needles on a densely pyramidal tree.

Upright Scotch pine (*Pinus sylvestris* 'Fastigiata').

JAPANESE BLACK PINE

Pinus thunbergii
PYE-nuss thun-BARE-jee-eye

- Large white terminal buds
- Easily trained into picturesque shapes
- Excellent for seashore
- Growth rate: fast
- Zones 6 to 8

15'
15'

Native to Japan, black pine can be a large tree, reaching 50 feet.

USES: Use as a stabilizer for sand dunes and seashore plantings (it is tolerant of salt spray) or as an irregular mass planting in a large landscape. Can also be used in a large border or backyard.

SITING AND CARE: Prevent drought by occasional deep watering. Prune only to retain natural shape.

RECOMMENDED VARIETIES: 'Thunderhead' has heavy, dense, dark green needles and a dwarf, broad habit. 'Monina' (Majestic Beauty is the more common, trademark name) has lustrous dark green needles and a growth habit like the species but is denser and more compactly shaped.

Japanese black pine can be trained into a sculptural form.

CHINESE PISTACHIO

Pistacia chinensis
piss-TAH-shee-uh chih-NEN-siss

Fall color of Chinese pistachio.

- Bright red or orange foliage in fall
- Habit a bit gangly when young, becoming more rounded and controlled with age
- Growth rate: medium to fast, 6 to 12 inches per year (depends on moisture availability)
- Zones 7 to 9

15' 15'

Chinese pistachio is an overlooked but reliable tree with a good growth rate and strong fall color. Native to China. With age, it can grow to 50 feet tall and 35 feet wide.

USES: Plant it in a corner garden or use it for a patio background or street tree. Able to withstand adverse conditions, it is a good tree for urban conditions, especially drought or dry soil.

SITING AND CARE: Stake and prune when young to develop structure and a strong central leader. Once established, Chinese pistachio is a fairly low-maintenance tree, resistant to most pests and diseases.

LONDON PLANE TREE

Platanus ×acerifolia
PLAH-tuh-nuss ah-sir-ih-FOH-lee-uh

London plane tree adapts well to both cities and pruning.

- Naturally gray-and-white peeling bark
- Develops a wide, open outline with age
- Growth rate: medium to fast, 12 to 24 inches per year
- Zones 6 to 8 (and milder parts of Zone 5)

75' 35'

London plane tree grows well in nearly all parts of the United States. This tree is a hybrid of sycamore (*P. occidentalis*) and Oriental plane tree (*P. orientalis*). It has the hardiness of sycamore and the anthracnose resistance of Oriental plane tree. It can reach 100 feet tall and wide.

USES: Excellent street tree and often pruned for formal effects.

SITING AND CARE: Adapts to a wide variety of soils.

RECOMMENDED VARIETIES AND RELATED SPECIES: 'Liberty' has good resistance to powdery mildew and anthracnose. 'Bloodgood' is rapid-growing and especially resistant to anthracnose. Native *P. occidentalis* is very susceptible to anthracnose and is messy, so it is best for large or wild areas.

YEW PINE

Podocarpus macrophyllus
poh-doh-CAR-pus mah-kroh-FILL-us

Yew pine is a useful screen plant in mild-winter areas.

- Upright to oval to columnar evergreen tree or large shrub
- 4-inch-long needlelike leaves grow on slightly drooping branches
- Growth rate: slow, 6 to 10 inches per year
- Zones 8 to 10

12' 3'

This striking conifer has a graceful, Oriental effect. Native to Japan and southern China. With age, it can reach 30 feet tall and 10 feet wide.

USES: Grow as an espalier or in patio tubs and in courtyards. Also good for hedges, screens, and small gardens. Be sure to consider its mature size when planting near walks and buildings

SITING AND CARE: Grows well in full sun or partial shade; good drainage is a must.

RECOMMENDED VARIETIES: 'Maki', a shrubby form growing slowly to 10 feet tall, is most commonly used.

COTTONWOOD

Populus deltoides
PAH-pyoo-luss del-TOY-deez

- Pyramidal as young tree; spreading branches as tree ages
- Dark green leaves flutter in the wind; sometimes with good golden fall color
- Prefers moist situations but tolerates dry soils
- Growth rate: fast, up to 3–4 feet per year
- Zones 3 to 9

Eastern cottonwood (*P. deltoides*) is a fast-growing shade tree for the

70'
50'

eastern United States. Wood is weak and subject to breakage during storms.

USES: Except in plains states where few choices of shade trees are available, best left for river bottoms and wild areas. Tolerates saline soils.

SITING AND CARE: Prune out deadwood as it develops.

RELATED SPECIES: Lombardy poplar (*Populus nigra* 'Italica') and white poplar (*Populus alba*) are short-lived screening trees.

Like its relatives, Eastern cottonwood is fast-growing.

QUAKING ASPEN

Populus tremuloides
PAH-pyoo-luss trem-yoo-LOY-deez

- Brilliant yellow fall foliage
- Narrow and upright, good for groves
- Slightest breeze flutters the leaves
- Smooth, pale trunks and limbs
- Growth rate: fast, 12 to 18 inches per year
- Zones 2 to 6

25'
8'

With its leaves in constant motion, quaking aspen offers an interesting animation in the landscape. It grows best at higher elevations

and in cool climates. Native from western mountains to the east, it grows 35 feet tall and 10 feet wide.

USES: Use for quick groves in a new landscape or in natural areas.

SITING AND CARE: Susceptible to cankers and borers. Produces many seedlings and suckers. Inspect trunk for evidence of pests.

RECOMMENDED VARIETIES AND RELATED SPECIES: European aspen (*P. tremula*) is the European equivalent of our quaking aspen; 'Erecta' is as columnar as Lombardy poplar (*Populus nigra* 'Italica') but much more trouble-free.

Quaking aspen is a signature tree of the Rocky Mountains.

CHERRY PLUM OR MYROBALAN PLUM

Prunus cerasifera
PROO-nuss sare-uh-SIH-fur-ah

- Red-purple cultivars
- White to pink flowers
- Useful, shrubby tree
- Growth rate: medium, 6 to 12 inches per year
- Zones 4 (southern half) to 8

12'
12'

A versatile, small tree, cherry plum is native to western Asia. Cultivars may be preferred over the species. Can grow to 20 feet tall and wide.

USES: Use as an anchor in the shrub border. Grows nicely in the small patio garden; scales down the size of tall brick walls and softens vertical corners.

SITING AND CARE: A full-sun plant, it adapts to a range of soil types. Susceptible to many pests, especially cankers, aphids, caterpillars, borers, and leaf spots. Routine pest inspection is a must.

RECOMMENDED VARIETIES: 'Atropurpurea' has an upright, dense form with reddish-purple foliage. 'Newport' is a hardy purple-leaved selection. 'Thundercloud', another purple-leaved cultivar, bears pink flowers before the foliage.

Cherry plum at peak bloom.

Prunus maackii
PROO-nuss MACK-ee-eye

- Unusual reddish-brown bark with a metallic luster
- White flowers in spring
- Medium-sized tree with rounded crown
- Growth rate: medium to fast, 15 to 18 inches per year
- Zones 3 to 6

AMUR CHOKECHERRY

20'

20'

Amur chokecherry has an interesting shape and habit, small flowers and fruit, and is very cold-hardy. Native to Manchuria and Siberia. Will eventually reach up to 35 feet tall and as wide.

USES: Use as a specimen or accent tree, as a framing tree, or for shade for the patio or deck.

SITING AND CARE: Requires well-drained soil. This tree is more trouble-free in the far north (Zones 3 and 4) than farther south, and more valuable there as a substitute for the less-hardy paperbark maple (*Acer griseum*). *P. serrula* is a related species, also known for its shiny bark, with narrow leaves and single white flowers (Zones 6 to 8).

RECOMMENDED VARIETIES: 'Amber Beauty' is a symmetrical tree with slightly ascending branches.

Spring flowers of Amur chokecherry.

Prunus sargentii
PROO-nuss sar-JEN-tee-eye

SARGENT CHERRY

- Clouds of pink flowers cover the tree in early spring
- Foliage turns bronzy red in fall
- Lustrous reddish-brown bark
- Growth rate: medium to fast, 15 to 18 inches per year
- Zones 5 to 8

25'

25'

An attractive harbinger of spring that grows well in northern climates, Sargent cherry is a tree with multiseason interest. Native to Japan and Korea. With age, it can reach 60 feet tall and wide.

USES: This is an ideal-size tree for any part of the landscape: island planting, corner of the house, patio garden, or in a lawn as a specimen.

SITING AND CARE: Hardy tree that requires little maintenance or disease prevention. Prune to keep upright shape.

RECOMMENDED VARIETIES AND RELATED SPECIES: 'Columnaris' is narrow and upright. 'Accolade', a hybrid between Sargent cherry and Higan cherry (*P. subhirtella*), is a vigorous, upright tree 20 to 30 feet tall, with semidouble blush pink flowers. Useful in Zones 5 through 8.

Bronze red fall leaf color of Sargent cherry.

Soft pink flowers of Sargent cherry are followed by red fruits.

Prunus hybrids
PROO-nuss

- Gorgeous, fragrant white or pink flowers in spring
- Most cultivars are vase-shaped and upright
- Growth rate: usually medium, but can be variable
- Zones 6 to 9, depending on species and cultivar

FLOWERING CHERRY

12'
12'

Flowering cherries are the landmark tree for the Washington, D.C. area and are among the most popular of flowering trees. Native to Japan, China, and Korea. Most reach 20 to 25 feet tall.

USES: Good for softening harsh corners; when massed in open areas, they attract birds and bring color and texture to the landscape.

SITING AND CARE: Plant in moist, well-drained soil. Inspect frequently for cankers.

Fall color of snow goose flowering cherry (*Prunus* 'Umineko').

Higan cherry (*Prunus subhirtella* 'Stellata').

Higan cherry (*Prunus subhirtella* 'Eureka Weeping') regularly inspires poets.

FLOWERING CHERRY VARIETIES

Name	Flower Color	Tree Form	Height	Key Features
Japanese cherry (*P. serrulata*)	Pink	Vase-shaped	15 feet	Beautiful flowers and fall color
SATO-ZAKURA HYBRIDS				
'Amanogawa'	Pale pink	Upright	25 feet	Single to semidouble flowers
'Kwanzan'	Pink	Vase-shaped	30 feet	Large, very double flowers
'Shirotae'	White	Spreading	20 feet	Single to semidouble flowers
Higan cherry (*P. subhirtella*)	Pink	Spreading	15–25 feet	May have fall color some years
'Autumnalis'	White	Spreading	15 feet	May rebloom in fall in warm areas
'Pendula' (*P. subhirtella*)	Pale pink	Weeping	25 feet	Very popular for weeping form
'Whitcombii'	Pink	Globose	30 feet	Large cherry with single pink flowers
Yoshino cherry (*P. ×yedoensis*)	White or pink	Open	40 feet	Washington, D.C.'s cherry
Okame cherry (*P. okame*)	Carmine-rose	Open	25 feet	Can color well in fall

Pseudotsuga menziesii
soo-dot-SOO-guh men-ZEE-see-eye

Douglas fir cones and foliage.

Douglas Fir

- Dark green to blue-green needles and small, feathery cones
- Upright, evergreen conifer with stately size and form
- Growth rate: medium, 8 to 12 inches per year
- Zones 4 to 6

18'

10'

Native to the Rocky Mountains and the Pacific coast, Douglas fir is used commercially for timber production and Christmas trees. Grows to 75 feet tall and 30 feet wide.

USES: Makes a good screen for patios, or use it as a single backyard specimen, an upright accent, in mass plantings, or in groups.

SITING AND CARE: Needs full sun and well-drained, moist soil; struggles otherwise.

RECOMMENDED VARIETIES AND RELATED SPECIES: Bluish-green

P. menziesii glauca is a slower-growing and more cold-hardy than the coastal form, and the one to use in the north, midwest, and colder areas of the west. 'Fastigiata' is a columnar variety and is useful for a vertical accent.

Douglas fir is a large, majestic tree.

Pyrus calleryana
PYE-russ cah-lare-ee-AY-nuh

Fall color of Callery pear.

Callery Pear

- White blossoms cover the tree before leaves emerge in midspring
- Lustrous medium-green leaves turn red to purple in fall
- Growth rate: medium to fast
- Zones 5 to 8

15'

10'

A medium-sized tree with many fine features, callery pear is native to Korea and China. Can reach 30 feet tall and 20 feet wide.

USES: Use in corner plantings, in parks, or as a street tree. Plant near small patios and backyard corners for immediate landscape impact.

SITING AND CARE: Best in full sun. Most cultivars of this species are highly resistant to fire blight.

RECOMMENDED VARIETIES: 'Aristocrat' is a large, narrowly pyramidal tree with strong crotch angles. Its fall foliage color is not quite as good as other cultivars, but

it flowers nicely. 'Chanticleer' is a smaller, upright, symmetrical tree. 'Redspire' is also pyramidal, with glossy dark green leaves. In the north, its fall color is not as dependable. 'Bradford' was the first selection made of callery pear. For the first 15 years of its growth, it is a symmetrical, oval tree, but it has weak crotch angles and can easily lose limbs. It has excellent flowers and fall foliage, but the flowers are sometimes killed by late frost.

Spring bloom of Bradford callery pear.

COAST LIVE OAK

Quercus agrifolia
KWER-kus ag-ri-FOH-lee-ah

- Gnarly, picturesque form with age
- Dense, hollylike, evergreen foliage
- Growth rate: medium, 12 to 15 inches per year.
- Zone 9

Coast live oak is a good tree for shade, much loved for its picturesque, gnarly form in old age. Native to the hills and mountains of coastal California. Can reach 50 feet tall and wide.

USES: A good shade tree and a must for natural landscapes. This is not a good choice for lawns.

SITING AND CARE: Plant in well-drained soil and full sun to part shade; avoid overwatering in any season. Inspect tree for oak moth larvae. Acorns and leaf drop can be annoying. Oak root fungus can be devastating; always use mulch over root zone, never turf or flowers.

RELATED SPECIES: Southern live oak (*Q. virginiana*, Zones 8 and 9) is the signature tree of the Deep South for its spreading branches dripping with Spanish moss.

Coast live oak is a stately tree.

WHITE OAK

Quercus alba
KWER-kuss AL-buh

- Dark green leaves in summer, reddish-purple in fall
- Large tree with outstanding durability and form
- Growth rate: slow to medium, 8 to 12 inches per year
- Zones 5 to 8 (and milder parts of Zone 4)

A majestic tree with a good shape and ruggedness, white oak is long-lived and nearly pest-free. Native to the East Coast, and west to the center of the United States. Can grow to 75 feet tall and wide.

USES: Good for shade and as a specimen if a large space is available. Needs the open space of estates, acreages, parks, and very large backyards.

SITING AND CARE: Grows best in well-drained soils.

RELATED SPECIES: Swamp white oak (*Q. bicolor*) is almost as large and handsome as white oak, with greater tolerance of wet soils. It is hardy to Zone 4.

White oak has round-lobed leaves.

WILLOW OAK

Quercus phellos
KWER-kuss FEH-lohss

- Willow-shaped, light, bright green leaves
- Pryamidal when maturing; rounded with age
- Growth rate: medium, 10 to 15 inches per year
- Zones 6 to 9

Native from the eastern seaboard west to Missouri and Texas, willow oak is one of the best oaks from the south. With age, it grows up to 50 feet tall and 40 feet wide.

USES: A magnificent street tree, entryway marker, or backyard shade tree, and is useful in other large spaces. Similar in shape to pin oak (*Quercus palustris*).

SITING AND CARE: Grows best in moist, well-drained soils but adapts to most soils.

RELATED SPECIES: Scarlet oak (*Q. coccinea*) is rounded and open at maturity, reliably produces red fall color, and has good tolerance of high-pH soils. Pin oak (*Q. palustris*) grows to 75 feet and makes an excellent shade or street tree.

Willow oak has willow-like foliage.

Quercus robur
KWER-kuss ROH-burr

English oak forms a rounded tree.

ENGLISH OAK

- Best known in the United States for good columnar forms
- Coarse texture
- Deeply furrowed and fissured bark
- Growth rate: slow, 6 to 8 inches per year
- Zones 6 to 8 (and milder areas of Zone 5)

A grand and stately tree, English oak is native to Europe. With age, it can reach 60 feet tall and as wide.

USES: Good for the small- to medium-sized landscape, this oak will mature so slowly that landscape renovation will likely be called for by the time it is too large. For most of the United States and Canada, native oaks are faster growing and perform better, but the narrow cultivars of English oak are useful.

SITING AND CARE: Requires full sun and moist, well-drained soil.

RECOMMENDED VARIETIES: 'Fastigiata' is a fine columnar tree for a strong vertical accent. Varieties with the trademark names Skymaster and Skyrocket have similar columnar shapes.

Quercus rubra
KWER-kuss ROO-brah

Northern red oak in fall.

NORTHERN RED OAK

- Lustrous, dark leaves turn red in fall
- Upright and rounded when young, rounded and symmetrical when older
- Foliage canopy is moderately open in youth, denser with age
- Growth rate: medium to fast, 12 to 15 inches per year
- Zones 4 to 8

One of the best oaks for growing in the midwest, red oak is native from Maine and Minnesota to Georgia. Mature trees can reach 75 feet tall and as wide.

USES: This fast-growing, large specimen makes an excellent shade tree for the backyard, patio, or deck area, or for use as a specimen.

SITING AND CARE: Best in full sun and moist but well-drained soil. Relatively pest-free.

RELATED SPECIES: Shumard oak (*Q. shumardii*), native from the midwest and east to the Carolinas, is strongly pyramidal but spreads with age. In most locations, it will grow to 50 to 55 feet tall. Fall color can be russet red to bright red.

Robinia pseudoacacia
rob-BIN-ee-ah soo-doh-uh-KAY-see-ah

Black locust is a tough tree that thrives where other trees cannot.

BLACK LOCUST

- Clusters of fragrant white flowers in spring
- Rough and fissured bark; young can be covered with large thorns
- Growth rate: medium to fast, 10 to 15 inches per year
- Zones 4 to 8

Black locust is a good tree for poor soils and other difficult conditions. Native from the Ohio River valley west to Iowa and naturalized elsewhere. Mature specimens can be 75 feet tall and 30 feet wide.

USES: Parks, cemeteries, and reclaimed sites such as landfills and strip mines. Named varieties are best.

SITING AND CARE: Adapts to dry and unfertile soils. Although it can sucker profusely, no special care is needed to maintain health.

RECOMMENDED VARIETIES AND RELATED SPECIES: 'Frisia' has golden yellow leaves in summer. Globe black locust ('Umbraculifera') is a small tree to 15 feet. *R. ×ambigua* includes hybrids of black locust, such as 'Idahoensis' and 'Purple Robe', which are rose-pink flowering trees 30 to 40 feet tall.

GOLDEN WEEPING WILLOW

Salix ×alba var. vitellina
SAY-licks sep-ull-CRAY-lis

- Large, rounded, weeping form
- Yellow-gold branches
- Growth rate: fast to extremely fast, 18 to 24 inches per year
- Zones 3 to 8

25'

25'

A tree for wet sites, golden weeping willow is native to Europe and some parts of Africa and Asia. Can grow to 75 feet tall and as wide. **USES:** Not really for the home landscape except on large acreages.

SITING AND CARE: Most vigorous in moist soil. Requires constant cleanup of fallen limbs; roots invade and damage drainage and septic lines. **RELATED SPECIES:** Laurel willow (*S. pentandra*) is a medium-sized, oval tree with shiny branches and stems and lustrous dark green foliage. In the humid south, foliar disease can completely defoliate the tree by midsummer, which limits its use. Babylon weeping willow (*S. babylonica*), milder areas of Zones 6 to 8) is a medium-sized, 35- to 50-foot tree with similar characteristics and form.

Golden weeping willow requires a large space away from the home.

CORKSCREW WILLOW

Salix matsudana 'Tortuosa'
SAY-licks matt-soo-DAH-nuh

- Narrow, bright green leaves, 3 to 4 inches long and contorted
- Curiously twisted and contorted branches and stems
- Grows 25 feet tall
- Growth rate: fast, 18 to 24 inches per year
- Zones 5 to 8

25'

25'

Corkscrew willow is a good conversation piece with an interesting winter appearance. Its foliage

and stems are used in flower arrangements. The species is native to northern China. Can rapidly reach up to 25 feet tall and wide. **USES:** Place this medium-sized tree near a patio or along a path with its contorted branches and stems in full view (but not near a pool, due to extensive limb and stem droppage). **SITING AND CARE:** Tolerates a wide range of soils. Experiences dieback in winters with fluctuating temperatures, as in Nebraska, Iowa, Kansas, and Illinois.

Twisted branches of Corkscrew willow create interest.

CHINESE TALLOW TREE

Sapium sebiferum
SAY-pee-um seb-BIH-fer-um

- Dense, thick foliage, yet has a slightly open, airy appearance
- Dark green leaves coupled with stringlike yellow flowers
- Good fall color
- Medium-sized, rounded tree
- Growth rate: fast, 12 to 18 inches per year
- Zones 8 to 10

Chinese tallow tree is rapid-growing and a good replacement for poplars (*Populus*) because it encounters

25'

15'

fewer pests. Fall color can be quite strong in some years. Native to China, Japan, and Korea. Can grow to 40 feet tall. **USES:** A fast-growing, medium-sized tree for quick shade. Over decks and patios or in terrace gardens, flower and fruit litter can be a problem. Useful as screening on property lines due to its rapid growth. **SITING AND CARE:** Prune when young to produce a single trunk with a strong central leader, or allow

it to grow in its natural form. Relatively pest-free. Can become weedy in the south.

Chains of yellow flowers contrast with the green foliage of *Sapium sebiferum*.

SASSAFRAS

Sassafras albidum
SASS-uh-frass al-BYE-dum

Sassafras in fall color.

- Bright green leaves in summer change to neon colors in fall
- Haze of yellow flowers is effective in early spring before leaves
- Growth rate: medium to fast, 12 to 18 inches per year
- Zones 5 to 9

25'
20'

Common to hedgerows and woodlands of the eastern United States, sassafras is a native tree best known for its blazing fall color. Will grow as a multitrunked thicket if not pruned back. Native from Canada to Florida and west to Texas. Grows to 60 feet tall.

USES: Use it along paths and in thickets, mass plantings, and corner landscape plantings, where the fall colors and early spring flowers can be seen up close.

SITING AND CARE: Can be difficult to transplant; acquire container-grown plants. Prefers moist, well-drained, slightly acidic soils. Remove suckers if single tree form is desired.

PEPPER TREE

Schinus molle
SKY-nuss moll

Leaves and berries of Pepper tree.

- Picturesque form and shape; gracefully drooping branches
- Fine-textured, bright, evergreen leaves
- Attractive red berries
- Can be messy with dropping leaves, fruits, and stems
- Growth rate: fast
- Zones 9 and 10

20'
20'

A fast-growing, ornamental shade tree native to Peru, Bolivia, and Chile. Can grow up to 50 feet tall.

USES: Good for fast shade and asymmetrical form. Can also be planted closely and sheared for a hedge. Fine tree for informal patios, to shade play areas, or in areas with poor soil. Unfortunately, drawbacks include weak wood that drops branches and much litter, and greedy roots that will seek out septic and sewer lines.

SITING AND CARE: Has surface rooting habit and will drop litter, making it a poor choice next to sidewalks and driveways. Susceptible to scales and aphids.

JAPANESE UMBRELLA PINE

Sciadopitys verticillata
sky-uh-DAW-pi-tis ver-tih-sih-LAY-tuh

Japanese umbrella pine is very slow-growing.

- Small, refined conifer
- Whorled needles create an umbrella-shaped terminal
- Growth rate: very slow, 3 to 5 inches per year
- Zones 5 to 8

10'
4'

An outstanding specimen, this native of Japan has been gaining in popularity for its slow, restrained growth and easy-care nature. It can be grown as bonsai. Can reach 25 to 40 feet tall after many years.

USES: Its slow growth makes it easy to incorporate into rock gardens and shrub borders and near patios. Be sure to site it with closeup viewing in mind.

SITING AND CARE: Locate it in moist, rich soil in areas where morning and midday sun give way to late-afternoon shade. Provide some wind protection.

COAST REDWOOD

Sequoia sempervirens
seh-KWOY-yuh sem-per-VYE-renz

- Narrow, pyramidal form
- Small, attractive needles grow in spirals
- Extremely large on the West Coast
- Fresh-looking and woodsy-smelling
- Growth rate: fast initially, slower with age
- Zones 7 to 9

Useful only on the Pacific coast, where it is native to northern

 20' / 15'

California. Mature trees can be more than 100 feet tall. **USES:** Plant it where it has room to grow—on the perimeter of a large lawn or other expansive area. **SITING AND CARE:** Grows well in cool locations and in moist, acidic soils. Needs frequent watering; does not tolerate drought. **RELATED SPECIES:** Giant sequoia (*Sequoiadendron giganteum*, Zones 7 to 9) is useful both in the west and in the Middle Atlantic area as well as California, where it is native. It reaches 75 feet tall in the east, with a handsome, buttressed trunk and red bark.

Giant sequoia is the largest tree on Earth.

JAPANESE PAGODA TREE

Sophora japonica
soh-FOR-ruh ja-PON-ih-kuh

- Creamy white flowers in summer
- Good filtered shade
- Medium-sized tree requiring little care
- Growth rate: medium to fast, 12 to 15 inches per year
- Zones 6 to 8 (and milder areas of Zone 5)

 20' / 20'

This wonderful summer-blooming tree with large white flowers is native to China and Korea. Can grow to 75 feet tall and wide.

USES: Good choice over patios for shade and late-summer flowers. **SITING AND CARE:** Best in sun and average, well-drained soil. Tolerates urban sites with poor soils. **RECOMMENDED VARIETIES AND RELATED SPECIES:** 'Pendula', a weeping form with bright green branches in winter, is a good accent tree. 'Regent' has a fast growth rate and a large, rounded crown. Mescal bean (*S. secundiflora*, Zones 8 and 9) is a small, 25-foot tree with long clusters of violet-blue flowers in early spring.

Japanese pagoda tree blooms with pealike white flowers in late summer.

EUROPEAN MOUNTAIN ASH

Sorbus aucuparia
SORE-buss awk-yoo-PARE-ee-uh

- Good reddish fall foliage
- White spring flowers
- Bright orange fruit in summer and fall
- Fine foliage texture
- Growth rate: medium, 10 to 12 inches per year
- Zones 3 to 6

 20' / 15'

Small, with an upright habit, European mountain ash is native to Europe and western

Asia. Best in Zones 3 and 4. Can grow to 30 feet. **USES:** Accent the patio, garden, or courtyard with this tree. **SITING AND CARE:** Plant in cool, moist, well-drained soils. Cankers and borers are serious problems, especially in Zones 5 and 6. Wrap young trunks to protect from scald. **RECOMMENDED VARIETIES AND RELATED SPECIES:** 'Cardinal Royal' is a vigorous grower with an upright, narrow-oval habit. Korean mountain ash (*Sorbus alnifolia*) is larger, to 50 feet tall, free of borers but susceptible to fire blight in some areas. Has red-orange fall foliage and silvery-gray bark in addition to bright fruit.

Colorful berries of European mountain ash.

Stewartia pseudocamellia
stew-AHR-tee-uh soo-doh-kah-MEE-lee-uh

Japanese stewartia has showy, white summer blooms.

JAPANESE STEWARTIA

- Dark green leaves turn bronze to purple in fall
- White camellia-like flowers in midsummer
- Outstanding, multicolored bark
- Growth rate: slow, 8 to 12 inches per year
- Zones 6 and 7

15'
12'

A magnificent ornamental tree, offering interest in every season of the year. Native to Japan. Can reach 40 feet tall and as wide.

USES: This small- to medium-sized beauty has a number of uses: in the patio, landscape border, and shrub border. It can be wonderful in a mixed flower garden for a strong vertical effect.

SITING AND CARE: Grows best in acidic soils that are well-drained. Check pH and correct if needed.

RECOMMENDED VARIETIES AND RELATED SPECIES: 'Korean Splendor' (also called *S. koreana*) is exceptional in its flowers and bark interest and is cold-hardy in the mildest areas of Zone 5.

Styrax japonicus
STY-racks ja-PON-ih-kuss

Plant Japanese snowbell in small groves.

JAPANESE SNOWBELL

- Pendulous white flowers bloom in early summer
- Lovely rounded, low-branched tree
- Small, clean and tidy, with dense foliage
- Growth rate: slow
- Zones 7 and 8 (and milder areas of Zone 6)

20'
25'

This little-known tree deserves more use. With age, it reaches 20 to 25 feet tall.

USES: Branches hanging over a patio can be impressive. Use it in small gardens, near decks, and in courtyards where you can look up into the flowers.

SITING AND CARE: Needs frequent watering and pruning to retain desired shape.

RECOMMENDED VARIETIES AND RELATED SPECIES: 'Pendula' ('Carillon') is semiweeping and has striking flowers and foliage. Semipendulous 'Pink Chimes' has pink flowers. Fragrant snowbell (*S. obassia*; Zones 6 to 8) is more upright, to 35 feet tall, with larger, rounded leaves and large clusters of fragrant flowers.

Syringa reticulata
sih-RING-guh reh-tick-yoo-LAY-tuh

Japanese tree lilac is a flowering tree for cold climates.

JAPANESE TREE LILAC

- Covered with plume-shaped white flowers in early summer
- Thick, oval-to-slightly-heart-shaped dark green leaves
- Dense, upright to pyramidal, small tree
- Growth rate: medium, 8 to 10 inches per year
- Zones 3 to 7

15'
15'

This is a care-free, reliable, tough performer for the midwest, the east, and some western climates. Native to Japan and parts of China. Grows to 30 feet tall.

USES: Excellent for the shrub border, in masses for screening, or as an accent; also good as a small street tree and for the entryway or corner of a home. Tends to flower well only every other year.

SITING AND CARE: In full sun for best flowering. Relatively pest-free.

RECOMMENDED VARIETIES: 'Ivory Silk' flowers at a young age and is sturdy and compact. 'Summer Snow' is compact, with a rounded crown and abundant flowers.

BALD CYPRESS

Taxodium distichum
tack-SOH-dee-um DISS-tih-kum

- Foliage turns russet-red in late fall
- Attractive reddish-brown bark on a buttressed trunk
- Deciduous conifer
- Growth rate: medium to fast, 18 to 24 inches per year
- Zones 5 to 10

30'
15'

Bald cypress is a good tree for wet sites and has many other fine features for use in the landscape.

Native to the southeastern United States. It can reach 100 feet tall and 40 feet wide. **USES:** Requires room to grow. Excellent specimen tree, especially near stream banks or the edge of a lake or pond. **SITING AND CARE:** Grow in full sun. May be a bit iron-chlorotic under high-pH conditions. Knees will pop up several feet from the tree, so it should be planted away from regularly mowed areas.

Fall color of Bald cypress.

AMERICAN ARBORVITAE

Thuja occidentalis
THOO-ya ock-sih-den-TAL-is

- Flat, bright, evergreen leaves
- Upright, cylindrical form
- Growth rate: slow to medium, 8 to 10 inches per year
- Zones 3 to 8

12'
3'

A good evergreen for adding upright form in the landscape. Its dense foliage makes an effective screen. Native to northeastern North America from Nova Scotia south to North Carolina. Can reach 40 feet tall and 15 feet wide. **USES:** Makes a good screen but not

a good windbreak; it will burn with excessive cold winter wind and summer sun. It is good for the larger shrub or garden border and will tolerate wet or poorly drained sites. **SITING AND CARE:** Grows best in partial sun with wind protection. Can be sheared if desired. **RECOMMENDED VARIETIES AND RELATED SPECIES:** 'Techny' is pyramidal with very dark leaves. 'Emerald' ('Smaragd') has bright green foliage and a symmetrical, pyramidal form. Giant or western arborvitae (*Thuja plicata*) has slender, drooping branches. Reaches 200 feet in Pacific coastal areas,

usually 80 feet in gardens. Varieties selected from inland individuals of giant arborvitae perform well in the midwest as windbreaks and are not eaten by deer, unlike American arborvitae.

American arborvitae (Thuja occidentalis 'Emerald').

LITTLELEAF LINDEN

Tilia cordata
TILL-ee-uh kor-DAY-tuh

- Extremely fragrant flowers in early summer attract bees
- Medium-sized tree, strong pyramidal shape
- Growth rate: medium, 10 to 12 inches per year
- Zones 4 to 7 (and milder areas of Zone 3)

75'
40'

In addition to its pleasing, pyramidal shape and fine foliage, littleleaf linden casts

dense shade and grows well in most conditions.
USES: A good framing tree for the backyard or shade from the street if enough root space is provided. **SITING AND CARE:** Needs well-drained, loose soil. Tolerates periods of dry weather; plant in low-maintenance landscapes. Will develop girdling roots in compacted sites, and it is severely damaged by Japanese beetles. **RECOMMENDED VARIETIES AND RELATED SPECIES:** Shamrock (a trademark name) has a more open

crown than the species but retains its strong, pyramidal shape. 'Greenspire' is a popular cultivar with dark green foliage; it is a hardy tree that grows well in difficult conditions.

Littleleaf linden has a classic conical shape.

Tilia tomentosa
TILL-ee-uh toh-men-TOH-suh

Leaves of Silver linden are silvery underneath and when new.

SILVER LINDEN

- Very fragrant, small flowers
- Silver undersides of dark green leaves
- Classic, pyramidal linden shape
- Growth rate: medium, 10 to 14 inches per year
- Zones 5 to 7

75'
40'

Silver linden adds a silvery sheen to the landscape in summer. Native to southeastern Europe and western Asia. **USES:** A good shade or framing tree for larger landscapes, especially where the silver leaves are easily seen. Also a good street tree.

SITING AND CARE: No special care is required. May develop girdling roots in compacted soils.

RECOMMENDED VARIETIES AND RELATED SPECIES: 'Wandell' ('Sterling Silver') has lustrous dark green leaves and is resistant to Japanese beetle and gypsy moth. Green Mountain (a trademark name) is a rapid grower, with a dense canopy, and is heat- and drought-tolerant. Redmond linden (*Tilia americana* 'Redmond') has dense green foliage on a rounded, broad canopy. It grows eventually to 40 to 50 feet.

Tsuga canadensis
SOO-guh can-uh-DEN-siss

Canadian hemlock (*Tsuga canadensis* 'Golden Splendor').

CANADIAN HEMLOCK

- Flattened, deep green sprays of short needles
- Evergreen with upright, conical habit
- Outer branches droop gracefully
- Growth rate: medium, 10 to 12 inches per year
- Zones 3 to 7

25'
10'

With its slightly weeping, evergreen foliage, it goes well with other plants grouped in semishade. Native from southern Canada south to Georgia along mountain ranges. Can grow to 90 feet tall.

USES: Grows well in groupings in odd-numbered masses, and makes a fine formal hedge, background planting, or screen. Goes well in semishaded gardens with astilbe, fothergilla, summersheet clethra, or coral bells planted nearby.

SITING AND CARE: Needs cool, moist conditions in full sun with protection, or in medium shade. Some native stands of Canadian hemlock in the northeast have been badly damaged by wooly adelgid insects. Inspect for them in landscape plantings.

Ulmus americana
UHL-muss uh-mare-ih-KAY-nuh

Once common, American elm has been decimated by Dutch elm disease.

AMERICAN ELM

- Vase-shaped winter silhouette
- Thick, dense foliage produces heavy shade
- Growth rate: fast, 14 to 20 inches per year
- Zones 3 to 9 (and milder areas of Zone 2)

30'
20'

A classic, American elm is a stately tree for large areas. Native from the eastern seaboard west to the Rocky Mountains. Mature specimens can grow up to 100 feet tall or more.

USES: Useful on large estates where it can grow without too much competition.

SITING AND CARE: Susceptible to elm leaf miners, elm leaf beetles, stem cankers, bacterial wet wood, and especially Dutch elm disease and elm yellows (phloem necrosis). Best to keep trees healthy through judicious pruning and debris removal.

RECOMMENDED VARIETIES AND RELATED SPECIES: It remains to be seen how resistant new cultivars will be to Dutch elm disease and elm yellows. Large-scale planting is not advised.

CHINESE ELM OR LACEBARK ELM

Ulmus parvifolia
UHL-muss pahr-vih-FOH-lee-uh

- Good bronze-red fall color
- Magnificent bark mottled gray, green, orange, and brown
- American elm shape without susceptibility to most elm diseases
- Growth rate: medium to fast, 8 to 12 inches per year
  - Zones 6 to 9 (and milder areas of Zone 5)

30'
20'

Native to China, Korea, and Japan, Chinese elm

is a good, medium-sized tree for patio shade. It can reach 50 feet tall and 30 feet wide.

USES: Plant Chinese elm where one can view the bark easily.

SITING AND CARE: Best in moist, well-drained soils but tolerant of poor, dry soils. Shows considerable resistance to Dutch elm disease and to elm leaf beetle.

RECOMMENDED VARIETIES: Several cultivars were introduced in the 1990s and are under evaluation for cold hardiness in different regions. Check with your local nursery.

Chinese elm (*Ulmus parvifolia* 'Seiju').

CHASTE TREE

Vitex agnus-castus
VYE-tex ag-nuss-KASS-tuss

- Prominent 6-inch lavender flower spikes appear in summer
- Broad and spreading, usually multitrunked
- Growth rate: slow in the north, fast in warmer areas, 1 to 3 feet per year
- Zones 7 to 9

20'
20'

Native to southern Europe and western Asia, chaste tree is good for patio shade when trained as a tree instead of a bush. Flowers and foliage exude a spicy fragrance.

Can reach 25 to 30 feet tall.

USES: Good for the patio and for summer color in the shrub border.

SITING AND CARE: Best flowering in full sun and hot conditions; pale flowers result from cool shade. Tolerates arid soils, but growth is best with adequate water. Prune to a single stem for patio shade or for the shrub border. Will die back to the ground periodically north of Zone 7 but will return to flower as a shrub, and is useful in this way to Zone 5.

RECOMMENDED VARIETIES: Cultivars with blue, pink, and white flowers are seldom available.

Spring flowers of Chaste tree.

JAPANESE ZELKOVA

Zelkova serrata
zel-KOH-vuh sare-AH-tuh

- Deep summer greens turn shades of red and yellow in fall
- Vase-shaped form similar to American elm
- Somewhat resistant to Dutch elm disease
- Growth rate: medium, 8 to 12 inches per year
- Zones 6 to 8 (and milder areas of Zone 5)

Native to Japan and Korea, consider this tree if elm shape is desired.

75'
50'

USES: Good tree for framing and for shade in the urban landscape.

SITING AND CARE: Select specimens with good branching structure in the nursery; this can be variable in zelkova. Prune to retain desirable shape.

RECOMMENDED VARIETIES AND RELATED SPECIES: 'Green Vase' is vase-shaped with upright, arching branches. 'Halka' is fast-growing with a graceful vase-shaped form similar to American elm.

Leaf shape and plant form of Japanese zelkova are similar to American elm.

Shrub
SELECTION GUIDE

Warm creams, pinks, and reds of azaleas enliven this woodland garden.

Part of the joy of gardening is trying new shrubs. Nursery catalogs are full of gorgeous photographs and enticing descriptions that beckon you to buy. But which shrubs will thrive in your backyard? This book provides tips on creating a garden specifically for your site.

In the plant selection guide, you get the facts you need before choosing a shrub. Included is a cross section of the best garden plants, classic favorites, promising new and unusual varieties, including species and varieties that are reliable, widely adapted, and easy to grow. At a glance, you'll be able to name the

SPRING SHRUBS WITH COOL COLORS

Camellia sasanqua 'White Dove'
Ceanothus cuneatus
Ceanothus 'Julia Phelps'
Hebe 'Amy'
Iberis sempervirens
Magnolia stellata
Rhododendron 'Boule de Neige'
Spiraea prunifolia 'Plena'
Syringa ×persica
Syringa vulgaris 'Sensation'

SPRING SHRUBS WITH WARM COLORS

Cytisus ×praecox 'Allgold'
Daphne cneorum 'Eximia'
Hamamelis ×intermedia 'Jelena'
Kerria japonica
Pieris japonica 'Flamingo'

Rhododendron degronianum yakushimanum
Rhododendron 'Hino-crimson'
Rhododendron 'Klondyke'
Rhododendron 'Orange Cup'
Ribes sanguineum

plant, understand how much cold it can tolerate, and find reasons why that plant is garden-worthy. More detailed information describing the shrub's landscape uses, growth rate, and cultural requirements follows.

Even if you do your research, follow planting directions, and provide appropriate care, not every plant will necessarily flourish. That's OK; change is an inevitable part of the gardening adventure. Exceptionally harsh winter weather or unexpected heat and drought may kill one plant, and another may succumb to a pest or disease. Before giving up on a shrub, however, check its cultural requirements. Did you plant a shade-loving plant in the sun, or a sandlover in heavy, wet clay? Move the plant to a better location and try again. Half the fun of gardening is seeing what does well where and using that information to find plants to buy. Your extension service or the staff of a local nursery or garden center can also recommend plants that will thrive in your community.

But don't forget that choosing plants is primarily about beauty. So to start this chapter, shrubs are listed by ornamental qualities: seasonal flowers and foliage colors, late-season attractions, and shrubs with exceptional long seasons of color. From there, you can explore descriptions of more than 100 favorite shrubs.

Showy flowers

When you see a shrub in bloom at a nursery or public garden and decide that you must have it, remember

that the floral display that attracts you will probably last a month or less. Choose shrubs for their foliage and branching structure, not just for their flowers.

There are several considerations for designing a planting of flowering shrubs. First, try to find shrubs that flower at the same time, creating attractive combinations. Be sure their colors also harmonize with bulbs and other flowers on the property, as well as with the house and other structures. Second, think about which shrubs should be planted in masses or in small groups, rather than individually, for best effect.

Then consider the details of flower size and prominence, fragrance, and the shrub's size and growth habit. Be sure they are compatible in their soil and environmental needs. If your soil is not acidic, keep all ericaceous plants, such as rhododendrons and azaleas, in an area of soil that can be acidified without having to treat all the soil.

SUMMER SHRUBS WITH COOL COLORS

Buddleia davidii 'Dartmoor'
Calluna vulgaris 'Mair's Variety'
Calycanthus floridus
Caryopteris ×*clandonensis* 'Longwood Blue'
Clerodendrum thomsoniae
Hydrangea macrophylla 'Nikko Blue'
Hydrangea quercifolia 'Snow Queen'
Lavandula angustifolia
Rosa 'Iceberg'
Viburnum macrocephalum

In the charts on these two pages, you will find examples showing the range of colors possible with flowering shrubs in spring and summer.

SUMMER SHRUBS WITH WARM COLORS

Calluna vulgaris 'J.H. Hamilton'
Hydrangea 'Forever Pink'
Kalmia latifolia 'Weston Redbud'
Lagerstroemia 'Seminole'
Paeonia 'Age of Gold'

Potentilla fruticosa 'Gold Star'
Rosa 'Abraham Darby'
Rosa 'Europeana'
Rosa 'Graham Thomas'
Rosa 'Playboy'

Shrubs with Showy Leaves

Dwarf blue spruce combines with crimson barberry
for a dramatic effect.

SHRUBS WITH SHOWY FOLIAGE (BLUE AND GRAY)

Buxus sempervirens 'Newport Blue'
Chamaecyparis 'Dragon Blue'
Cornus alba 'Elegantissima'
Hebe 'Pewter Dome'
Juniperus horizontalis 'Blue Rug'
Juniperus squamata 'Blue Star'
Picea pungens 'Montgomery'
Picea pungens 'Procumbens'
Pittosporum tobira 'Variegatum'
Rosa glauca

Although seasonal gardens benefit from the careful use of flowering shrubs, it's not the color of the flowers but of the leaves that has the greater impact on the landscape. Leaves are present throughout the growing season and, on evergreen shrubs, year-round. By using foliage color to paint the landscape, you can create a long-lasting, harmonious setting for your home.

A leaf color of emerald green has a restful, neutral effect. Likewise, shades of cool blue, gray, and variegated green and white tend to recede visually in the border. Variegated shrubs, such as Japanese aucuba, can enliven a shady corner of the garden, the green of the leaves blending the plant into its surroundings while the white reflects the dim light and stands out. The typical yellow-leaved deciduous or evergreen shrub has a golden-greenish tint that can be jarring if overused in the garden but makes an outstanding highlight in a sunny border.

Red, another accent color, is the complement of green on standard color charts. Therefore, a shrub with bright red leaves creates a vibrant contrast against a green background. The exception is a shrub with dark purple leaves, which, from a distance, has a blackish effect on the landscape and creates a dramatic visual hole in a bed or border.

Fall foliage color is as arresting as the color of flowers. It may not last long, but while it does, red, orange, purple, and yellow leaves weave a spectacular tapestry of brilliant color.

SHRUBS WITH SHOWY FOLIAGE (RED AND BRONZE)

Albelia grandiflora 'Francis Mason'
Berberis thunbergii 'Bagatelle'
Berberis thunbergii 'Golden Nuggett'
Calluna vulgaris 'Wickwar Flame'
Cotinus coggygria 'Royal Purple'
Ilex crenata 'Golden Gem'
Photinia ×fraseri
Pieris japonica 'Christmas Cheer'
Pinus sylvestris 'Aurea Nana'

SHRUBS WITH SHOWY FOLIAGE (YELLOW)

Acuba japonica 'Picturata'
Buxus sempervirens 'Elegantissima'
Chamaecyparis obtusa 'Nana Aurea'
Chamaecyparis obtusa 'Nana Lutea'
Daphne ×burkwoodii 'Carol Mackie'
Euonymus fortunei 'Aureo-variegatus'
Juniperus communis 'Gold Cone'
Platycladus orientalis 'Aurea Nana'
Spiraea japonica 'Goldmound'
Taxus baccata 'Dovastoniana'

The fall foliage colors of shrubs are every bit as dramatic as those of trees.

Shrubs with Late-Season Appeal

The brilliant red berries of winterberry last until February or March.

Many deciduous shrubs still look terrific after the last fall leaf has dropped. Some bear flashy fruit in red, yellow, orange, purple, or blue that will last until spring. Others carry vibrant berries for hungry birds and visiting wildlife to devour.

SHRUBS WITH EDIBLE FRUIT

Shrubs often produce enticing fruits, some of which are edible and some of which are toxic. Don't sample the flavors in your landscape without knowing with certainty which species produce fruit edible to humans. Fruit may be red, orange, or yellow to green, blue, or purple, thus integrating colorfully

into your landscape design. Fruit also may attract birds and other wildlife, adding another dimension to the garden. But if you want the fruit for your own table, you may need to cover the shrubs with netting while they ripen.

Attractive shrubs with edible fruit include flowering quince, pomegranate, beach rose, highbush and lowbush blueberry, and American cranberrybush viburnum.

Winter color also shows in stems and bark, not only in berries, as the red bark of this dogwood (*Cornus alba* 'Siberica') demonstrates.

WINTER FLOWERS

Jump-start the growing season by planting shrubs that blossom in winter or by forcing branches of early-spring-flowering shrubs indoors. Winter-blooming deciduous shrubs include familiar plants such as witch hazel, (pictured at left) and pussy willow.

Among favorite winter-blooming evergreens are common camellia and winter daphne.

Shrubs that bloom in early spring are the best for forcing. Border forsythia, buttercup winter hazel, and lilac all work well. Forcing time varies, but the nearer it is to a plant's natural flowering time, the faster the stems will bloom. Simply cut the stems up to 3 feet long, then set them in a tall container of clean water until they flower. For quicker forcing, use warm water and set the container in bright, warm, indirect sunlight. Continue to add warm water as necessary. To delay blooming, place the vase in a cooler part of the room and, if necessary, add ice to the water.

Colorful or textured bark also makes an effective winter display in the home landscape. Japanese kerria, for example, boasts vivid arching green stems that stand out against winter's palette of whites, browns, and grays in the woodland garden.

Late-season interest is not confined to berries and bark. Harry Lauder's walking stick rises like an expressionist sculpture from the landscape. It is a shrub with greater impact in winter than in summer, when coarse leaves cover and, to a large extent, hide its curious, twisted branches. What's more, the branches are useful for indoor arrangements.

SHRUBS WITH SHOWY FRUIT

Berberis thunbergii
Berberis thunbergii 'Atropurpurea'
Callicarpa dichotoma
Clerodendrum trichotomum
    var. *fargesii*
Cotoneaster horizontalis
Hippophae rhamnoides
Ilex verticillata 'Red Sprite'
Mahonia bealei
Myrica pensylvanica
Nandina domestica
Punica granatum
Pyracantha coccinea
Pyracantha 'Santa Ana'
Pyracantha 'Soleil d'Or'
Rhus typhina 'Dissecta'
Viburnum davidii
Viburnum dentatum
Viburnum dilatatum
Viburnum setigerum 'Aurantiacum'
Viburnum trilobum

Shrubs with Year-Round Effect

American cranberrybush viburnum with white flower clusters in spring.

months of seasonal interest. For instance, dwarf fothergilla produces three seasons of beauty, with charming white bottlebrush flowers in spring, attractive medium-textured bright green leaves during the growing season, and luminous orange foliage in fall. Cream-edged tatarian dogwood stands out all four seasons with its spring flowers, variegated foliage, and colorful bark (in this case, glowing red stems) after the leaves drop.

Sometimes bark, like dead skin, peels off shrubby stems, giving them a lively three-dimensional look.

Broadleaf evergreens can have striking flowers and unusual leaves. For example, yaku rhododendron bears white, pink, or rose flowers in May on a shrub covered with leaves that are glossy green on

Choosing shrubs for year-round interest guarantees the everchanging beauty of a garden for the longest possible time. Moreover, because top-quality plants can also be expensive, selecting shrubs that are attractive for more than a few weeks a year gives value for your money.

Whereas evergreens offer year-round color and greater consistency, deciduous shrubs change from season to season. Some are noticeable only for a few weeks when in bloom. Others provide

American cranberrybush viburnum berries develop red coloration by mid-summer and remain colorful on the shrub through fall and winter.

DECIDUOUS SHRUBS FOR MORE THAN ONE-SEASON EFFECT

Red chokeberry (*Aronia arbutifolia* 'Brilliantissima')
Cream-edged tatarian dogwood (*Cornus alba* 'Argenteomarginata')
Variegated golden-twig dogwood (*Cornus stolonifera* 'Silver and Gold')
Harry Lauder's walking stick (*Corylus avellana* 'Contorta')
Warminster broom (*Cytisus ×praecox*)
Enkianthus (*Enkianthus* spp.)
Dwarf fothergilla (*Fothergilla gardenii*)
Large fothergilla (*Fothergilla major*)
Seven-son flower (*Heptacodium miconioides*)
Oakleaf hydrangea (*Hydrangea quercifolia* 'Snow Queen')
Flame azalea (*Rhododendron calendulaceum*)
Royal azalea (*Rhododendron schlippenbachii*)
Lowbush blueberry (*Vaccinium angustifolium*)
Highbush blueberry (*Vaccinium corymbosum*)
Double-file viburnum (*Viburnum plicatum* f. *tomentosum* 'Mariesii')
American cranberrybush viburnum (*Viburnum trilobum*)

top and felted with heavy brown hair below. The effect of the color and textural contrasts within each leaf gives this shrub a subtle richness. Oregon grapeholly and leatherleaf mahonia add showy berries to the winning combination of yellow flowers and evergreen leaves.

Because conifers add year-round color to the garden, you may be tempted to overuse them. Their density, however, can mire the composition in textural sameness. Especially in foundation plantings, use conifers with rounded forms to bring the gaze back to the earth. Conifers with pyramidal shapes sometimes grow tall and lead the gaze up the walls of the house, emphasizing the disparity between the elements in constructed and natural environments. When designing with conifers,

check their mature size before buying. Given their many colors and the proliferation

of dwarf varieties, conifers are fundamental to the well-landscaped home.

EVERGREEN SHRUBS FOR MORE THAN ONE-SEASON EFFECT

Heathers (*Calluna* spp.)
Sawara cypress (*Chamaecyparis pisifera* 'Golden Mop')
Wintergreen cotoneaster (*Cotoneaster conspicuus*)
Heaths (*Erica* spp.)
Salal (*Gaultheria shallon*)
Common juniper (*Juniperus communis* 'Berkshire')
Rocky Mountain juniper (*Juniperus scopulorum* 'Table Top Blue')
Drooping leucothoe (*Leucothoe fontanesiana* 'Girard's Rainbow')
Firethorn (*Pyracantha* spp.)

Abelia ×grandiflora
ab-BEE lee-a gran-di-FLO-ra

Trumpet-shaped pink flowers dangle from branches of glossy abelia.

GLOSSY ABELIA

- Pinkish-white flowers
- Medium-fine texture with lustrous leaves
- Rounded habit
- Zones 6 to 9

This easy, pest-free, 6-foot-tall plant has a graceful, arching silhouette that looks handsome even when not smothered in fragrant, pink-tinged white flowers from midsummer to midfall. Hybrid origin; species native to Asia.

USES: Abelia has glossy green summer foliage that turns bronze in fall. Use it as a specimen, an informal hedge, a grouping, or a mass; it combines well with broadleaf evergreens such as *Ilex* and *Pieris*.

GROWTH RATE: Moderate to fast.

CULTURE: Thrives in well-drained, acid soil with half to full sun and average watering. Experiences winter dieback, so prune any dead branches in northern zones. New growth comes back quickly.

RECOMMENDED VARIETIES: 'Prostrata' and 'Sherwoodii' are ground covers. 'Francis Mason' has green leaves with yellow margins.

Acacia farnesiana
a-KAY-sha farns-ee-AY-na

Blooming sweet acacia grows beautifully in a desert garden.

SWEET ACACIA

- Fragrant yellow flowers in early spring and after
- Shrub to 10 feet high and wide; tree to 20 feet with ample moisture
- Tiny, compound leaves and small spines
- Zones 9 and 10

This native of Texas and Mexico has globose 1- to 2-inch flower clusters that open in a burst in spring and continue in smaller numbers until fall.

USES: Accent or street tree (it is longer-lived than *A. baileyana*.).

CULTURE: Grows well in average soils and tolerates alkaline soils better than many acacias. Best in full sun to medium shade.

RELATED SPECIES: There are at least 80 species of acacia in commerce. The commonly planted Bailey acacia (*A. baileyana*), from Australia, has pale yellow flowers. It grows at least as tall as sweet acacia with adequate moisture but seldom lives longer than 20 years. Catclaw acacia (*A. greggii*) has delicately fragrant, creamy white flowers but is too thorny for public areas.

Aesculus parviflora
ES-kew-lus par-vi-FLOR-a

Upright flower spikes of bottlebrush buckeye punctuates the shade.

BOTTLEBRUSH BUCKEYE

- Late-season flowers
- Trouble-free foliage
- Suckering habit
- Zones 5 to 8

Give this wide-spreading shrub room to grow, and it will reward you with profuse, spectacular, 1-foot-long flower spikes that are white with protuberant red anthers. Leaves start bronze and turn an attractive yellow in autumn. Native to the woods of the U.S. coastal plains.

USES: Use it as a specimen or for massing and clumping in shady areas, such as under oak, ash, or maple trees.

GROWTH RATE: Slow to moderate.

CULTURE: Moist, well-drained soil amended with organic matter in sun to heavy shade. Suckering habit can be troublesome if the tree is not given room (8 to 15 feet) to grow.

RECOMMENDED VARIETIES AND RELATED SPECIES: 'Rogers' produces flower clusters 18 to 24 inches long. Red buckeye (*A. pavia*) has bright red flowers and disease-resistant foliage.

BEARBERRY

Arctostaphylos uva-ursi
ark-toe-STAFF-i-los oo-va ER-si

- Low, mat-forming ground cover
- Evergreen foliage
- Drought-tolerant
- Zones 2 to 7

1' 5'

With drooping, tiny, bell-shaped white to pink flowers followed by bright red berries, bearberry makes a useful, pleasing ground cover for poor, sandy soil. Transboreal native.
USES: Cultivate for a slow-growing, fine-textured evergreen ground cover, particularly suitable for the beach. Plant it with *Rosa rugosa* and *Juniperus conferta*.
GROWTH RATE: Slow.
CULTURE: Because it tolerates salt, and drought, bearberry is suited for a sunny location at the beach. Set plants 2 feet apart for complete cover in about two seasons.
RECOMMENDED VARIETIES: 'Massachusetts' and 'Vancouver Jade' form mats and are resistant to disease. 'Point Reyes', from California, is heat- and drought-tolerant. All have urn-shaped pale pink flowers and red berries.

Pink flowers of bearberry contrast nicely with its glossy green foliage.

RED CHOKEBERRY

Aronia arbutifolia
ah-ROW-nee-a ar-bew-ti-FOH-li-a

- Profuse red berries
- Red to purple fall color
- Easy to grow
- Zones 4 to 9

8' 10'

Ideal for massing, this care-free, leggy, upright shrub offers white spring flowers, good fall color, and gorgeous berries. Native to thickets in bogs, swamps, wet woods, and some dry soil from Nova Scotia to Florida, and west to Michigan, Missouri, and Texas.
USES: Use in large groups at a woodland's edge or around sunny ponds to accentuate fruit display and diminish its legginess. Plant it with *Ilex verticillata* and *Clethra alnifolia*.
GROWTH RATE: Slow.
CULTURE: Grows well in problem wet areas and heavy soil but tolerates prairie drought. Does not do well in dry, shallow, alkaline soil. Fruits best in full sun. No pruning is usually necessary.
RECOMMENDED VARIETIES AND RELATED SPECIES: 'Brilliantissima' (also known as 'Brilliant') has glossy dark green leaves that turn bright scarlet in autumn, profuse blooms, and a fuller habit and bigger berries than the species. Black chokeberry (*A. melanocarpa*) has white flowers followed by conspicuous, large black berries, wine red fall color, and a vigorous suckering habit.

Fall leaf color of chokeberry is amplified by large red berries.

ANGELS-HAIR WORMWOOD

Artemisia spp.
Ar-tay-MIS-ee-a

- Evergreen perennial
- Up to 2 feet tall
- Full sun
- Zones 5 to 9

2' 3'

These hardy, shrubby or herbaceous plants are grown for their ornamental, fragrant leaves or flowers. 'Silver Mound' (*A. schmidtiana*) forms fine-textured, 12-inch-tall silvery mounds. It grows best in well-drained, infertile soil. Roman wormwood (*A. pontica*) has feathery leaves that are whitish or ash gray underneath and fragrant when crushed. Its creamy white flowers bloom in September. Soft gray-green leaves look silky and produce dense, spreading coverage. Small, insignificant yellow flowers appear within foliage in summer.
USES: Hard-to-water or drought areas; good firebreak plant.
CULTURE: Water in dry weather. Propagate shrubby artemisia from cuttings taken in August or September. Perennial types can be propagated by division.

Angels-hair wormwood leaves are soft, threadlike, and silvery.

JAPANESE AUCUBA

Aucuba japonica
a-KEW-ba ja-PON-i-ka

Gold and green variegated leaves and red berries of Picturata Japanese aucuba.

- Large, leathery, evergreen leaves
- Good container plant
- Adaptable
- Zones 7 to 10

6'
5'

Available in different leaf colors and variegations, this broadleaf evergreen is a choice plant for dry shade.

USES: Does well in dim, north-facing entryways or under densely foliaged shade trees.

GROWTH RATE: Slow.

CULTURE: Grows in the shade of buildings, in containers, and under shade trees, where it competes well with tree roots. Cut branches back to keep it dense and rounded and to prevent it from becoming leggy. Variegated forms maintain their color best in open sites.

RECOMMENDED VARIETIES: 'Mr. Goldstrike', a male, has prominent gold markings on the leaves. 'Picturata' has leaves with a central golden blotch and are yellow-spotted within the margin. 'Sulphurea' has serrated leaves with broad gold edges and a dark green center.

COYOTE BRUSH

Baccharis pilularis
BA-ka-ris pill-you-LAR-us

Twin Peaks coyote brush grows in low mounds in dry soils.

- Adaptable to dry soils
- Dense, dark green ground cover
- Zones 8 to 10 (West)

2'
10'

This mounded shrub grows up to 2 feet tall and spreads 6 feet or more. Glossy green leaves densely cover its branches. Native to coastal California.

USES: Good for hot, dry areas, especially slopes.

GROWTH RATE: Slow to moderate.

CULTURE: Coyote brush does well in many soil types and climates, although it is best adapted to the western United States. It prefers well-drained soil and full sun but can thrive in damp, foggy climates in sandy soil or in heavier or alkaline soil and desert heat. Water during extremely hot and dry summers. Prune old, woody branches and upright stems in late fall. Buy plants propagated from seedless male plants. Female plants have messy, cottony seeds.

RECOMMENDED VARIETIES: 'Twin Peaks', with small dark green leaves, and lighter green 'Pigeon Point' are improved male selections.

JAPANESE BARBERRY

Berberis thunbergii
BER-ber-is thun-BARE-jee-eye

Rose Glow Japanese barberry leaves are rose-pink mottled with purplish-red.

- Shearable foliage
- Outstanding fall color
- Red, yellow, and variegated cultivars
- Zones 4 to 8

6'
8'

This upright, arching, rounded shrub has a dense profusion of thorny stems and finely textured foliage. Native to Japan.

USES: It makes a good formal or informal hedge. Plant red-leaved varieties with pink lilacs, and 'Crimson Pygmy' or 'Aurea' with sedum 'Autumn Joy'.

GROWTH RATE: Moderate.

CULTURE: Drought-tolerant, deciduous shrub grows in nearly any soil and in full sun to partial shade. Take care when near this plant because the thorns are dangerous. Also tends to be invasive.

RECOMMENDED VARIETIES AND RELATED SPECIES: 'Crimson Pygmy' is a good red-leaved ground cover or low hedge up to 2 feet tall and 3 feet wide for hot, sunny areas. 'Aurea' has intense yellow leaves that do not burn in the sun. Use mentor barberry (*B. ×mentorensis*) for hedging in the east and midwest.

BUTTERFLY BUSH

Buddleia davidii
BUD-lee-a dah-VID-ee-eye

- Fragrant flowers
- Attracts butterflies
- Coarse-textured
- Large flower spikes
- Zones 5 to 9

This sprawling shrub produces flowers in pink, blue, or purple. **USES:** Arching stems and gray-green leaves make a delightful addition at the back of the perennial border. It's an excellent companion to taller plants, such as cleome and sunflowers.

GROWTH RATE: Fast.

CULTURE: Plant this tender shrub in well-drained, fertile soil in full sun. Prune it every year to within a few inches of the ground in fall after it flowers or in early spring before growth begins.

RECOMMENDED VARIETIES AND RELATED SPECIES: 'Black Knight' is a robust dark purple. 'Nanho Blue' is slow, spreading, and mauve-blue. 'Pink Delight' produces huge, fragrant pink flowers and has silvery leaves. *B.* 'Lochinch' has fragrant blue flowers with an orange eye and silvery leaves.

Arching flowers of butterfly bush are attractive to butterflies.

COMMON BOXWOOD

Buxus sempervirens
BUK-sus sem-per-VIR-ens

- Hedges and topiary
- Evergreen leaves
- Dense habit
- Zones 6 to 10, some cultivars to Zone 5

Boxwood hedges are staples of formal gardens. Native to southern Europe, northern Africa, and western Asia.

USES: Hedging, massing, or topiary. Suitable companions include *Pyracantha coccinea* and shrub roses.

GROWTH RATE: Slow.

CULTURE: To thrive, boxwood needs a warm, moist climate without extremes of heat or cold. Plant in well-drained, moist soil amended with organic matter. Mulch heavily. Remove inner dead twigs and fallen leaves in branch crotches to prevent twig canker. Protect it from drying winds, and provide partial shade in hot climates. Do not cultivate around this plant's shallow roots.

RECOMMENDED VARIETIES AND RELATED SPECIES: 'Northern Find' and 'Vardar Valley' are hardy to Zone 5. Littleleaf boxwood (*B. microphylla*) and *B. m. koreana* are very hardy. Leaves turn yellow-brown in winter. *B. m.* 'Wintergreen' has superior winter color and is the boxwood most used in the north.

Common boxwood responds well to shearing and shaping.

CHINESE BEAUTYBERRY

Callicarpa dichotoma
kal-i-KAR-pa dye-COT-oh-ma

- Abundant, lilac-colored berries
- Long, slender, arching branches
- Pink flowers
- Zones 5 to 8

Attractive in early autumn, when the conspicuous clusters of small purple fruit are at their peak against a green background of leaves. Flowers are small and clustered.

USES: Use it massed in the mixed or shrub border, where its fruit contrasts beautifully with shades of green on other plants. Plant it with *Viburnum dilatatum* and *Heuchera* 'Palace Purple'.

GROWTH RATE: Fast.

CULTURE: Plant in well-drained soil in full sun or dappled shade. Tip-prune to tidy it up, or prune it to the ground in late winter.

RECOMMENDED VARIETIES AND RELATED SPECIES: *C. d. albifructus* is a white form. Taller-growing *C. bodinieri* 'Profusion' (Bodiner beautyberry) has 30 to 40 violet fruits per cluster, but they are not as persistent as Chinese beautyberry.

Distinctive lilac-violet berries cover the stems of Chinese beautyberry in fall.

Calycanthus floridus
kal-i-KAN-thus FLOR-i-dus

CAROLINA ALLSPICE

- ■ Flowers in late spring
- ■ Easy and adaptable
- ■ Sturdy
- ■ Neat, rounded habit
- ■ Zones 5 to 9

8'
8'

Allspice produces reddish-brown flowers with a spicy fragrance and numerous straplike petals. Native to the southeastern United States' woodlands. The dark green leaves, 2 to 8 inches long, have a camphor or clovelike scent when crushed.

Carolina allspice, an 8-foot-tall shrub, is prized for its fragrant flowers.

USES: Plant allspice around outdoor living areas, under windows, beside screen doors, in shrub borders, or wherever its distinctive strawberry scent will be appreciated in summer. **GROWTH RATE:** Slow. **CULTURE:** Allspice is a bushy, spreading shrub that grows in nearly any soil but does best in deep, moist loam. It's adaptable to sun or shade but doesn't grow as tall in sun. Pest-resistant. Prune after flowering. **RECOMMENDED VARIETIES:** 'Athens' has deeply fragrant, greenish-yellow flowers and yellow fall color.

Camellia japonica
ka-MEAL-i-a ja-PON-i-ka

JAPANESE CAMELLIA

- ■ Flowers December to March
- ■ Evergreen foliage
- ■ Often pyramidal
- ■ Zones 8 to 10

10'
6'

Camellias bear large flowers in shades of white to red against lustrous dark green leaves.

USES: A fine specimen, it is also excellent in mixed borders and massed in shady gardens. It blends well with other broadleaf evergreens, such as *Kalmia* and *Rhododendron*.

Camellia flowers are appreciated for their classic forms.

GROWTH RATE: Slow. Can be grown in containers. **CULTURE:** Grow in slightly acid soil high in organic matter. Avoid over-fertilization, salt buildup, and cultivation around shallow roots. No pruning is usually needed except to remove deadwood in spring. **RECOMMENDED VARIETIES AND RELATED SPECIES:** 'Debutante' is light pink, double, and early-flowering. 'Governor Mouton' has variegated red-and-white blossoms, cold-hardy buds. Sasanqua camellia (*C. sasanqua*) blooms from autumn to early winter.

Caragana arborescens
kara-GANE-a ar-bo-RES-enz

SIBERIAN PEASHRUB

- ■ Bright yellow flowers in May
- ■ Rapid-growing
- ■ A good windbreak
- ■ Zones 2 to 7

The weeping Pendula Siberian peashrub grows to 6 feet tall.

20'
15'

Siberian peashrub is extremely hardy with arching branches to the ground. Native to Siberia, Manchuria, and Mongolia.

USES: Plant it with *Arctostaphylos uva-ursi* and *Cornus alba*. **GROWTH RATE:** Medium to fast. **CULTURE:** Tough and easy to grow, peashrub tolerates poor soils,

drought, and alkalinity. Shear it for denser growth, although it is not suited for formal hedges. Peashrub is often trained as a small tree. It is valued as one of the most adaptable of all plants, even in exposed areas and in all types of soils. **RECOMMENDED VARIETIES:** 'Nana' is a dwarf form with contorted branches. 'Lorbergii' is extremely graceful, with fine-textured foliage. 'Pendula' has weeping branches grafted to a standard. The popular 'Walker', a hybrid of 'Lorbergii' and 'Pendula', combines their fine foliage texture and weeping habit.

NATAL PLUM

Carissa macrocarpa
CAR-ee-sa mac-row-CARP-a

- Glossy foliage
- Fragrant white flowers year-round
- Edible red fruit
- Barrier plant
- Zones 9 to 10

Natal plum has dark green, shiny leaves, sharp spines, and fragrant white or pink flowers, which are often followed by edible, plumlike fruits. Most natal plums grow 6 feet tall, but several varieties have a prostrate, ground-hugging habit and make fine ground covers. Native to South Africa.

USES: Coastal areas; barrier plant. Prostrate varieties for ground covers.

GROWTH RATE: Fast.

CULTURE: Full sun and any soil but prefers well-drained. Plants do well in coastal areas.

RECOMMENDED VARIETIES: Ground cover varieties include 'Horizontalis', which grows to about 2 feet; 'Green Carpet', which reaches about 18 inches; and 'Prostrata', which also grows to about 2 feet. 'Tuttlei' grows 3 feet tall and is semi-prostrate.

Flowers and maturing fruit of natal plum, an evergreen shrub.

BLUEBEARD

Caryopteris ×clandonensis
kar-i-OP-ter-is klan-doe-NEN-sis

- Flowers from mid-August to frost
- Beautiful against yellow or white flowers
- Loose, airy habit
- Zones 5 to 8

Bluebeard is valued for its compact size and delicate blue haze of flowers during late summer and early fall. It is a hybrid. Aromatic foliage.

USES: Bluebeard can be massed in front of sunny borders to emphasize its gray-blue misty effect, or use it as a perennial in the mixed border and with 'Moonbeam' *Coreopsis verticillata* and 'Sunny Border Blue' *Veronica*.

GROWTH RATE: Fast.

CULTURE: Put bluebeard in good garden soil with average water. Cut to the ground before new growth begins in early spring to keep it compact (2 to 3 feet high) and to increase blossoms.

RECOMMENDED VARIETIES: 'Azure' and 'Heavenly Blue' produce bright blue blooms. 'Blue Mist' has light blue flowers. 'Longwood Blue' has medium blue flowers on a gray-green mound of leaves and a long flowering period.

Deciduous bluebeard produces copious blue flowers in late summer.

CALIFORNIA LILAC

Ceanothus spp.
see-a-NO thus

- Best on West Coast
- Fragrant, lilac-like
- Glossy, dark evergreen leaves
- Zones 8 to 10 (west)

California lilac is grown for its fragrance and beautiful, fluffy panicles of blue, pink, or white flowers that are reminiscent of the lilac's conelike blooms in miniature.

USES: Mass as a ground cover on rocky slopes, or plant as a specimen.

GROWTH RATE: Moderate.

CULTURE: Plant in full sun in well-drained, rocky or sandy soil away from sprinklers and sheltered from cold, dry winds. Does not tolerate hot, alkaline soils. Prune only during dry summer months to avoid spreading disease. Repeated pruning will shorten its life.

RECOMMENDED VARIETIES AND RELATED SPECIES: 'Julia Phelps' produces dark blue flowers on a large evergreen shrub. Carmel creeper (*C. griseus horizontalis*) develops 2-inch blue flowers on 2- to 3-foot-high spreading evergreen shrub with lustrous, glossy leaves.

California lilac is a signature shrub of California's chaparral.

Chaenomeles speciosa
kee-NAH-ma-leez spee-see-OH-sa

Jane Taudevin flowering quince blooms early in spring.

COMMON FLOWERING QUINCE

- Early spring flowers
- Thorniness good for barriers
- Fragrant fruit used in jams and jellies
- Zones 5 to 9

8'

8'

Early blooms of red, scarlet, pink, or white flowers have long endeared quince to gardeners and flower arrangers. **USES:** Use as a hedge or barrier. Grow in a border or on a bank or train against a wall. Combine with bulbs such as *Narcissus* 'February Gold' and *Scilla siberica*.

GROWTH RATE: Moderate.
CULTURE: Flowering quince likes full sun and is adaptable to many types of soil, including prairie drought. Will thrive against a slightly shaded wall, but performs best, and produces fruit best, in full sun. Prune annually after spring bloom. May be renewed by pruning to 6 inches from the ground after blooming. Tolerant of pollution and urban environments.
RECOMMENDED VARIETIES: *C. ×superba* 'Cameo' develops prolific double apricot-colored flowers on a nearly thornless, low-growing shrub.

Chamaecyparis spp.
kam-ee-SIP-a-rus

Koster's false cypress develops an intriguing form and texture.

FALSE CYPRESS

- Evergreen foliage
- Size ranges from small shrubs to trees
- Medium texture
- Dwarf cultivars
- Zones 5 to 8, depending on species

3'

4'

Foliage may be bright yellow, deep green, gray, or blue. Some are adapted to moist coastal climates, others the harsher conditions of the midwest. **USES:** Use false cypress as a specimen or in a border.

GROWTH RATE: Slow.
CULTURE: Give it rich, well-drained soil; needs full sun in moist, mild climates and partial shade elsewhere. Transplant it in spring. Protect it from hot, drying winds.
RECOMMENDED VARIETIES AND RELATED SPECIES: Sawara cypress (*C. pisifera*) prefers acid soil and loses its inner foliage with age. 'Boulevard' grows to 15 feet with silver-blue foliage. 'Golden Mop' has threadlike bright gold foliage. Hinoki cypress (*C. obtusa*) is excellent in the midwest. 'Nana Gracilis' dwarf hinoki cypress eventually grows conical, to 7 feet tall and 3 feet wide.

Choisya ternata
CHOY-zy-a ter-NAH-ta

Evergreen Mexican orange produces many and very fragrant flowers.

MEXICAN ORANGE

- White flowers
- Potent fragrance
- Compact form
- Zones 8 (southern) to 10

8'

10'

Grow Mexican orange for its sweetly scented white flowers and handsome, glossy dark green evergreen foliage. Native to Mexico. **USES:** Plant it for fragrance near entryways, outdoor living areas, windows, walkways, and paths, wherever fragrance can be enjoyed. Good in a shrub border or against a wall. Plant it with *Daphne odora* 'Marginata' and *Lagerstroemia indica*.
GROWTH RATE: Moderate.
CULTURE: Grow Mexican orange in well-drained, acid soil rich in organic matter, and in full sun at the coast but in partial shade in climates with hot summers. Too much shade makes it leggy and prone to insect attacks. Water infrequently but deeply, and prune yearly to maintain a compact form about 4 to 5 feet tall and wide.
RECOMMENDED VARIETY: 'Sundance' has golden foliage and fragrant white flowers.

ROCK ROSE

Cistus spp.
SIS-tus

- Fragrant foliage
- Low-maintenance
- Five-petaled flowers
- Gray-green foliage
- Zones 8 to 10

Evergreen produces white, pink, rosy red, or purple flowers. **USES:** Rock rose is a colorful, drought-resistant, salt-tolerant, large-scale bank and ground cover that grows as an irregular mound 1 to 6 feet tall.

GROWTH RATE: Moderate.
CULTURE: Rock rose does best on the West Coast in fast-draining soil. Pinch tips of young plants to encourage denser growth. Do not move it once it's established, and avoid hard pruning.
RECOMMENDED VARIETIES AND RELATED SPECIES: 'Peggy Sammons' has delicate pink blooms and downy gray-green stems on a midsize shrub. Laurel rock rose (*C. laurifolius*) is the largest (reaching up to 6 feet in height) with 2- to 3-inch white blossoms with a yellow center and gray-green foliage.

Sunset rock rose produces 2-inch-wide flowers on a 3-foot-tall plant.

HARLEQUIN GLORYBOWER

Clerodendrum trichotomum
clare-oh-DEN-drum try-ko-TO-mum

- Tubular flowers
- Blue berries
- Vigorous
- Zones 6 to 9

Very fragrant mid- to late-summer white flowers, enclosed in a maroon calyx, with brilliant blue berries in early autumn make this an excellent addition to the garden. This upright, bushy shrub is native to eastern China and Japan.

USES: Useful in the shrub or mixed border for late-season interest. Can be trained over a trellis, pergola, or other support. Combine it with *Clethra alnifolia* 'Paniculata' and 'Pink Spire'.
GROWTH RATE: Fast.
CULTURE: Plant harlequin glorybower in moist, well-drained soil in full sun to partial shade. Especially in northern parts of Zone 6, treat it like a perennial, and cut it back before new growth begins in spring. May become invasive by suckering.
RELATED SPECIES: *C. ugandense* bears striking blue to violet flowers.

Showy flowers and berries are the prime attractions of harlequin glorybower.

SUMMERSWEET CLETHRA

Clethra alnifolia
KLETH-ra all-ni-FOH-lee-a

- Fragrant flowers
- Yellow fall color
- Attracts bees
- Broad, oval habit
- Zones 5 to 9

Summersweet clethra has a medium texture and fragrant white flower spikes in late summer.
USES: It can be used in wet, shady areas of the garden but thrives just about anywhere. Perfect for a mixed border or woodland. Summersweet clethra combines well with *Itea virginica* and *Ilex glabra*.
GROWTH RATE: Slow.
CULTURE: Grows best in moist, acid soil. Plant in early spring. When transplanting into wet soils, ease the transition by planting 3 to 4 inches higher than the soil level and by mulching. Prune after flowering in late summer, allowing the shrub to keep its dense, oval shape.
RECOMMENDED VARIETIES: 'Paniculata' is superior for its abundant, longer flower spikes.

'Rosea' has pink-tinged spires of fragrant flowers.

Flower spikes of Rosea summersweet clethra bloom in summer.

Coprosma repens
co-PROZ-ma REE-penz

Marble Queen mirror plant has glossy, variegated leaves.

MIRROR PLANT

- Glossy, evergreen foliage
- Inconspicuous flowers and fruit
- Upright habit
- Zones 9 and 10

6'
8'

Native to New Zealand, mirror plant is grown for its orange-red berries in late summer and its showy, fleshy foliage.
USES: Hedge, screen, foundation plant, or espalier. Good in rock gardens or as the border.
GROWTH RATE: Fast.
CULTURE: Salt- and drought-tolerant when established, it does well in virtually any soil. Mirror plant needs full sun on the coast and partial shade in hot inland areas. Will survive only in areas with little frost. Prune regularly.
RECOMMENDED VARIETIES AND RELATED SPECIES: *C. ×kirkii* is a wide-spreading, 2- to 3-foot-tall irregular shrub that makes a tough evergreen ground cover, especially where erosion is a problem. In autumn, it produces oblong berries that are translucent white, flushed or flecked with red. 'Variegata' has white-margined gray-green leaves and white berries.

Cornus alba 'Sibirica'
KOR-nus AL-ba sigh-BEER-i-ca

Notably red stems of redtwig dogwood stand out in winter landscapes.

REDTWIG DOGWOOD

- Red stems in winter
- Loose, open, erect
- Medium texture
- Easy to grow
- Zones 3 to 8

10'
15'

Brightly colored stems are an arresting sight in the winter landscape.
USES: Use it in the shrub border or massed on a large scale along drives, on banks, or naturalized around a pond.
GROWTH RATE: Fast.
CULTURE: Adapts to nearly any soil in sun or light shade. Remove at least one-third of the old growth every spring to encourage new growth with bright red stems.
RECOMMENDED VARIETIES AND RELATED SPECIES: Cream-edged tatarian dogwood (*C. a.* 'Argenteo-marginata') has leaves with creamy white edges and green centers. Red-osier dogwood (*C. stolonifera*) has red winter stems and takes soggy soils. 'Flaviramea' has yellow winter stems but is disease-prone. 'Isanti' is dwarf. 'Silver and Gold' has yellow stems and cream-colored leaf margins.

Cornus canadensis
KOR-nus can-a-DEN-sis

Bunchberry is a charming woodland ground cover.

BUNCHBERRY

- White flowers in spring
- Edible red berries
- Bright yellow to red fall color
- Zones 3 to 6

6"
3'

This ground cover has creeping, woody roots. Its leaves radiate around the stems in whorls. As is typical of its dogwood cousins, bunchberry has small flowers surrounded by four to six showy white bracts in spring. After flowering, small bunches of edible bright red fruits appear in late summer. Foliage turns bright yellow to red in autumn.
USES: Mass planting; to attract wildlife. Slow-growing round cover.
CULTURE: Plant in partial sun to full shade. Bunchberry spreads by underground runners but not invasively so. Plants can be difficult to establish; site preparation is the key to success. It prefers loose, moist, acid soil with plenty of organic matter mixed in. Protect plants from strong winds. Hard pruning may be needed to prevent overgrowth. Propagate from seed or hardwood cuttings, or by layering in fall.

Corylopsis pauciflora
kor-i-LOP-sis paw-si-FLOR-a

- Fragrant flowers
- Yellow fall color
- Fine to medium texture
- Zones 6 to 8

5'
8'

This small shrub is valued for its delicate, soft, yellow flowers, fine zigzag twigs, and dainty, horizontally spreading habit. Native to Japan.

USES: Mass it in a woodland setting or against a dark background to

BUTTERCUP WINTER HAZEL

show off its lovely spring flowers. Winter hazel looks good with Robusta Green Chinese juniper and *Rhododendron mucronulatum*.

GROWTH RATE: Moderate.

CULTURE: Plant buttercup winter hazel in well-drained, moist, somewhat acid soil in partial, dappled, or afternoon shade. If well-placed, it requires little care. Renew by pruning off oldest wood after or during bloom.

RELATED SPECIES: Spike winter hazel (*C. spicata*) is hardy to Zone 5 and is similar in size to buttercup

winter hazel, but its fragrant yellow blossoms hang in drooping clusters of 6 to 12 in spring.

Buttercup winter hazel produces yellow flowers in spring.

Corylus avellana 'Contorta'
KOR-i-lus a-vel-LAN-a con-TOR-ta

- Strikingly gnarled and curly stems
- Interesting winter silhouette
- Showy yellow catkins
- Zones 5 to 7

6'
6'

Harry Lauder's walking stick becomes a dramatic living sculpture with autumn leaf drop. Native to Europe, northern Africa, and western Asia.

USES: It's good as a focal point in an entryway or a courtyard, especially against a light-colored

HARRY LAUDER'S WALKING STICK

wall, which silhouettes its contorted branches. Particularly effective in winter and useful in flower arrangements. Plant it with European wild ginger (*Asarum europaeum*) and glory of the snow (*Chionodoxa*).

GROWTH RATE: Fast.

CULTURE: It adapts to a wide range of soils, acidity, and sunlight. This plant is easy to grow when you buy plants on their own roots. For grafted plants, prune vigorous suckers from below the graft union right away, or they may overtake the shrub's conspicuously twisted growth.

Curling branches of Harry Lauder's walking stick provide winter interest.

Cotinus coggygria
ko-TYE-nus ko-GIG-ree-a

- Cloudlike flowers
- Low-maintenance
- Medium texture
- Zones 5 to 8

12'
15'

Blossoms-like puffs of pinkish, whitish, and smoke-like, and an open, rounded, irregular habit give smoke tree exotic appeal.

USES: Plant in shrub borders as a textural and color accent and in masses and groups. Some have

SMOKE TREE

blue-green leaves, and some have outstanding fall color in reds, yellows, and purples. Combine with black-eyed Susan (*Rudbeckia*).

GROWTH RATE: Moderate.

CULTURE: Adapts to a variety of soils, including dry, rocky ones. Needs full sun. Water it often and deeply when young; it is drought-tolerant when established. Prune to remove dead branches.

RECOMMENDED VARIETIES: 'Velvet Cloak' retains its purple leaf color as the season progresses and has good red-purple fall color. 'Royal Purple'

is the darkest purple nonfading cultivar. 'Day Dream' is an especially floriferous form with pink flower stalks.

Deep purple leaves of smoke tree contrast with pinkish blooms.

COTONEASTER

Cotoneaster spp.
ka-TOH-nee-as-ter

- Lustrous leaves
- Pink or white flowers followed by red berries
- Spreading habit
- Zones 5 to 8, depending on species

A handsome and versatile shrub, cotoneaster suits many garden styles and conditions. Native to China.

USES: Use it as a ground cover, in masses, or in the shrub border.

GROWTH RATE: Fast.

CULTURE: Cotoneaster is adaptable to many soils but prefers well-drained soil in a sunny, airy location.

RECOMMENDED VARIETIES AND RELATED SPECIES: Bearberry

 cotoneaster (*C. dammeri*) is one of the best broadleaf evergreens for ground covering because of its hardiness, attractive leaves, good fruiting color, rapid growth, and low, prostrate habit. White flowers bloom in May, followed by small red berries. It spreads to 6 feet or more and remains less than 1½ feet tall. It is a good choice for dry, rocky soil in a sunny place. 'Lowfast' is hardy to southern Zone 5. 'Coral Beauty'

Cotoneaster conspicuus branches are cloaked with white flowers in spring.

flowers and fruits freely. 'Streibs Finding' has a low, prostrate habit.

 Spreading cotoneaster (*C. divaricatus*) is one of the most handsome cotoneasters for summer and fall foliage, fruit, and graceful form. It grows 5 to 6 feet tall and 6 to 8 feet wide. Rose-colored flowers in May are followed by red fruit from September to November. Fall colors are fluorescent in yellow and red. It prefers moist, well-drained soil but also performs well on dry, rocky, windy sites, making it a good choice for the seashore.

 Rock cotoneaster (*C. horizontalis*) can be planted to spill over walls, down slopes, and over rocks. The angular, layered form and herringbone branches add an unusual texture to the garden. It can control erosion. Fall color is red except in mild climates, where the leaves remain a green all winter.

By fall, *C. conspicuus* flowers have turned into red berries.

 Many-flowered cotoneaster (*C. multiflorus*) is one of the most trouble-free of the cotoneasters, as well as one of the most beautiful. May flowers are followed by red berries that persist through October. This is a graceful, arching, mounded or fountainlike shrub growing 8 to 12 feet tall and 12 to 15 feet wide. Use it in the shrub border or for massing. Blue-green leaves have little to no fall color.

Willowleaf cotoneaster (*C. salicifolius*, Zones 6 to 8) is another large, arching cotoneaster similar to many-flowered cotoneaster, but with elongated dark green leaves. Good for large-scale massing in southern gardens. Bright red berries are attractive all winter.

Cotoneaster horizontalis 'Variegatus' makes a handsome groundcover.

Rock cotoneaster branches grow in a herringbone fashion.

Cotoneaster salicifolius 'Autumn Fire' can be trained to a weeping form.

WARMINSTER BROOM

Cytisus ×praecox
SIT-i-sus PREE-koks

- Year-round color
- Profuse pale yellow flowers
- Medium-fine texture
- Zones 6 to 8

This large shrub has grasslike, evergreen stems, sparse deciduous leaves, and pale yellow flowers. Hybrid origin.

USES: Plant it anywhere for evergreen accent in winter and a showy spring display. Plant it with evergreen candytuft *(Iberis sempervirens),* and ornamental grasses.

GROWTH RATE: Fast.

CULTURE: Dry, infertile, poor soil. Tip-pinch young plants, but older plants should develop their own natural form.

RECOMMENDED VARIETIES AND RELATED SPECIES: 'Goldspeer' produces abundant yellow blooms. 'Hollandia' is a 4-foot shrub with prolific pink blossoms. *C. decumbens* (prostrate broom) is a low, creeping form with golden yellow flowers in spring and is useful for ground cover. Common broom *(C. scoparius)* is a 6-foot shrub with golden yellow flowers.

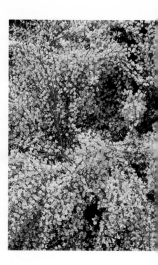

Allgold warminster broom at peak flower.

TRAILING INDIGO BUSH

Dalea greggii
DAY-lee-ah GREG-ee-eye

- Lavender flowers
- Drought gardens
- Stabilizes soil
- Zones 8 to 10 (desert only)

This evergreen plant's low, spreading, rooting branches typically reach 1 foot in height but occasionally grow as high as 2 feet; plants spread 4 to 8 feet wide. Leaves are small, gray, and evergreen. Clusters of small rose-lavender flowers appear from spring to early summer. Very drought-tolerant, this desert plant is native to western Texas, and it grows well throughout dry areas of the western United States.

USES: Desert regions, moderate to large areas; erosion-control ground cover on level or sloping sites.

GROWTH RATE: Watering deeply once a week will increase growth rate. Propagate from stem cuttings. Young plants and cuttings may succumb to an unidentified fungal pathogen.

CULTURE: It tolerates dry, hot climates and a wide range of soils if well-drained.

Lavender flowers contrast beautifully with gray leaves of trailing indigo bush.

ROSE DAPHNE

Daphne cneorum
DAF-nee nee-OH-rum

- Finely textured evergreen foliage
- Perfumed flowers
- Low, trailing mass
- Zones 5 to 7

This spring bloomer is one of the most fragrant shrubs available. Native to central and southern Europe.

USES: Rose daphne can serve as a small-scale ground cover, in a rock garden, in shady spots, near entrances, or in groupings. It looks good with winter honeysuckle *(Lonicera fragrantissima).*

GROWTH RATE: Slow.

SITING AND CARE: It performs best in well-drained, pH-neutral soil, protected from hot sun and drying winds. Plant high to reduce chance of crown rot. Don't cultivate or move it after it is established.

RECOMMENDED VARIETIES AND RELATED SPECIES: *D. c.* var. *variegata* has cream-edged foliage. *D. ×burkwoodii* (Zones 4 to 7) has extremely fragrant flowers that open white in May. Compact, rounded to about 3 feet tall and wide. 'Carol Mackie' has green leaves edged in pale yellow, grows in sun or light shade.

Evergreen rose daphne is very fragrant.

Daphne odora
DAF-nee oh-DOH-rah

Fragrant flowers of Aureomarginata winter daphne.

WINTER DAPHNE

- Rosy pink flowers
- Lustrous leaves
- Compact shrub
- Zones 7 to 10

3'
3'

Winter daphne blooms in February and March and has 3-inch-long leaves. Sweet, lemony scent.

USES: A sometimes difficult plant that can thrive in shady woodland conditions. Excellent in foundation plantings or in borders near walks or patios.

GROWTH RATE: Slow.

CULTURE: Give winter daphne

perfect drainage, water it infrequently during the summer, and plant it high. In colder regions, this evergreen should be sheltered by a wall. Protect from winter sun and wind. May be short-lived.

RELATED SPECIES: *D. o. alba* has white flowers. 'Aureomarginata' has yellow-margined green leaves and is a little more cold-hardy. February daphne (*D. mezereum*, Zones 5 to 8) produces purple flowers in late March or early April, before the leaves sprout on this vertically branched, 3- to 5-foot-tall shrub. Red fruits are poisonous.

Deutzia gracilis
DOOT-see-a gra-SIL-iss

White flowers cover low-growing slender deutzia in spring.

SLENDER DEUTZIA

- Low, broad, mounded shrub with arching branches
- Pure white flowers
- Medium texture
- Zones 5 to 8

5'
6'

Dependably lavish white blossoms in May.

USES: Plant easy-to-grow slender deutzia in the mixed shrub border where its plain appearance when not in bloom can blend with other shrubs.

GROWTH RATE: Slow to medium.

CULTURE: Grow in any good garden soil in full sun to light shade. Prune

winter dieback immediately after flowering. Growth starts quite early in some areas and may be damaged by late-spring frosts.

RECOMMENDED VARIETIES AND RELATED SPECIES: *D. crenata* 'Nikko' is a dwarf variety that grows 12 to 18 inches tall and 2 to 3 feet wide. *D. ×rosea* 'Carminea' is dwarf with rosy pink flowers on arching branches. *D. lemoinei* is a twiggy shrub 5 to 7 feet tall with white flowers that appear after those of slender deutzia. *D. scabra* 'Codsall Pink' grows to 5 to 7 feet tall, with double pink flowers and orange-brown bark.

Elaeagnus pungens
ell-ee-AG-nus PUN-jens

Maculata silverberry displays a prominent gold blotch.

SILVERBERRY

- Evergreen foliage
- Powerfully fragrant flowers in October
- Zones 7 to 10

10'
15'

Silverberry, a thorny evergreen with olive-colored leaves (speckled with brown beneath), is an excellent barrier shrub for hot, dry climates and poor soil.

USES: Use it as a hedge or barrier. Good in heat, wind, and drought. Provides excellent shelter in exposed and coastal situations.

GROWTH RATE: Very fast.

CULTURE: Prefers poor, infertile soil. Without pruning, it rapidly becomes a rigid, sprawling, angular shrub 6 to 16 feet tall. Should be pruned as necessary to restrict its vigorous growth.

RECOMMENDED VARIETIES: 'Aurea' has yellow edges on the leaves. 'Fruitlandii' has rounder, larger, wavy-edged leaves with silver below and a more symmetrical outline than the species. 'Maculata' has a large golden blotch in the center of each leaf. 'Variegata' is similar to 'Aurea' but with paler yellow margins.

Enkianthus campanulatus
en-kee-AN-thus cam-pan-u-LAY-tus

- Flowers in May
- Red fall color
- Interesting horizontal branching structure
- Zones 5 to 8

10'
8'

Redvein enkianthus produces delicate yellowish clusters of bell-like flowers that are veined with red. Leaves turn shades of orange-red in autumn. **USES:** Use as a specimen near

REDVEIN ENKIANTHUS

entryways and outdoor living areas. Perfectly suited to an open position in the woodland garden. Flowers last a long time in arrangements.
GROWTH RATE: Slow.
CULTURE: Needs moist, well-drained acid soil. Plant it in full sun to partial shade. Water well during times of drought.
RECOMMENDED VARIETIES AND RELATED SPECIES: 'Albiflorus' has whiter flowers than the species. White enkianthus (*E. perulatus,* Zone 6) grows to 7 feet with dark green leaves, scarlet fall foliage, and urn-

shaped, small white flowers in spring.

Red Bells redvein enkianthus has more intense flower color than most cultivars.

Escallonia rubra
ess-ka-LONE-ee-a ROO-bra

- Red flowers in summer and fall
- Evergreen foliage
- Medium texture
- Zones 8 to 10

10'
8'

This South American native is a tough, virtually foolproof shrub for warm coastal gardens.
USES: Screen or windbreak, or for massing and integrating into the shrub border. Plant it with Darwin's barberry (*Berberis darwinii*) and blue passion flower (*Passiflora caerulea).*

ESCALLONIA

GROWTH RATE: Fast.
CULTURE: Plant it away from highly alkaline soils. Provide partial shade in hot inland gardens. It tolerates short periods of drought but performs best with adequate watering. Prune lightly to keep its form compact. Otherwise, it grows 6 to 13 feet tall with a dense, mounded, upright habit.
RELATED SPECIES: *Escallonia ×exoniensis* 'Balfourii' (Zones 9 and 10) grows up to 10 feet tall with drooping branchlets and pink blossoms. 'Frades' (Zones 9 and 10) produces abundant pink flowers and retains a compact 5 to 6 feet height.

Closeup of pink escallonia flowers, which cover the plant in late spring.

Euonymus alatus
yew-ON-i-mus a-LAY-tus

- Exceptional fall color
- Vase-shaped habit
- Big, corky ridges or wings on stems
- Zones 4 to 7

12'
15'

Brilliant scarlet fall foliage color.
USES: Makes a good unclipped hedge or screen, in groups, in the shrub border, or as a specimen.

BURNING BUSH

GROWTH RATE: Slow.
CULTURE: Adaptable to many soils and growing conditions except wet ones. Full sun to heavy shade. Needs moister soil in full sun. Grows 12 to 15 feet tall and wide, so leave plenty of room for it to expand. Pruning destroys its neat outline and causes uneven growth. All parts of the plant are mildly toxic.
RECOMMENDED VARIETIES: Dwarf burning bush (*E. a.* 'Compactus', Zones 5 to 7) is more compact and dense than one species and grows 10 feet tall; pinkish-red fall color.

'Rudy Haag' grows 4 to 5 feet tall with rosy red fall color.

Burning bush is always noticed and much loved for its brilliant fall color.

Euonymus fortunei
yew-ON-i-mus for-TOO-nee-eye

Moonshadow wintercreeper euonymus.

WINTERCREEPER EUONYMUS

- One of the hardiest broadleaf evergreens
- Spreading and bushy forms
- Disease-prone
- Zones 5 to 8

3'

5'

An extremely versatile landscape shrub.

USES: Plant it as a ground cover, vine, wall cover, or low hedge.

GROWTH RATE: Fast.

CULTURE: Tolerant of all but the wettest soil; withstands full sun to heavy shade. Susceptible to several pests and diseases, especially euonymous scale. Avoid harsh, windy locations where the foliage is prone to browning in winter.

RECOMMENDED VARIETIES AND RELATED SPECIES: Japanese euonymus (*E. japonicus*) is hardy in Zones 8 to 10. It becomes a small tree 15 feet tall and 8 feet wide and can make a tough, low-maintenance shrub. Spreading euonymus (*E. kiautschovicus*) is an 8- to 10-foot-tall shrub in Zones 8 and 9, lower in Zones 6 and 7. 'Dupont' is hardier and more compact, with a more robust habit, but it is susceptible to disease.

Exochorda racemosa
eks-oh-KOR-da ra-se-MOH-sa

Deciduous pearlbush covers itself with flowers in spring.

PEARLBUSH

- Covered in pearl-like white buds
- Medium texture
- Irregular habit
- Zones 5 to 8

4'

4'

A large, spreading shrub that is lovely in spring, when stems are cloaked with white flowers and blue-green leaves.

USES: Useful as a specimen or for the spring-flowering mixed border and for the shrub border, where its rather unruly habit will be hidden after flowering.

GROWTH RATE: Moderate.

CULTURE: Plant in well-drained, acid soil in full sun to partial shade; provide average watering. Prune annually after flowering to remove weak or crossing stems and to maintain a more compact habit and reduce crowding.

RECOMMENDED VARIETIES AND RELATED SPECIES: *E. ×macrantha* 'The Bride' grows 3 to 4 feet tall and wider with a somewhat weeping habit and profuse white flowers in mid- to late spring; it's less cold-hardy than pearlbush. Wilson's pearlbush (*E. giraldii* var. *wilsonii*) is showy and hardy to Zone 5.

Forsythia ×intermedia
for-SITH-ee-a in-ter-MEE-dee-a

Golden blooms of forsythia signal the arrival of spring.

BORDER FORSYTHIA

- Spectacular pale to deep yellow flowers
- Medium texture
- Upright, arching, vigorous habit
- Zones 5 to 9

9'

12'

Long popular for forcing branches; it blooms in early spring.

USES: When allowed room to grow and to maintain its natural massive, mounded habit, forsythia is dramatic in the distant landscape.

GROWTH RATE: Fast.

CULTURE: It grows in any soil but requires full sun, water, and feeding. Plant it in protected areas to shield flower buds from spring frosts. Prune annually after flowering by removing one-third of the oldest canes. Do not shear. Renew old plants by cutting to the ground.

RECOMMENDED VARIETIES AND RELATED SPECIES: 'Lynwood' and 'Spring Glory' are the most popular varieties. Hybrids 'Meadow Lark' and 'Northern Gold' are cold-hardy to Zone 4 and floriferous with an erect form. *F. suspensa* (Zones 5 to 8) has a gracefully pendulous form that cascades over banks.

Fothergilla major
faw-ther-GIL-la MAY-jer

- Profuse, honey-scented blooms
- Long-lasting fall color
- Neat, rounded habit
- Zones 5 to 8

Blooms in April or May and has fluorescent orange, yellow, and red fall foliage.

USES: Use in groups, borders, or as specimens in the woodland garden.

LARGE FOTHERGILLA

GROWTH RATE: Medium.

CULTURE: It does best in acid, well-drained soil. Grows well in partial shade, but full sun encourages more flowers and improves autumn color.

RECOMMENDED VARIETIES AND RELATED SPECIES: Dwarf fothergilla (*F. gardenii,* Zones 5 to 8) is similar except for size (3 to 5 feet tall) and flowers, which are smaller and appear before the leaves. It is an attractive plant for smaller spaces. 'Blue Mist' has blue-green leaves. 'Mount Airy' grows to 5 feet tall with outstanding fall color and flowers.

White flower clusters cover large fothergilla in spring.

Fuchsia ×hybrida
FEW-shya HIBE-rid-a

- Flamboyant, multicolored flowers
- Shrubby to cascading
- Medium texture
- Zones 10 and 11

Fuchsia flowers from early summer to frost and attracts hummingbirds.

USES: As an espalier, an upright specimen for the rock garden, or in the shrub border.

GROWTH RATE: Fast.

CULTURE: Best in areas with cool summers, high atmospheric moisture,

HYBRID FUCHSIA

filtered shade, and moist, rich soil. Mulch heavily, mist, and water frequently in dry climates. Protect from hot, searing winds. Apply liquid fertilizer lightly every 10 to 14 days throughout the growing season. Pinch stems back frequently to encourage dense growth. Prune annually in early spring before new growth starts, keeping at least two healthy buds on each branch.

RELATED SPECIES: Hardy fuchsia (*F. magellanica,* Zones 6 to 10) grows to a graceful, rounded, 3-foot shrub each year in the north after dying back in winter (4 to 8 feet tall in the Deep South). It bears profuse

bright red flowers with blue inner petals, smaller than those of common fuchsia.

Gartenmeister Bonstedt fushia produces flowers year-round.

Gardenia augusta
gar-DEE-nee-a a-GUST-a

- Magnificent fragrance
- Large, waxy white flowers in summer
- Glossy, evergreen leaves
- Zones 8 to 10

An intensely fragrant, beautiful shrub worth the maintenance it requires.

USES: Use as a specimen in containers, and in raised beds, hedges, low screens, or espaliers.

GROWTH RATE: Moderate.

GARDENIA

CULTURE: Avoid alkaline soil, poor drainage, and drought. Plant crowns high in acid soil rich in organic matter in a site protected from full sun. Mist regularly in early morning while plant is not in bloom. Feed every 3 to 4 weeks with an acid plant food. Spray to control sucking insects. Best in areas with warm evenings; gardenias do not bloom well in cool-summer climates.

RECOMMENDED VARIETIES: 'Radicans' has a prostrate habit that makes it an effective ground cover on a limited scale. 'Radicans

Variegata' is similar but with creamy white to pale yellow leaf margins. 'August Beauty' is a robust shrub 4 to 6 feet tall with big, profuse, double white flowers.

Enjoy classic form with an unforgettable scent in Veitchii gardenia.

Gaultheria procumbens
gawl-THE-ree-a pro-KUM-benz

Fragrant wintergreen makes an ideal woodland ground cover.

WINTERGREEN

- Aromatic green foliage
- White flowers
- Red berries attract birds
- Burgundy fall color
- Zones 3 to 10

Wintergreen is a beautiful, herblike, woody evergreen ground cover that grows 3 to 10 inches tall. Its round leaves become leathery with age and turn a rich burgundy in spring and fall. Crushing them releases aromatic wintergreen oil. Small, bell-shaped white flowers are followed by edible red berries that are attractive to birds and other wildlife.

USES: Ground cover in bogs, woodland, or shady areas.
GROWTH RATE: Moderate.
CULTURE: Shady location with well-drained, moist, acid soil. Propagate from seed sown in spring, from stem cuttings, or by division.
RELATED SPECIES: Creeping pearlberry (*G. hispidula*) grows 2 to 3 inches tall. It has white flowers and white berries.

Genista spp.
jen-IS-ta

Broom at peak bloom.

BROOM

- Yellow flowers in spring
- Tough ground cover
- Zones 6 to 9

Evergreen or deciduous, depending on the species, its common name is from the whiplike branches. All species have sparsely covered branches and masses of pealike yellow to golden flowers from late spring to late summer.
USES: Hot, dry settings (except desert) and coastal areas; drought-prone slopes or banks.

CULTURE: Brooms prefer dry, well-drained, poor-quality, slightly acid to alkaline soil, and full sun. Brooms do not transplant well. Shelter them from wind. Pinch shoots annually to encourage bushiness. Propagate from seed sown in early spring.
RELATED SPECIES: Lydia broom (*G. lydia*) is a dwarf deciduous species with drooping branches. Silky-leaf broom (*G. pilosa*) is deciduous and grows to 18 inches; it has silky hairs on its flowers and foliage. Dyer's greenwood (*G. tinctoria*) grows up to 2 feet tall and is hardy to Zone 4.

Hamamelis ×intermedia
ham-a-MEAL-is in-ter-MEE-dee-a

Sunburst witch hazel has spidery flowers in spring.

HYBRID WITCH HAZEL

- Red, orange, and yellow foliage in fall
- Yellow, red flowers
- Spicily fragrant
- Zones 5 to 8

Spider-shaped flowers are produced in early spring on leafless branches and can withstand long periods of extreme cold.
USES: Excellent woodland shrub.
GROWTH RATE: Slow.
CULTURE: Plant in rich, moist soil in full sun to partial shade. Needs watering during droughts. Prune to remove dead wood.
RECOMMENDED VARIETIES AND RELATED SPECIES: 'Arnold Promise' medium-sized, bright yellow flowers. 'Jelena' has yellow flowers with copper, and orange, red, and scarlet foliage in fall. 'Diane' has deep red flowers and rich red fall color. *H. virginiana*, Zones 5 to 9, grows 15 to 20 feet tall and wide, with tiny yellow flowers in late winter and clear yellow fall foliage. Japanese witch hazel (*H. japonica*; Zones 5 to 8) has fragrant yellow flowers and yellow fall color.

Calluna, Daboecia, Erica
ca-LUN-a, da-BEE-see-a, AIR-ee-ka

Blooming Scotch heather makes a carpet of pink.

Scotch heather (*Calluna vulgaris*) is a true heather. It is 6 to 24 inches tall (depending on species) and spreads 2 to 8 feet with dark green, sometimes gold to brown, foliage on dense branches. It has a mounding, spreading growth habit. Small, bell-shaped flowers in pink, purple, or white on spikes appear in mid- to late summer and, in some varieties, to fall. Flowers attract bees. Grow in acid, well-drained soil in sun or light shade. Plants do best in cool, moist climates. They will grow in poor, well-drained, acid soil.

Before new growth begins in spring, prune previous year's growth at its base. In cold climates, mulch plants with evergreen branches in

HEATHS AND HEATHERS

winter. Space plants 12 to 18 inches apart. Apply acid fertilizer in late winter, again in early spring. Do not add lime. In hot, dry climates, water frequently to keep soil moist. Hardy in Zones 5 to 9.

Irish heath (*Daboecia cantabrica*) is a 2-foot-tall evergreen perennial shrub with thin stems and small, oval leaves that are dark green on top, white underneath. Spikes of bell-shaped flowers in white, purple, mauve, and red come early summer to late fall. Some have bicolored or double-petaled flowers. Plants like moist, well-drained, organic soil and a sunny location. They do fine in partial shade, but sprawl and may need more frequent pruning. Space plants 2 feet apart and protect from cold winds. They need low to moderate watering. Hardy in Zones 6 to 10.

Most true heaths (*Erica carnea*) are 12 to 18 inches tall. Evergreen foliage ranges from gold and silver to lime green. Scented, bell-shaped flowers are white to lavender to scarlet. Plants prefer full sun and acid, organic, well-drained soil. Prune after flowering to promote bushiness. Add peat moss to soil before planting to enhance growth. Plants generally do not need fertilizer. Protect them from cold, drying winds. Plants grow best in cool, moist climates in Zones 6 to 8.

Erica ×*darleyensis* 'Mediterranean Pink'.

Heather blooms are often shades of pink or white.

Hebe spp.
HEE-bee

- Bottlebrush flower
- Long bloom period
- Green, silver, or creamy variegated evergreen foliage
- Invaluable for seashore areas
- Zones 8 to 10

Shrubby veronica produces mauve, red, purple, blue, or white flowers from early summer to late fall.
USES: Cultivated for its flowers and evergreen foliage, shrubby veronica is useful for bedding, containers, and

SHRUBBY VERONICA

difficult sites, including rock gardens, where few other plants will thrive.
GROWTH RATE: Fast.
CULTURE: It is adaptable to any well-drained soil in full sun, including seashore conditions. Prune to renew every four to five years.
RECOMMENDED VARIETIES AND RELATED SPECIES: Autumn Glory grows 2 feet tall and wide with 2-inch deep lavender-blue flowers in late summer. *H. buxifolia* is a rounded form to 5 feet tall and wide, with white flowers in small clusters in summer, and is one of the hardier

(to Zone 8) shrubby veronica; 'Patty's Purple' has deep purple flowers.

Autumn Glory shrubby veronica is a low-growing shrub that blooms in late summer.

Heptacodium miconioides
hep-ta-KOH-dee-um mi-ko-nee-OY-deez

Fragrant white flowers appear on seven-son flower in late summer.

SEVEN-SON FLOWER

- Exfoliating tan bark
- Fragrant, delicate white flowers
- Rose to purple sepals
- Zones 6 to 8

12'
8'

An increasingly popular shrub from western China, seven-son flower has an upright, multi-stemmed habit and provides year-round interest. White flowers in late summer are followed by showy rose-purple sepals that remain effective for a month or more. Prized for its attractive, peeling light tan to brown bark. Dark green leaves become purple-tinged in fall.

USES: Attractive in shrub borders, where its legginess can be faced down with shorter shrubs. Works well in urban gardens; good tolerance for drought and salt conditions. Plant with blue hydrangeas and azaleas.

GROWTH RATE: Fast.

CULTURE: Flowers best in well-drained, acid soil in full sun, but tolerates partial or dappled shade and alkaline soil, occasional drought. Water sparingly in winter. Cut out dead or broken branches.

Hibiscus syriacus
high-BISS-kus see-ree-AY-kus

Closeup of Red Heart rose of sharon flower shows its relation to hibiscus.

ROSE OF SHARON

- Flowers in white, red, purple, and violet
- Medium texture
- Shrub or small tree
- Zones 5 to 9

12'
10'

Grow this popular, round-topped shrub for late-season flowers 2 to 4 inches wide.

USES: Use grouped or massed in a border. Combine with shore juniper (*Juniperus conferta*).

GROWTH RATE: Moderate.

CULTURE: Salt- and wind-tolerant. Thrives in well-drained soil and in full sun; tolerates partial shade. Susceptible to insects in humid climates. Prune to two or three buds per stem each spring for increased flowers.

RECOMMENDED VARIETIES AND RELATED SPECIES: 'Diana' has ruffled clear white flowers; 'Blue Bird' has light violet-blue flowers. 'Minerva' has a dark red eyespot and lavender petals tinged pink. Chinese hibiscus (*H. rosa-sinensis*, Zones 9 and 10) has huge flowers in many shades and grows fast to 30 feet tall with moist, well-drained soil, sun, heat, and protection from wind and frost.

Hippophae rhamnoides
HIP-o-figh ram-NOY-deez

Use sea buckthorn berries to make a vitamin-C-rich beverage.

SEA BUCKTHORN

- Orange fruit clusters
- Lancelike leaves
- Spreading, suckering, thorny habit
- Zones 3 to 7

20'
15'

A valuable addition to seaside gardens, with female plants producing tiny yellow-green flowers followed by edible bright orange fruit (both male and female plants are needed to produce fruit.). Leaves are dark gray-green on top and lustrous silver on bottom.

USES: Good, low-maintenance plant for borders and massing. Plant in a mixed border, as a specimen plant, as well as in the wild garden. Plant sea buckthorn in combination with spreading cotoneaster (*Cotoneaster divaricatus*).

GROWTH RATE: Fast.

CULTURE: It grows best in full sun. Tolerates salty and wet conditions. Succeeds in almost any soil. For fruit, plant one male buckthorn for every half-dozen females. Prune in late summer if necessary. Because it is difficult to transplant, use care and consideration when siting.

SMOOTH HYDRANGEA

Hydrangea arborescens
by-DRAN-jya ar-bor-ESS-enz

- Rounded, creamy flower cluster 4 to 6 inches wide
- Bold texture
- Low, clumpy habit
- Zones 3 to 9

4'
6'

Long-lasting, lavish flowers from midsummer to early fall grow on a tough, multistemmed shrub. Flowers can be used in dried arrangements.

USES: Smooth hydrangea is good for a range of garden sites. It works well in group plantings or as a single specimen, in a shrub border, or even in containers.

GROWTH RATE: Fast.

CULTURE: Prefers well-drained, moist soil rich in organic matter. It does best in partial shade but adapts well to full sun if kept watered. Salt-tolerant and pH adaptable. It flowers on new growth, so prune in late fall or early spring to keep it compact. Provide shelter from cold, drying winds. Contact with the foliage may irritate skin.

RECOMMENDED VARIETIES: 'Grandiflora' bears 4- to 6-inch creamy white snowball clusters from midsummer to early autumn. 'Annabelle' is the most commonly grown variety. It is a showy, compact, 4-foot shrub with huge, spectacular, rounded heads of white, as much as 12 inches or more across. Blooms best in full sun. Leaves are medium green and large.

Pom-pom flowers of Annabelle smooth hydrangea may span one foot.

BIGLEAF HYDRANGEA

Hydrangea macrophylla
by-DRAN-jya mak-row-FILL-a

- Rounded, suckering shrub
- White, pink, or blue flowers
- Coarse-leaved
- Zones 7 to 10 (Zone 6 along the East Coast)

6'
8'

Bigleaf hydrangea is valued for its late-summer floral display and lustrous, neat leaves in mild-winter areas. Native to Japan.

USES: Good for foundations and facing down taller, leggy shrubs, as well as in the shrub border. Excellent seaside plant, especially in the south. Combine it with *Lagerstroemia indica* and *Clethra alnifolia*.

GROWTH RATE: Fast.

CULTURE: Plant in full sun at the shore or in partial shade and in moist, rich, well-drained soil high in organic matter. The soil's acidity affects the plant's uptake of aluminum, which in turn determines whether the flowers are pink or blue. For bluer flowers, provide extra acidity and aluminum (aluminum sulfate is good). For pink flowers, apply lime to decrease soil acidity. Prune after flowering only to remove flower heads. It flowers on the previous year's growth.

RECOMMENDED VARIETIES: Many are available, differing by hardiness (some are hardy to Zone 5, whereas others have been bred as pot plants for greenhouses), length of bloom (some begin blooming earlier for a longer season), size (dwarf 2-foot mounds to large 5-foot shrubs), foliage color (some are variegated), flower color (blue, white, pink, and red), and flower form (the Hortensia group bears globe-shaped flower clusters composed of many large, sterile florets; the lacecap group bears tight clusters of tiny florets circled by a ring of large, sterile florets). Some of the most garden-worthy varieties are 'All Summer Beauty', a compact (to 3 feet) early bloomer with dark blue flowers; 'Endless Summer' with repeat blooms on new wood; 'Forever Pink', a compact, 3-foot Hortensia with flowers that remain pink even in acid soils; 'Glowing Embers', a bright red Hortensia; 'Mariesii Variegata', a blue lacecap with ivory-variegated leaves; and 'Nikko Blue', a large bright blue Hortensia.

Acid soil around bigleaf hydrangea shifts flower color from pink to blue.

Lacecap hydrangea has a cluster of tiny flowers encircled with large, sterile flowers.

Hydrangea paniculata
by-DRAN-jya pa-nik-u-LAY-ta

PANICLE HYDRANGEA

- Conical flower panicles 6 to 8 inches long
- Coarse texture
- Spreading shrub
- Zones 4 to 8

This large shrub or small tree is an old-fashioned favorite for its long season of bloom, with branches that arch from the weight of its cone-shaped flower clusters. The white flowers appear in midsummer, changing through shades of pink, buff, and rust from late summer into fall. Native to Japan.

Pink Diamond panicle hydrangea can grow 20 feet tall.

USES: Plant it in the shrub border, where its coarseness will not be as prominent, or prune it to form a small tree. Combine it with plumbago (*Ceratostigma plumbaginoides*), sedum 'Autumn Joy', and Japanese holly (*Ilex crenata* 'Helleri').

GROWTH RATE: Fast.

CULTURE: Moist, well-drained soil with plenty of organic matter in sun or partial shade. It flowers on new growth, so prune in winter or early spring, removing weak or dead stems. Vigorous and trouble-free.

RECOMMENDED VARIETIES: 'Grandiflora' (sometimes called peegee hydrangea) has snowball-type clusters, elongated to 8 to 10 inches, which turn pink in late summer and brown in autumn. 'Unique' bears especially large, 12-inch-long flower clusters over an even longer period than the species.

Hydrangea quercifolia
by-DRAN-jya kwer-si-FOH-lee-a

OAKLEAF HYDRANGEA

- Bold leaves
- Flowers to 1 foot long
- Shaggy bark is decorative in winter
- Zones 5 to 8

Burgundy and purple leaves provide fall color, and dry flowers stay on the plant into winter. Flowers are white changing to greenish-pink to brown, and leaves are shaped like oak leaves. Native to the southeastern United States.

USES: A fine addition to the shrub border, oakleaf hydrangea also provides a strong accent in large masses. It performs well in sun or shade and in mass or as a specimen.

Oakleaf hydrangea has panicle-like flowers.

Plant it with large fothergilla (*Fothergilla major*) and fringed bleeding heart (*Dicentra eximia*).

GROWTH RATE: Slow to moderate.

CULTURE: Plant in moist, fertile, well-drained, acid soil in sun or half shade. Also tolerates dense shade but produces fewer flowers and less intense fall color. In Zones 7 and 8, it requires shade. Mulch well in dry climates to keep the roots cool and moist.

RECOMMENDED VARIETIES: 'Snow Queen' has larger flower heads than the species (with larger individual florets) that are held more upright for greater show. Plant is more compact (5 to 7 feet tall and wide), and fall color is good. 'Snowflake' has double florets, with a set of smaller sepals within the larger ones, making a unique display. 'Pee Wee' is 30 to 40 inches and produces excellent flowers.

Hypericum prolificum
by-PEAR-i-kum pro-LIH-fi-kum

- Bluish-green leaves
- Dense, rounded shrub
- Bright yellow flowers
- Medium-fine texture
- Zones 4 to 9

3'
4'

Compact shrub flowers from mid-June through August.

USES: Foundation plantings, shrub borders, mixed borders, or in masses.

GROWTH RATE: Slow.

SHRUBBY ST. JOHNSWORT

CULTURE: Grows best in full sun and light, well-drained soil. Prune in late spring after new growth hardens.

RECOMMENDED VARIETIES AND RELATED SPECIES: *H. frondosum* 'Sunburst' (Zones 5 to 9) has handsome blue-green foliage. It is a 3- to 4-foot-tall shrub with large bright yellow flowers. *H. patulum* (Zones 7 to 10) is a semievergreen or evergreen shrub 3 feet tall and wide. 'Hidcote' is an 18-inch shrub in Zones 5 and 6, with large yellow flowers from late June to September. In Zones 7 to 9, it is less likely to kill back and reaches 3 to 4 feet, flowering from May to October.

Hidcote is a popular form of this low-growing shrub.

Iberis sempervirens
IH-ber-is sem-per-VY-renz

- Showy, pure white flowers in spring
- Dwarf evergreen
- Low, spreading habit
- Zones 5 to 10

1'
2'

This handsome plant forms a mat of fine-textured dark green foliage. Native to southern Europe and western Asia.

USES: Candytuft can be planted as a ground cover with woody shrubs and spring bulbs. Combine with *Abelia ×grandiflora* 'Prostrata' and

EVERGREEN CANDYTUFT

Ajuga reptans 'Burgundy Glow'. Excellent with rhododendrons.

GROWTH RATE: Slow to moderate.

CULTURE: It prefers light, well-drained soil with average fertility, in sun to light shade. Prune it hard each year after flowering, and do not overfertilize. Removing spent flowers increases the next year's bloom and keeps plants dense.

RECOMMENDED VARIETIES: 'Autumn Snow' blooms again in autumn. 'Little Gem' is shorter and hardier than the species. 'Purity' and 'Snowflake' have larger flower clusters. 'Snowmantle' is an especially vigorous variety.

White flowers of evergreen candytuft cover the plant in early spring.

Ilex cornuta
EYE-leks kor-NOO-ta

- Evergreen leaves
- Profuse red berries
- Upright, rounded shrub
- Zones 7 to 9

12'
12'

Bold, handsome, glossy foliage.

USES: Use for foundations, hedges, and shrub borders.

GROWTH RATE: Slow to moderate.

CULTURE: Moist, well-drained, slightly acid soils in sun or shade.

CHINESE HOLLY

Tolerates drought, heat, variable pH, and pollution. Male and female plants are needed for berries.

RECOMMENDED VARIETIES: 'Burfordii' is dense and rounded, grows 10 feet tall, fruits without pollination. 'Dwarf Burford' grows to 6 feet. 'Dazzler' is a compact female, less than 10 feet, with superb fruit display. *I. ×merserveae* is an 8-foot evergreen hardy to Zone 5 (some varieties to Zone 4), with glossy dark blue-green foliage. Blue Princess and China Girl are popular trademarked varieties.

Rotunda Chinese holly is an 18-inch-tall shrub for mild climates.

Ilex crenata
EYE-leks kren-AH-ta

JAPANESE HOLLY

- ■ Lustrous, dark, evergreen foliage
- ■ Neat, rounded shape
- ■ Fine texture
- ■ Zones 6 (south) to 10; some cultivars to Zone 5

10'
12'

Native to Japan.
USES: Excellent for hedges, foundation plantings, massing, and shrub borders. Fruit is black and inconspicuous.
GROWTH RATE: Slow.
CULTURE: Best in moist but well-drained, slightly acidic soil in sun or shade. Pollution-tolerant. It can be sheared into formal shapes. Prune after new growth matures in spring.
RECOMMENDED VARIETIES: 'Beehive' is a rounded dwarf with bright green foliage. 'Convexa' has small, convex leaves that sparkle; it is hardy to Zone 6. 'Dwarf Pagoda' is a picturesque dwarf with closely packed leaves, suitable for bonsai. 'Glory' has small, flat leaves and is unusually cold-hardy to Zone 5. 'Helleri' has small leaves and is very dwarf, 2 to 3 feet tall. 'Hetzii' is similar to 'Convexa' but with larger leaves, hardy to Zone 6.

Hetzii Japanese holly has small, oval, glossy leaves.

Ilex glabra
EYE-leks GLAY-bra

INKBERRY

- ■ Black fruit
- ■ Dense and compact when young
- ■ Hardiest broadleaf evergreen
- ■ Zones 5 to 10

8'
12'

Valued by northern gardeners for bringing green year-round to the landscape. Native to swamps from Nova Scotia to Florida and Mississippi. Small, shiny, nearly black berries are ⅓ inch in diameter. They ripen in fall and persist to the following spring.
USES: A fine shrub for massing, hedges, and foundation planting. Salt-tolerant; excellent for the seashore. Plant it with northern bayberry (*Myrica pensylvanica*) and rugosa rose (*Rosa rugosa*).
GROWTH RATE: Slow to medium.
CULTURE: It grows well in moist but well-drained soil, in full sun to part shade. Responds well to shearing. Pinch to keep plants dense; prune heavily to renew leggy, old plants. Generally pest-resistant and trouble-free.
RECOMMENDED VARIETIES: 'Compacta', 'Densa', 'Nordic', and 'Shamrock' are all compact forms, the latter one the most popular.

Tiny black berries of inkberry are much loved by birds.

Ilex verticillata
EYE-leks ver-tih-sih-LAY-ta

COMMON WINTERBERRY

- ■ Deciduous holly
- ■ Outstanding bright red berries
- ■ Happy in wet soil
- ■ Zones 4 to 8

8'
10'

Fruit of winterberry persists into the winter on bare branches, attracting birds in the eastern United States. Native to North American swamps in the east and midwest.
USES: Effective in masses in the shrub border and by water.
GROWTH RATE: Slow.
CULTURE: It does best in moist to wet soil, high in organic matter, and in full sun to partial shade. Male plants required for pollination.
RECOMMENDED VARIETIES: 'Afterglow' grows 4 to 6 feet tall with large, orange-red fruits. 'Aurantiaca' grows 3 to 5 feet tall with red, then yellow-orange fruits. 'Jim Dandy' is a low-growing male that will pollinate 'Afterglow', 'Aurantiaca', and 'Red Sprite'. 'Red Sprite' (also called 'Nana') grows to only 2 to 4 feet tall with very large red fruits. 'Winter Red' grows 8 to 10 feet tall and wide.

Birds wait until late winter to feast on the fruit of winterberry.

JUNIPERS

Juniperus spp.
joo-NIH-pur-us

- Fine texture
- Low-maintenance
- Shrubby, prostrate, or columnar cultivars
- Zones vary with the species

Worldwide, there are about 70 species of junipers, 17 of which are native to the United States. They have two types of leaves: sharp, needlelike juvenile leaves, or blunt, scalelike mature leaves, varying with the species. Junipers are adaptable to almost any conditions, notably to hot, dry sites, but sometimes are infested with mites and bagworms. Some are susceptible to juniper blight *(Phomopsis).*

USES: Varieties make good ground covers, accents, and border plants. Plant shrubby and spreading junipers with maiden grass *(Miscanthus)* and mondo grass *(Ophiopogon).*

GROWTH RATE: Slow, variable.

CULTURE: Best in well-drained soil and full sun, but adaptable to average moisture and partial shade. Place them away from lawn sprinklers and in general avoid overwatering.

RELATED SPECIES: Chinese juniper *(J. chinensis,* Zones 4 to 10) tolerates alkaline soil. It is slightly susceptible to juniper

blight, moderately so in very wet years. Native to China, Mongolia, and Japan. 'San Jose' is a low form, 2 feet tall and 8 to 10 feet wide.

 Common juniper *(J. communis,* Zones 3 to 7, depending on geographical origin) typically grows 5 to 10 feet tall and 8 to 12 feet wide. It has only spiny juvenile foliage, dull to blue-green in summer and brownish to purplish in winter. Common juniper is native to more places than any other shrub or tree, including northern and central Europe, the Mediterranean region, Asia Minor, Iran, Afghanistan, the western Himalayas, Canada, and the United States from New England to North Carolina and west to the Rockies, and California. *J. c.* ssp. *alpina* is a low-growing alpine plant with good blue-green color year-round or purplish color in winter. Varieties include 'Berkshire' (Massachusetts) and 'Gold Beach' (California); both are fine ground covers. *J. c.* ssp. *depressa* includes vase-shaped plants, a few of which are useful. 'Compressa' is a slow-growing conical form 2 to 3 feet tall; 'Depressa Aurea' is more vigorous, with golden branch tips.

Gold Cone common juniper.

Shore juniper *(J. conferta,* Zones 6 to 10) is an excellent ground cover, especially for coastal sites. It has soft-looking but prickly bluish-green foliage and a dense, matlike growth habit, 1 to 2 feet tall and 6 to 8 feet wide. Shore juniper is native to the seacoast of Japan.

Hetzii Chinese juniper provides an effective screen if grown as an unpruned hedge.

Blue Pacific shore juniper.

6"

4'

Creeping juniper (*J. horizontalis*, Zones 3 to 9) is a low-spreading ground cover with silvery blue-green foliage that turns purple in winter. Some varieties are highly susceptible to juniper blight. It is native from Nova Scotia to British Columbia and south to Montana and Massachusetts. 'Bar Harbor', 'Wiltonii' ('Blue Rug'), 'Douglasii', and 'Blue Chip' are blue-green in summer, silvery blue or purple in winter, and grow 6 to 8 inches tall.

Blue Chip creeping juniper.

4'

8'

Hybrid juniper (*J. ×media*, Zones 4 to 9) includes varieties that once were assigned to *J. chinensis* but now are believed to be hybrids with *J. sabina*. 'Armstrongii' is upright to 5 to 6 feet, with olive-green foliage. 'Hetzii'

grows 8 to 10 feet and taller and 20 feet or more wide, with silvery blue-green foliage. Mint Julep grows 2 to 3 feet tall, spreading 6 feet wide, with bright green foliage. 'Pfitzeriana' grows 6 to 8 feet tall and 15 feet wide, with olive-green foliage.

2'

15'

Japanese garden juniper (*J. procumbens*, Zones 5 to 9) is a ground cover that grows 1 to 2 feet tall and spreads very wide. It has soft, needlelike, blue-green juvenile foliage. It is a popular ground cover but is very susceptible to juniper blight. 'Nana' grows to 1 foot.

2'

6'

Savin juniper (*J. sabina*, Zones 5 to 9) has bright to deep green foliage that turns brown in winter. Pollution-tolerant and blight-resistant. It varies from 1 to 6 feet tall and much broader. Low forms are good for massing and ground cover. It is native to the mountains of central and southern Europe. 'Arcadia' is a ground cover just over 1 foot tall with bright green foliage. 'Broadmoor' is a low form, about 1 to 2 feet tall and 6 feet wide, with fine-textured bright green foliage. 'Skandia' is similar to 'Broadmoor' but with feathery, needlelike, blue-green foliage.

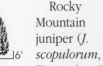

3'

6'

Rocky Mountain juniper (*J. scopulorum*, Zones 4 to 8) has an upright growth habit, to 10 to 20 feet tall, and silvery to blue-green foliage. Varieties are useful for vertical

Plumosa Aurea hybrid juniper.

Japanese garden juniper.

accent, hedges, screens, and windbreaks. It is native to dry ridges of the higher elevations of the Rocky Mountains from Alberta to Texas. 'Skyrocket' is columnar and slow-growing, reaching about 12 feet tall. It has silvery blue foliage.

3'

6'

Singleseed juniper (*J. squamata*, Zones 4 to 7) was known for many years only as the shapeless 'Meyeri'. Now represented by new varieties, this species is reputedly not as heat-tolerant as other junipers. It is native to China. 'Blue Star' is a dwarf that forms a mound 2 to 3 feet tall and 5 to 6 feet wide, with blue needles and scalelike, yellow-tipped, blue-green foliage. It grows like a smaller version of 'Meyeri'.

MOUNTAIN LAUREL

Kalmia latifolia
KAL-mee-a la-ti-FOH-lee-a

- Not a good choice for dry gardens
- Flowers in clusters
- Dense, rounded habit
- Zones 5 to 8

9' / 7'

This eastern U.S. woodland native has spectacular white to deep pink flowers and evergreen foliage. Medium-textured, it becomes gnarled and open in old age. It is considered one of the finest of all American native shrubs.
USES: Use it as a specimen or as a companion for azaleas and rhododendrons.
GROWTH RATE: Slow.
CULTURE: Grow it in acidic, cool, moist soil high in organic matter, in full or half sun.
RECOMMENDED VARIETIES: 'Sarah' has a compact habit and red buds that open pinkish red. 'Elf' is a dwarf with pink buds opening white. 'Ostbo Red' has red buds that open lighter pink. 'Raspberry Glow' has maroon buds opening deep pink.

Clementine Churchill mountain laurel is a favored woodland shrub.

KERRIA

Kerria japonica
CARE-i-a ja-PON-i-ca

- Bright yellow flowers in spring
- Bright green stems
- Good in shade
- Zones 5 to 9

7' / 10'

A tough, care-free shade plant. Forcing its stems indoors provides color in winter. Native to western and central China.
USES: Use in borders, masses, groups, and where shade is an opportunity. Combine kerria with Oregon grapeholly (*Mahonia aquifolium*).

GROWTH RATE: Slow to establish, fast when established.
CULTURE: Plant in light to half shade because flowers fade in full sun. Plant in a protected location with good drainage to reduce the chance of winter damage. Prune directly after flowering because it flowers on last year's growth.
RECOMMENDED VARIETIES: 'Pleniflora' is double-flowered and showy. 'Variegata' (also known as 'Picta') has white-variegated foliage and slower growth. It is unstable, developing green-leaved shoots that must be cut out. 'Shannon' and 'Golden Guinea' have single flowers 1½ to 2 inches in diameter.

Pleniflora kerria is a double-flowered form of this tough shrub.

BEAUTYBUSH

Kolkwitzia amabilis
kole-KWIT-zee-a ah-MAH-bi-lis

- Low-maintenance
- Profuse, pale-pink flowers
- Medium texture in summer
- Zones 5 to 8

10' / 10'

This shrub has limited value when not in flower; it has somewhat ragged, peeling, light-brown bark on lower trunks. Native to central China.
USES: Best used in the rear of the shrub border in large gardens. Good companion plants include Crimson Pygmy barberry (*Berberis thunbergii* 'Crimson Pygmy') and Beacon Silver deadnettle (*Lamium maculatum* 'Beacon Silver').
GROWTH RATE: Fast.
CULTURE: Indifferent to soil type or pH. Give it a sunny location and plenty of room to grow. Prune out older stems every year after flowering; it flowers on old wood. Renew by cutting to the ground.
RECOMMENDED VARIETIES: 'Pink Cloud' and 'Rosea' have deeper pink flowers than species.

Pink Cloud beautybush makes a fountain of flowers.

LANTANA

Lantana spp.
lan-TAN-uh

New Gold lantana is a heat-tolerant shrub that flowers all summer.

- Long flower season
- Tough
- Zones 9 and 10

Evergreen shrub that bears rounded clusters of flowers in cream, white, yellow, gold, pink, lavender, orange, and red. Some types combine colors in the same flower cluster. Most grow 2 to 3 feet tall.

USES: Upright types can be pruned as hedges. Spreading types make tough, colorful ground covers for hillsides and coastal areas.

GROWTH RATE: Fast.

CULTURE: Plant in full sun; does well in almost all soils. Do not overwater. Prune deadwood in spring, and trim plants to control shape and growth. Spider mites, aphids, and whiteflies are common pests.

RECOMMENDED VARIETIES AND RELATED SPECIES: Hardier trailing lantana (*L. montevidensis*) has sprawling stems and lavender blooms. Shrub lantana (*L. camara*) and its hybrids offer the most diversity with numerous varieties: 'Miss Huff' has orange and pink flowers; 'Rainbow' is yellow-orange.

ENGLISH LAVENDER

Lavandula angustifolia
la-VAN-dew-la an-goose-ti-FOH-lee-a

Hidcote English lavender is both beautiful and delightfully scented.

- Evergreen
- Fragrant, lavender-purple flower spikes early to late summer
- Scented leaves
- Zones 5 to 8

Cultivated for centuries for its fragrance and beauty, lavender has silvery or bluish-green leaves, a fine texture, and a mounded habit. Native to the Mediterranean region.

USES: Use it in perennial or shrub borders or as a low hedge in a parterre or herb garden. Companions include sage, thyme, dwarf boxwood, and germander varieties.

GROWTH RATE: Slow.

CULTURE: Give it a well-drained, rather dry spot in the garden with neutral to alkaline pH. Prune off flower stalks after they've bloomed. Overwatering kills lavender.

RECOMMENDED VARIETIES: 'Hidcote' has deep purple flowers and silver leaves; it grows to 12 inches tall. 'Munstead' has lilac spikes and gray-green leaves; it reaches 18 inches tall. 'Nana' has lavender-purple flowers and is reputed to be more cold-hardy. 'Rosea' has soft pink flowers.

SAND MYRTLE

Leiophyllum buxifolium
li-o-FIL-um buk-si-FO-lee-um

Prostrata sand myrtle flowers well in partially shaded areas.

- Lovely white flowers in spring
- Dark green leaves turn bronze in fall
- Zones 6 to 10

Sand myrtle is an attractive evergreen shrub with a rounded habit and tiny, oval, dark green leaves that turn bronze in fall. In spring, large clusters of tiny, star-shaped white flowers open from pink buds. The species grows 1 to 2 feet tall by 4 to 5 feet wide. Native to northeastern United States.

USES: Good shady ground cover, especially near the coast.

GROWTH RATE: Slow.

CULTURE: Plant in partial shade. Plants need moist, well-drained, acid soil, well-amended with organic matter. Water as needed and top-dress with a peat-soil mix. Prune after flowering. Propagate by seed in spring or cuttings in summer.

RECOMMENDED VARIETIES AND RELATED SPECIES: 'Nanum' has pink flowers and is only 2 to 4 inches tall and 12 inches wide. Allegheny sand myrtle (*L. buxifolium prostratum*) is 4 to 10 inches tall by 18 inches wide.

NEW ZEALAND TEA TREE

Leptospermum scoparium
lep-toh-SPER-mum sco-PAR-ee-um

- ■ Evergreen
- ■ Good for West Coast
- ■ Red, pink, or white flowers
- ■ Zones 9 and 10

This versatile plant with fragrant, fine-textured, narrow leaves varies from a shrub 10 feet tall to an 8-inch ground cover. New Zealand tea tree blooms profusely from late winter to midsummer.

USES: It can serve as a specimen, accent, or focal point in coastal shrub borders. Prostrate forms make colorful ground covers but do not suppress weeds.

GROWTH RATE: Medium.

CULTURE: Needs thorough drainage and full sun. It is drought-tolerant and pest-free once established. Shear or prune lightly for a formal appearance. Never prune into bare wood, which prevents buds from breaking into new growth.

RECOMMENDED VARIETIES: 'Gaiety Girl' has double salmon-pink flowers. 'Red Damask' produces double cherry red flowers on a dense shrub 6 to 8 feet tall.

Nanum is a low, 2-foot-tall form of New Zealand tea tree.

DROOPING LEUCOTHOE

Leucothoë fontanesiana
lu-KOH-tho-ee fon-ta-nee-see-AN-a

- ■ Evergreen foliage
- ■ Graceful, drooping form
- ■ White flowers
- ■ Zones 5 to 7

Leucothoe makes a fine companion for rhododendrons, azaleas, and mountain laurels. Native to mountain streamsides from Virginia to Tennessee.

USES: Naturalize it in a shady woodland garden, or use it as a foreground plant for leggy shrubs, as a graceful ground cover for shady slopes, or in the shrub border. Its cascading form is lovely hanging over a wall.

GROWTH RATE: Slow to moderate.

CULTURE: Plant it in acid, moist, well-drained soil high in organic matter. It needs full shade, ample moisture, and protection from drought and drying winds. Prune after flowering. Rejuvenate by cutting to the ground.

RECOMMENDED VARIETIES: 'Girard's Rainbow' has yellow, green, and copper-variegated foliage. 'Nana' is a dwarf form.

Rollissonii drooping leucothoe naturalizes in sheltered woodlands.

PRIVET

Ligustrum spp.
li-GUS-trum

- ■ Low-maintenance, evergreen or deciduous
- ■ Strongly scented white flowers
- ■ Lustrous leaves
- ■ Zones vary with species

Highly adaptable and trouble-free, privet is one of the most popular hedge plants.

USES: Used most often as formal or informal hedges, backgrounds, and screens.

GROWTH RATE: Fast.

CULTURE: Adaptable to most soils in sun to partial shade. For flowers, prune just after it blooms in early summer. Otherwise, prune anytime.

RECOMMENDED VARIETIES AND RELATED SPECIES: Japanese privet (*L. japonicum*, Zones 7 to 10) is a 6- to 12-foot-tall evergreen. Golden privet 'Vicaryi', Zones 5 to 8) is a deciduous shrub with yellow-green leaves. Border privet (*L. obtusifolium*, Zones 4 to 8) has deciduous foliage and a horizontal growth habit. California privet (*L. ovalifolium*, Zones 6 to 10) is a popular, semievergreen hedge plant.

Vicaryi privet has bright golden leaves.

OREGON GRAPEHOLLY

Mahonia aquifolium
ma-HOH-nee-a a-kwi-FOH-lee-um

- Open, loose form
- Showy, bright yellow flowers in late April
- Spiny evergreen leaves
- Zones 5 to 9

A popular, hardy evergreen for shady areas, its hollylike leaves turn bluish purple in cold weather. Yellow spring flowers are followed by purple fruits. Native to damp forests from British Columbia to Oregon.

USES: Best integrated into a shrub border or foundation planting, or as a specimen. Combine with plantain lily *(Hosta)*.

GROWTH RATE: Slow.

CULTURE: Plant in moist, acidic soil and protect from hot sun and wind. Winter wind especially can dessicate and "burn" foliage, turning it brown, especially where snow cover is light. Prune annually after flowering to maintain a 3-foot height.

RECOMMENDED VARIETIES AND RELATED SPECIES: 'Compacta' remains less than 2 feet with little or no pruning. Creeping mahonia *(M. repens)* has blue-green foliage and tolerates dry soil.

Yellow flowers of Oregon grapeholly develop into purple berries.

LEATHERLEAF MAHONIA

Mahonia bealei
ma-HOH-nee-a BAY-lee-eye

- Vertical stems
- Large clusters of yellow flowers
- Grapelike fruit
- Zones 6 (south) to 10

Striking structural interest makes this plant worth growing. Native to China.

USES: Leatherleaf mahonia has an exotic, tropical effect when displayed against a wall or lit dramatically at night. Use it with deciduous azaleas *(Rhododendron)*, and lily-of-the-valley *(Convallaria majalis)*. It makes an excellent container plant.

GROWTH RATE: Slow.

CULTURE: Plant in rich, moist soil, and give it plenty of water. Consider its ultimate size before planting because it is difficult to prune correctly. Avoid planting it where spiny foliage can scratch.

RELATED SPECIES: Burmese mahonia *(M. lomariifolia*, Zones 8 to 10) grows to 10 feet or taller, if allowed. Its tropical-looking, 2-foot leaves have 20 to 40 leaflets; showy flowers and powdery blue fruit in clusters of 15 to 20.

Large leaves of leatherleaf mahonia produce a nearly tropical effect.

RUSSIAN CYPRESS

Microbiota decussata
mike-row-BUY-ott-a DAY-coo-saw-ta

- Evergreen coniferous shrub
- 20 inches tall
- Space 3 to 4 feet
- Sun to partial shade
- Moderate watering
- Zones 2 to 8

This low-growing conifer is a spreading shrub with flat sprays of leathery, scalelike leaves, almost like those of ground-cover junipers. The yellow-green leaves turn pinkish-bronze in winter. Russian cypress flowers are inconspicuous; they're followed by tiny, globe-shaped, yellowish-brown cones. One plant can spread as much as 9 to 12 feet in width.

USES: Moderate to large areas; foundation plantings; substitute for juniper in partially shaded sites.

CULTURE: This ground cover grows well in all soil types and can withstand drought. It also does well in part shade, providing an effect similar to that of ground-cover junipers, which do not take shade. Shear annually to keep growth compact. Propagate from cuttings.

Russian cypress is a very hardy evergreen ground-cover shrub.

Myrica pensylvanica
MIR-ih-ka pen-sil-VAN-i-ka

- **Aromatic**
- **Light gray fruits all winter**
- **Deciduous foliage**
- **Zones 2 to 7**

8'
8'

Valued for centuries for its fragrant berries, bayberry fixes its own nitrogen from the atmosphere and thus can grow in the poorest soils.
USES: Excellent for large-scale massing in poor soil, difficult urban

NORTHERN BAYBERRY

sites, and coastal areas. Also good for the shrub border or informal hedge or for combining with broadleaf evergreens.
GROWTH RATE: Medium from old growth, fast from root suckers.
CULTURE: Plant in any soil in full sun to partial shade, but it prefers dry, infertile, sandy soil. Pest-free, it is tolerant of salt spray and wind. Prune to renew branches, and renew old, leggy plants by pruning to the ground.
RELATED SPECIES: Wax myrtle (*M. cerifera,* Zones 7 to 10) grows

to 10 to 15 feet tall, making a fine specimen shrub or small tree.

Northern bayberry thrives in seaside locations.

Myrtus communis
MUR-tus co-MYOON-nis

- **Evergreen leaves are fragrant when bruised**
- **Sweet-scented flowers**
- **Smooth tan bark**
- **Zones 9 and 10**

10'
6'

Commonly grown in hot, dry areas of Arizona and the coastal gardens of California, this is a wide, round, bushy shrub that bears white flowers in summer and has lustrous dark green leaves. Native to Mediterranean regions.

MYRTLE

USES: Formal and informal hedges, screens, masses, or backgrounds. Combine in landscapes with lantana (*Lantana camara*) and oleander (*Nerium oleander*).
GROWTH RATE: Moderate.
CULTURE: Myrtle grows in any soil with fast drainage. Best in full sun to partial shade. It tolerates shearing well and is easily trained into a formal hedge.
RECOMMENDED VARIETIES: 'Compacta' is slow growing and compact, to 3 feet tall. 'Variegata' has small, white-margined leaves and is similar in size to 'Compacta'.

Myrtle's small white flowers in summer are followed by purple berries.

Nandina domestica
nan-DEE-na doe-MESS-ti-ka

- **Vertical form**
- **Erect panicles**
- **Purple foliage in fall and winter**
- **Zones 6 to 10**

7'
4'

Popular in southern gardens for its good looks and easy care. Creamy white flowers appear in June, followed by bright red clusters of berries.
USES: Heavenly bamboo is effective in a mass, as a specimen, or in a container.

HEAVENLY BAMBOO

GROWTH RATE: Moderate.
CULTURE: Grow heavenly bamboo in nearly any soil in sun or shade, but it requires protection in hot climates. It is drought-tolerant when established. Use it as a herbaceous perennial in the north. Plant heavenly bamboo in groups because cross-fertilization improves fruiting. Prune out leggy canes annually to increase density.
RECOMMENDED VARIETIES: 'Harbour Dwarf' grows into a dense 2- to 3-foot-tall mound with purplish winter color.

'Gulfstream' is a compact mound 2 to 3 feet tall.

Heavenly bamboo produces a striking crop of red berries in fall.

Nerium oleander
NEAR-ee-um OH-lee-an-der

Oleander is a tough utility plant for mild-climate regions.

OLEANDER

- Coarse, evergreen foliage
- Red, pink, white, or yellow flowers
- Broad, round habit
- Zones 8 to 10

15' / 15'

A no-fuss, drought-tolerant shrub that is popular west of the Rockies and in the south, oleander is native to the Mediterranean region. All parts of this plant are poisonous. **USES:** Takes high heat and drought. **GROWTH RATE:** Fast. **CULTURE:** Plant it in full sun, in any soil from dry sand to wet clay. It tolerates heat, salt, and drought. In shady or humid environments, it's prone to mildew, scale, aphids, and many other insects and diseases. Prune in early spring to control size and form. Remove old wood that has flowered each year. Tip-pinch to encourage density, or pull off suckers from the base to encourage more open height. All plant parts are toxic. Smoke from burning can cause severe skin and respiratory irritations. Contact with leaves can cause dermatitis. Ingesting small amounts can cause death.

Osmanthus fragrans
oz-MAN-thus FRAY-grans

Kembu sweet olive has white-variegated leaves.

SWEET OLIVE

- Powerfully fragrant, nearly year-round flowers
- Evergreen foliage
- Neat, compact habit
- Zones 8 to 10

15' / 10'

Native to eastern Asia. **USES:** Hedge, screen, background, espalier, or container plant. **GROWTH RATE:** Moderate. **CULTURE:** Plant it in any soil from sand to clay. Keep it low by shearing. Prune anytime of year. Pinch growing tips to keep dense.

RECOMMENDED VARIETIES AND RELATED SPECIES: 'Aurantiacus' has very fragrant orange blossoms mostly in October. Delavay osmanthus (*O. delavayi*, Zones 8 to 10) has finely textured leaves; graceful, arching habit; and large white flowers that are profuse and fragrant from late March to May. Holly osmanthus (*O. heterophyllus*, Zones 7 to 10), often confused with English holly, has lustrous, spiny, dark green leaves and fragrant, hidden, cream-colored flowers in fall; it is unusually shade-tolerant. 'Variegatus' has cream-colored leaf margins.

Paeonia suffruticosa
pee-OH-nee-a suf-fru-ti-KOH-sa

Impressively large flowers of tree peony are a springtime spectacle.

TREE PEONY

- Enormous flowers last up to 10 days
- 18-inch leaves
- Open, leggy habit
- Zones 5 to 9

4' / 4'

Although its deciduous foliage is attractive, this shrub is grown chiefly for its immense blooms in red, green, pink, purple, maroon, white, blue, or multicolors. **USES:** Perennial and shrub borders. **GROWTH RATE:** Slow. **CULTURE:** Plant in early fall in well-drained, moist, rich soil amended with ample organic matter. Locate carefully in full sun to light shade because it does not transplant well. Plant grafted forms with the graft union at least 4 inches below the ground to encourage the grafts to form their own roots. Protect from rabbits during the first year and mulch well. Don't mulch after the first year, and remove faded blossoms immediately to help control botrytis fungus. Largest flowers may need staking. **RECOMMENDED VARIETIES:** There are many varieties to select from for flower color and form.

Philadelphus coronarius
fil-a-DEL-fus co-ro-NAH-ree-us

- Deliciously fragrant flowers in late spring
- Coarse-textured
- Leggy, straggly habit
- Zones 4 to 8

6' / 5'

This shrub is popular for sweet-scented flowers. Native to Europe and southwestern Asia.

USES: Grow it where you can smell it: in the border, near patios, entryways, and windows.

SWEET MOCKORANGE

GROWTH RATE: Fast.

CULTURE: Easy to grow and pest-free, mockorange is not particular about soil; it takes sun or partial shade. Prune annually right after flowering by removing older wood or cutting to the ground.

RECOMMENDED VARIETIES: 'Miniature Snowflake' ('Double Snowflake') grows 2 to 3 feet tall, with fragrant, double white flowers. 'Galahad' grows to 5 feet tall and wide, with fragrant white flowers. Minnesota Snowflake mock orange (*P. ×virginalis* 'Minnesota Snowflake') is fragrant, grows 6 feet tall, and is hardy to Zone 4.

Sweet mockorange is famed for its flower's fragrance.

Photinia ×fraseri
fo-TIN-ee-uh FRAY-zer-eye

- Bronze-red new foliage
- Ivory flowers
- Red berries attractive to birds
- Zones 7 to 10

20' / 18'

Popular in southern gardens for its lustrous red-tipped leaves in spring, it produces malodorous flowers in clusters in late March and April. Hybrid origin.

USES: Use it as a screen, hedge, or single-trunked small tree. Combine it

REDTIP PHOTINIA

with oleander (*Nerium oleander*) and sunrose (*Cistus*).

GROWTH RATE: Moderate to fast.

CULTURE: Plant in well-drained soil amply amended with organic matter. Even though it is heat-resistant, water it generously, without splashing water on the leaves; foliage is susceptible to fire blight, which blackens the branch ends. Prune out diseased branches, sterilizing the shears in alcohol or bleach after each cut, and destroy the refuse.

RELATED SPECIES: Chinese photinia (*P. serratifolia*, Zones 7 to 10).

New growth of redtip photinia is bright coppery red.

Picea abies 'Nidiformis'
pie-SEE-a AY-bees ni-di-FOR-mis

- Dwarf conifer
- Often indented in the center like a bird's nest
- Finely textured, needled foliage
- Zones 3 to 5

3' / 6'

A versatile and popular dwarf spruce for the north. Native to northern and central Europe.

USES: Shrub borders, foundations.

GROWTH RATE: Slow.

CULTURE: It prefers full sun to light

BIRD'S NEST SPRUCE

shade in well-drained, sandy, moderately moist soil but tolerates other soils as long as they are moist. It also prefers deep winter cold and cool summers. Avoid hot, dry sites. Harmed by urban pollution.

RELATED SPECIES: There are numerous dwarf varieties of different species of spruces that are useful as shrublike masses. Conical white spruce (*P. glauca* 'Conica', Zones 5 to 7) is stiffly and densely conical. A slow-growing dwarf conifer, it reaches 6 to 8 feet in 50 years. *Picea pungens* 'Montgomery' forms a broad cone only 6 feet tall after years, with beautiful silvery blue foliage.

Bird's nest spruce is one of the most popular dwarf conifers.

Pieris japonica
pee-AIR-is ja-PON-i-ka

Clusters of dangling, bell-shaped flowers adorn Japanese pieris in spring.

JAPANESE PIERIS

- Delicate pinkish-white panicles
- Colorful new growth
- Upright habit
- Zones 6 to 9

This broadleaf evergreen blooms in early spring for 2 to 3 weeks and is attractive year-round. Native to Japan.

USES: Use as a specimen, in the shrub border, or combine with other acid-loving, broadleaf evergreens, including hollies (*Ilex* species) and drooping leucothoe (page 177).

GROWTH RATE: Slow.

CULTURE: Plant pieris in moist, acid soil, protected from wind and winter sun, especially in Zones 6 and 7. It seldom needs pruning. It sometimes has insect and mite problems.

RECOMMENDED VARIETIES AND RELATED SPECIES: There are many good varieties selected for colorful new spring growth, flower color, and overall form and size. 'Dorothy Wycoff' has dark red buds that open to pale pink flowers. Mountain pieris (*P. floribunda*, Zones 5 to 8) is more cold tolerant and shorter than Japanese pieris.

Pinus mugo mugo
pie-nus MEW-go

Dwarf mountain pine can become a large shrub.

DWARF MOUNTAIN PINE

- Dark-needled evergreen
- Medium texture
- Bushy, spreading habit
- Zones 3 to 8, except for the desert

Bought as a small cushion, it becomes a big bush. Native to the mountains of Europe from Spain to the Balkans.

USES: Use it for textural evergreen interest in a foundation planting.

GROWTH RATE: Slow.

CULTURE: Plant in moist, deep loam in full sun to part shade. To maintain a compact, dense form, prune annually by removing two-thirds of each young, expanding candle in spring. Be sure to grow truly dwarf varieties if you want a plant less than 15 feet tall and wide.

RECOMMENDED VARIETIES AND RELATED SPECIES: *Pinus mugo mugo* can eventually reach 16 feet tall and 20 feet wide. 'Enci', 'Gnom', and 'Mops' are smaller tall varieties. *P. strobus* 'Nana' (Zones 3 to 8) and *P. sylvestris* 'Beauvronensis' (dwarf Scotch pine, Zones 2 to 8) are a few of the many dwarf varieties of other pines.

Pittosporum tobira
pit-o-SPOH-rum to-BEER-ra

Japanese pittosporum is a low shrub for mild climates.

JAPANESE PITTOSPORUM

- Leathery leaves
- Rich fragrance in bloom
- Broad, dense habit
- Zones 8 (south) to 10

Pleasing foliage and creamy yellow spring flowers make this a popular plant in southern and western gardens.

USES: It's good for screens, massing, and in borders and is effective in containers or trained as small, crooked-stemmed trees.

GROWTH RATE: Slow.

CULTURE: Prefers full sun to partial shade but tolerates deep shade. Fairly drought-resistant, but water as needed during drought.

RECOMMENDED VARIETIES AND RELATED SPECIES: 'Variegatum' has white-variegated, gray-green foliage and grows to about 5 feet tall. 'Wheeler's Dwarf' grows only to about 2 feet in many years. Karo (*P. crassifolium*, Zones 9 and 10) is a large shrub up to 25 feet tall that can form a dense hedge 6 feet tall. Fine-textured, gray-green leaves respond well to shearing and tolerate wind and salt. 'Nana' is 3 feet tall.

Platycladus orientalis
(formerly *Thuja orientalis*)
pla-tee-CLA-dus o-ree-en-TAL-is

- Tall, evergreen conifer
- Branches in vertical, fan-shaped planes
- Bright yellow or blue foliage
- Zones 7 to 9

8'
5'

Popular in the south and west for its blue and yellow dwarf varieties. Native to China and Korea.

USES: In masses or groupings, or for textural evergreen interest

ORIENTAL ARBORVITAE

in a foundation planting. Combine it with *Prunus laurocerasus* 'Otto Luyken' and *Chamaecyparis pisifera* 'Filifera Aurea'.

GROWTH RATE: Slow to moderate.

CULTURE: It grows in all but wet soils and tolerates dry soil and atmosphere. Protect it from harsh, dry winds.

RECOMMENDED VARIETIES: 'Aurea Nana' is a rounded yellow dwarf, 2 to 3 feet tall. 'Blue Cone' is a pyramidal form that can grow to 8 feet tall with blue-green needles.

Aurea Nana Oriental arborvitae is a popular dwarf form.

Potentilla fruticosa
po-ten-TIL-la fru-ti-COH-sa

- Prolific, bright flowers in summer
- Deciduous foliage
- Neat, rounded habit
- Zones 3 to 7

3'
3'

A small, versatile shrub for most conditions. Native to meadows and bogs of northern and mountainous Asia, Europe, and North America.

USES: Suitable for shrub borders, foundations, massing, edging, informal low hedges, or facing down larger shrubs.

BUSH CINQUEFOIL

GROWTH RATE: Slow.

CULTURE: It tolerates most well-drained soils and extreme cold and drought. It is susceptible to mites. Flowers best in full sun but tolerates partial shade. Plant orange- and red-flowering varieties in partial shade because they fade in full sun.

RECOMMENDED VARIETIES AND RELATED SPECIES: 'Abbotswood' produces large white flowers on a spreading shrub. 'Goldfinger' is one of the best for bright yellow flowers. 'Primrose Beauty' has pale yellow flowers and silvery leaves. *P. atrosanguinea* 'Gibson's Scarlet' produces profuse red flowers.

Bush cinquefoil produces flowers well into summer.

Prunus laurocerasus
PROO-nus lohr-o-ser-ASS-sus

- Large, dark, evergreen leaves
- Large shrub or small tree
- Medium texture
- Zones 7 and 8

20'
18'

Cherry laurel is a popular hedge plant in southern gardens and in California. Unpruned, it can grow into a small tree or large shrub 20 feet tall.

USE: It makes a handsome formal hedge, screen, or background plant.

CHERRY LAUREL

GROWTH RATE: Medium.

CULTURE: Plant in any soil in partial shade. Prune it selectively and frequently because it grows fast, and shearing mutilates the large leaves. Beware of its greedy, far-reaching roots.

RECOMMENDED VARIETIES: A number of smaller varieties are available that are restrained in habit and size. 'Schipkaensis' has smaller leaves, grows 4 to 5 feet tall, and is hardy to Zone 6 with protection. 'Otto Luyken' is a low-growing form hardy to southern Zone 6 that

reaches only 3 to 4 feet tall after many years. It is also hardier than one species, surviving winters in Zone 6.

Upright flower clusters of cherry laurel become showy black berries by fall.

Prunus tomentosa
PROO-nus toh-men-TOH-sa

Nanking cherry is an outstanding spring-flowering shrub for harsh climates.

NANKING CHERRY

- Open, spreading, twiggy habit
- Top choice for the northern plains
- Pink buds
- Zones 3 to 7

9'
15'

Valuable for its extreme hardiness, fragrant white or pink spring flowers, and delicious scarlet fruit. Native to the Himalayas.

USES: Good for a specimen, hedge, in groups and masses, or in a shrub border.

GROWTH RATE: Medium.

CULTURE: Any soil in partial shade.

RELATED SPECIES AND HYBRIDS: 'Hally Jolivette' (Zones 5 to 8) is an airy shrub or small tree with pink-eyed white flowers that open over 3 weeks. *P.* ×*cistena* (purple-leaf sand cherry, Zones 4 to 7) is valued for extreme hardiness and light pink flowers against reddish-purple leaves. Flowering almond (*P. triloba* var. *multiplex*, Zones 4 to 9) is a large, treelike shrub 12 to 15 feet tall with 1- to 1½-inch, double pink flowers.

Punica granatum
PEW-ni-ka gra-NAY-tum

Pomegranate is an extremely drought-tolerant tree that produces fruit.

POMEGRANATE

- Red-orange flowers
- Delicious fruit
- Brilliant yellow autumn foliage
- Dense, twiggy, fountainlike
- Zones 8 to 10

15'
15'

An excellent desert shrub, it withstands heat, drought, and alkaline soils. A favorite landscape plant for California gardens. Native to southeastern Europe across Asia to the Himalayas.

USES: Selections for size range from container or edging plants to border shrubs 15 feet tall. The dwarf varieties make excellent low hedges.

GROWTH RATE: Moderate.

CULTURE: Plant in full sun for best flowers and fruit. Water regularly for best fruit.

RECOMMENDED VARIETIES: 'Wonderful' is the most popular form for fruit; it grows 8 to 12 feet tall. 'Nana' may grow to only 2 to 3 feet tall, with small flowers and tiny fruits in good proportion to its diminutive stature. It is also a good selection for growing in containers and will flower and fruit indoors.

Pyracantha spp.
py-ra-CAN-tha

Flowers of Watereri firethorn.

Berries of Orange Glow firethorn.

FIRETHORN

- White flowers, early summer
- Prostrate to upright
- Semievergreen to evergreen
- Red to yellow berries, early autumn well into winter
- Zones 6 to 10 (parts of Zone 5, depending on cultivar)

10'
12'

This shrub from southeastern Europe and Asia is irregularly open, with small flowers in large clusters, attractive against the dark green foliage. Its greatest attraction is its colorful fruit.

USES: Specimen, free-form, or trained as espalier, or barrier.

CULTURE: Best in well-drained soil, even if dry. Grows well and fruits in full sun to half shade. May need pruning to maintain desired habit. Susceptible to fire blight and scab, but resistant varieties are available.

RECOMMENDED VARIETIES AND RELATED SPECIES: *P. coccinea* 'Kasan' and 'Lalandei Thornless' grow to 5 feet, have orange fruits, are susceptible to scab, and hardy to Zone 5. *P. angustifolia* 'Gnome' and Yukon Belle are slightly hardier. For mild climates, 'Apache' and many others are scab-resistant.

INDIAN HAWTHORN

Rhaphiolepis indica
ra-fee-o-LEP-is IN-di-ka

- Evergreen foliage
- Flowers bloom in spring, repeat in fall
- Neat, dense habit
- Zones 8 (south) to 10

Low-maintenance shrub has leathery foliage and white or red flowers and serves a multitude of purposes. Native to southern China.

USES: Indian hawthorn can be planted for low background, in a mass, in an informal hedge, or as a large-scale ground cover. Use it as a foreground or a facing plant in a shrub border or as a container plant.

GROWTH RATE: Slow.

CULTURE: It prefers full sun but tolerates partial shade and a variety of soils. Reasonably drought-tolerant, it performs best when watered frequently. Minimize splashing water onto foliage because fire blight and leaf spots can be problems.

RELATED SPECIES: *R. umbellata* (Zones 8 to 10) is a larger version of Indian hawthorn, growing to 5 to 6 feet.

Rose-colored flowers of Indian hawthorn appear spring and fall.

STAGHORN SUMAC

Rhus typhina
ROOS TYE-fi-na

- Excellent fall color in red, orange, and yellow
- Red fruit
- Ferny foliage
- Zones 4 to 8

Exotic, almost tropical look in a hardy plant native to eastern North America. Outstanding fall color.

USES: A suckering, spreading habit, 15 to 25 feet tall, makes it good for massing in large, open areas.

GROWTH RATE: Slow from old growth, fast from suckers.

CULTURE: Adaptable to all but standing water, sumac prefers good drainage. When necessary, renew it by cutting to the ground in late winter.

RELATED SPECIES: *R. aromatica* 'Gro-Low' (fragrant sumac, Zones 3 to 9) has lustrous green leaves and spreads 2 feet tall and up to 8 feet wide. It makes an effective ground cover with often showy but variable orange-red fall color. *R. copallina* (Zones 5 to 8) rarely exceeds 10 feet tall in cultivation. A native of the eastern United States, it has good fall color and interesting silhouettes. *R. glabra* (smooth sumac, Zones 2 to 9) has brilliant red and yellow fall color and fuzzy, large red fruit clusters. Invasive but good for large areas.

Staghorn sumac produces outstanding fall color but needs space to spread.

ALPINE CURRANT

Ribes alpinum
RYE-beez al-PIE-num

- Upright, twiggy growth
- Fruit attracts birds
- Deciduous; little fall color
- Zones 2 to 7

This hardy European native grows easily in the northern United States.

USES: Companions include *Aster ×frikartii* 'Monch' and *Coreopsis verticillata* 'Zagreb'.

GROWTH RATE: Moderate.

CULTURE: It adapts to any soil in full sun to shade. Prune at any time.

RECOMMENDED VARIETIES AND RELATED SPECIES: 'Green Mound' is a dense, compact form 2 feet tall, 3 feet wide. Clove currant (*R. odoratum*, Zones 4 to 6) has yellow flowers that smell like cloves. Winter currant (*R. sanguineum* 'King Edward VII', Zones 5 and 6) has red flowers, is a compact 5 to 6 feet tall, and is native to the west.

Currants are good additions to both formal and informal gardens.

Rhododendron spp.
ro-do-DEN-dron

- Beautiful flowers
- Rounded form
- Evergreen or deciduous foliage
- Zones 3 to 10, depending on species

Balzac, an Exbury azalea, is noted for its fiery color.

RHODODENDRONS AND AZALEAS

Rhododendrons and azaleas differ in subtle ways, but all 900 species belong to the genus *Rhododendron*. Rhododendron flowers resemble bells, and azalea blossoms look like funnels. Most rhododendrons are evergreen, and most azaleas are deciduous. For convenience, we divided the genus into three groups: rhododendrons, evergreen azaleas, and deciduous azaleas.

USES: They are outstanding for shrub borders, woodland edges, foundation plantings, masses, groupings, and (for small species) in rock gardens.

GROWTH RATE: Usually slow.

CULTURE: Plant in well-drained, acid soil. In the south, rhododendrons need more shade than in the north, where light shade is adequate. Keep them away from alkaline soil, salt spray, and harsh winter sun and wind.

RECOMMENDED EVERGREEN RHODODENDRONS:

Carolina rhododendron (*R. carolinianum*; Zones 5 to 8) is a restrained, rounded shrub 3 to 6 feet tall with white or pink flowers against dark, medium-sized, evergreen leaves. Native to the Blue Ridge Mountains of the Carolinas and Tennessee.

Catawba rhododendron (*R. catawbiense*, Zones 5 to 7) grows 6 to 10 feet tall and wide in the garden. It produces prolific trusses of reddish-purple flowers against dark green leaves. Native to the Allegheny Mountains from West Virginia to Georgia and Alabama.

Rosebay rhododendron (*R. maximum*, Zones 5 to 7) reaches 4 to 15 feet tall in the garden; it has a loose, open habit. Flowers are white or rosy purple. It needs at least partial shade to thrive. Native from North Carolina to Alabama.

R. degronianum yakushimanum is compact, 3 feet tall and wide, with white flowers. Dark green leaves have fuzzy undersides. 'Yaku Princess' has red to pink buds that open pure white; leaves are densely hairy underneath. Native to Japan.

Album catawba rhododendron.

Purple flowers of rosebay rhododendron.

Red-flowered Kurume-type azalea.

Grandi

prevai
when
were (
white
and o
to mo
garder
hardy,
resista

CLASS

4'

centur
tend t
habits
robus
seem
Holm(
white
and b
Dagm
stands
petale
shiny

Abrah

P.J.M. hybrids, hardy to Zone 4, are rounded shrubs 3 to 6 feet tall. Dark green leaves turn purple in fall. Lavender-pink flowers last into autumn in the southeast.

Dexter hybrids are big and hardy and have dense leaves and beautiful flowers in yellows, pinks, and reds. 'Wheatley' bears yellow-blotched pink flowers on a shrub 6 feet tall and hardy to Zone 5. 'Scintillation', a pink, is the most famous Dexter.

An old, popular ironclad includes 'Boule de Neige', with glossy, dark, evergreen leaves; a compact, rounded habit; and lovely white flower trusses. Hardy to northern Zone 4, it is heat- and sun-tolerant.

RECOMMENDED EVERGREEN AZALEA HYBRIDS: Southern Indian hybrids (Zones 8 to 10) were developed for greenhouse forcing but now are a common landscape plant in southern and California gardens. There are tender Belgian Indian hybrids and more vigorous and sun-tolerant southern Indians. Flowers range from white to violet, pink, red, and salmon.

Kurume hybrids are Japanese hybrids popular in the landscape. Slow growing, they reach 6 feet tall and are hardy in Zones 6 to 9.

Gable hybrids (Zones 6 to 8) are bred for increased hardiness but should not be used north of Zone 6. Their evergreen leaves redden and fall in the northern part of their range. They are midsize shrubs with flowers in red to purple hues, with some light violets, orange-reds, and pinks available.

Torch azalea (*R. kaempferi*, Zones 6 to 8) flowers white to rose to red-orange and salmon on a shrub up to 10 feet tall. Foliage is semievergreen in the north, evergreen in the south, and often turns red in cold weather. It flowers well in the deepest shade but prefers light shade.

Girard hybrids produce large, lovely flowers in pink, purple, white, and red on a handsome, evergreen shrub about 4 to 6 feet tall. They are good for northern Zone 6 to southern Zone 9.

Glenn Dale hybrids are cold-hardy in Zones 6 (south) to 9 (north) and grow 3 to 8 feet tall. They bloom from early to late season, with large, varied flowers in pink, red, orange-red, and white with flecks or stripes in a darker, contrasting color.

Robin Hill hybrids are hardy and reliable to about 10° F. They have big, late flowers up to 4 inches in diameter in pale pink, lavender, white, salmon, and red.

Shammarello hybrids, bred for cold climates, are hardy in Zones 5 to 9.

Korean azalea.

Torch azalea.

A Knap Hill-Exbury hybrid azalea.

A yellow form of flame azalea.

Rosmarinus officinalis
rows MARE-i-nus oh-fi-si-NAL-is

Arp rosemary is an upright variety with gray-green foliage.

ROSEMARY

- ■ Evergreen with fragrant, edible foliage
- ■ Blue flowers
- ■ Attracts birds, bees
- ■ Zones 7 (south) to 10 (some hardy to Zone 6)

4'
6'

A Mediterranean native with a bushy, irregular habit. Flourishes on the West Coast and in the heat and humidity of the southeast. It flowers from fall to winter.

USES: Shears well, makes a good hedge, useful in the dry shrub border. Also a delicious kitchen herb.

GROWTH RATE: Moderate.

CULTURE: Tolerate of salt, heat, sun, infertile soil, and drought, rosemary can take any well-drained soil except a wet one. Plant in full sun only. Prune it for a low hedge. Don't give it too much water or fertilizer.

RECOMMENDED VARIETIES: 'Collingwood Ingram', 'Lockwood de Forest', and 'Tuscan Blue', selected for bright blue flowers and, in the case of 'Lockwood de Forest', a prostrate habit.

Spiraea japonica
spy-REE-ah ja-PON-i-ka

Goldflame spirea.

Little Princess spirea.

Vanhoutte spirea.

JAPANESE SPIREA

- ■ White to deep pink flowers
- ■ Medium-fine texture
- ■ Low, spreading habit
- ■ Zones 4 to 8

3'
4'

Flower clusters 6 inches wide appear over a long season, June to August.

USES: Spirea is good in masses and in the shrub border, where it makes a quick, easy-care filler, and where its dull, non-blooming appearance can be masked.

GROWTH RATE: Fast.

CULTURE: Plant in any soil in full sun and with good air circulation. It is susceptible to many pests and diseases, none of which is fatal. Prune it in late winter or early spring. Cut old, leggy plants to the ground in spring to renew them.

RECOMMENDED VARIETIES AND RELATED SPECIES: 'Albiflora' has white and 'Anthony Waterer' has

Snowmound spirea.

Bridalwreath spirea (*Spiraea prunifolia*).

deep rose flowers. 'Crispa' grows 2 feet tall with twisted leaves. 'Atrosanguinea' is a superior deep rose red cultivar 2 to 4 feet tall and hardy to Zone 4. 'Goldflame' is low-growing with brightly colored red, copper, and orange leaves in early spring and fall. 'Shibori' is an upright mound to 3 feet tall, with quantities of rose, pink, and white flowers. Vanhoutte spirea (*S. ×vanhouttei*) is a tough, fountainlike shrub 5 to 6 feet tall and wide. White flowers appear on old growth in mid- to late spring. *S. nipponica* 'Snowmound', (Zones 4 to 8) is a white-blooming species growing 3 to 5 feet tall and wide. Bridalwreath spirea (*S. prunifolia*, Zones 4 to 8) is a rangy, open shrub, 4 to 9 feet tall and 6 to 8 feet wide, with double white flowers in April on old growth. Leaves turn red-orange in autumn.

■ Beau
■ Thor
■ Vario
■ Zone
   on sp

Seductiv
flowers
make rc
garden
USES: I
roses fc
ground
or bedd
with bo
switchg
GROWT
CULTUR
slightly
amende
sun. Ga
feed ro
require
RECOM
RELATE
species
of hybr
fall intc
HYBRID
5'

3'

long st
regular
sprayin
   Gran

Alba rc

Common lilac.

COMMON LILAC

Syringa vulgaris
sur-RING-a vul-GARE-is

■ Powerful floral fragrance
■ Large, conical flower clusters
■ Bluish-green foliage
■ Zones 3 to 7

18'
15'

Lilacs are valued in spring for their beauty and for the scent of their violet, purple, pink, blue, magenta, yellow, and white flowers. Native to southern Europe.

USES: Long-lived and capable of surviving most conditions, common lilac has an upright, irregular habit that's good in the back of the border. Plant it with linden viburnum *(Viburnum dilatatum)*.

GROWTH RATE: Slow.

CULTURE: Plant in full sun in neutral, rich soil high in organic matter. Provide a location with good air circulation to help reduce problems with powdery mildew, to which these shrubs are susceptible. Some varieties produce good flowers only every other year. Remove spent blossoms immediately to increase next year's flowering; prune out 50 to 75 percent of the basal suckers each year. Renew old plants by cutting them back to within a few inches of the ground.

RECOMMENDED VARIETIES AND RELATED SPECIES: Hundreds are available, selected mostly for color. Most lilacs do best in cold climates. 'Lavender Lady', 'Blue Boy', 'Chiffon', 'Mrs. Forrest K. Smith', and 'Sylvan's Beauty' do well in mild climates. *S. meyeri* 'Palibin' has pink flowers on a compact, floriferous, low-maintenance shrub. *S. patula* 'Miss Kim' is a tidy, blue-flowered, oval shrub 6 to 8 feet tall and 4 to 5 feet wide. *S. ×persica* is a low shrub with smaller leaves and nearly scentless pale lavender flowers.

Miss Kim lilac.   **Persian lilac.**

Palibin lilac.

YEW

Taxus spp.
TAK-sus

■ Dark evergreen foliage
■ Hardy, trouble-free
■ Many varieties available
■ Zones 4 to 7, depending on species

7'
8'

This versatile, needled evergreen has many uses in the home landscape, but the seeds are toxic, as is the foliage.

USES: Yew is good for formal hedges, massing, topiary, shrub borders, screens, and foundation plantings.

GROWTH RATE: Slow.

CULTURE: Plant in soil with excellent drainage in sun or shade. In hot, dry climates, place it with a northern exposure. Water on dry sites and protect from sweeping wind. It may be browsed by deer. The red fruits of the female plants contain highly toxic bronze seeds.

RECOMMENDED VARIETIES AND RELATED SPECIES: *T. baccata* (English yew, Zones 6 and 7) is good for southern gardens. 'Adpressa Fowle' is a shade-tolerant, compact yew, with distinctive short needles, growing 7 feet tall and twice as wide. 'Repandens' is a graceful, low form for massing, useful in Zones 5 to 7. *T. cuspidata* (Zones 4 to 7) has many excellent varieties. 'Aurescens' is a dwarf with yellow new growth. 'Densa' is a thick mass of upright stems 2 to 3 feet tall and 3 to 4 feet wide. *T. c.* 'Capitata' is a botanical variety quite variable from seed. *T. ×media* (Zones 5 to 7) is a hybrid between the previous two species. 'Beanpole' has bright red fruit and stands 3 to 4 feet tall and 6 to 8 inches wide. 'Hatfieldii' (Hatfield yew) is a broad, upright hedging plant, 12 feet tall and 10 feet wide. 'Hicksii' (Hick's yew) is a good hedging plant with dark green leaves and a columnar habit, 15 to 20 feet tall and 10 to 15 feet wide.

An upright shrub, Fastigiata yew grows slowly and stays narrow.

Thuja occidentalis
THOO-ya ok-si-den-TAL-is

AMERICAN ARBORVITAE

- Large, upright
- Fine-textured, dark green leaves
- Foliage yellow-brown in cold weather
- Zones 3 to 7

25'
10'

Varieties range from rock-garden plants only inches tall to 20-foot columns useful for screens. Native from Nova Scotia south to the Carolinas and Tennessee.

USES: Varieties are found in foundation plantings, hedges, and screens. Plant it with evergreen candytuft (*Iberis sempervirens*) and false cypress (*Chamaecyparis* species.)

Golden Globe American arborvitae grows to about 4 feet tall.

GROWTH RATE: Slow for compact varieties.

CULTURE: Plant in well-drained, moist soil in full sun. It tolerates alkaline soils and performs best in areas of high atmospheric moisture. Low-maintenance; it needs some protection from winter winds, snow, and ice.

RECOMMENDED VARIETIES AND RELATED SPECIES: 'Nigra' and 'Techny' retain dark green leaves all winter. 'Golden Globe' is a dwarf, dense, evergreen shrub with a rounded, globular form. Most often seen as a 2- to 4-foot-tall shrub, it may reach twice that height after many years. 'Emerald' maintains a compact, pyramidal form to nearly 15 feet, and it retains its green color in winter. Giant arborvitae (*T. plicata*) varieties are better adapted to the central midwest than American arborvitae, and are reportedly not as palatable to deer.

Vaccinium corymbosum
vak-SIN-i-um ko-rim-BOW-sum

HIGHBUSH BLUEBERRY

- Colorful fall foliage
- Blue fruit
- Dark purplish-red stems
- Zones 5 to 8

2'
2'

Primarily grown for its fruit, this is a choice, four-season landscape plant that has white flowers and yellow, bronze, orange, or red fall colors. Native from Maine to Minnesota and south to Florida and Louisiana.

USES: Good for shrub borders, foundation plantings, and massed naturally in large areas. Blueberry grows well with *Viburnum trilobum* 'Compactum' and *Ribes* species.

GROWTH RATE: Slow.

CULTURE: Blueberries do best in sandy, acid soil in full sun, but they

Highbush blueberry produces small, edible fruit. Leather leaves turn bronze-red in winter.

also produce in moist, acid, well-drained soil high in organic matter. Mulch well to promote a cool, moist root run, and water during drought.

RECOMMENDED VARIETIES AND RELATED SPECIES: *V.* 'Blueray' grows 5 to 8 feet tall but is easily kept lower. Berries are ½ inch in diameter and ripen in midsummer. Dark green leaves turn attractive shades of red in fall. 'Bluecrop' is the favored commercial variety in North America. 'Bluetta' is more compact, at only 4 feet, and 'Georgiagem' needs little winter chill. Many other varieties are available: Check with your local extension service for the best ones for your locale. *V. angustifolium* (lowbush blueberry, Zones 2 to 5) has blue-green leaves and an open habit up to 2 feet tall and 2 feet wide. It thrives in poor, thirsty, acid soil, and provides bright red fall color and delectable berries.

VIBURNUM

Viburnum spp.
vy-BUR-num

- Some are fragrant
- Flowers and fruit
- Evergreen and deciduous species
- Zones 3 to 9, depending on the species

This diverse genus contains a range of valuable shrubs for the garden, and some species have fine fall color.

USES: They can be used in shrub borders, in groups, or for massing. They also can be used as landscape specimens or, depending on the species, as bird-attracting shrubs in a wildlife garden. Plant them with oak leaf hydrangea *(Hydrangea quercifolia)* and shining sumac *(Rhus copallina)*, as well as other viburnums.

GROWTH RATE: Moderate.

CULTURE: Plant in moist, well-drained, slightly acid soil, although they're generally adaptable to other soils. If kept vigorous, these shrubs are usually untroubled by pests and diseases.

RELATED SPECIES:

 Burkwood viburnum *(V. ×burkwoodii,* Zones 5 to 8) is an upright, somewhat straggly shrub 8 to 10 feet tall and 5 to 7 feet wide, grown for its fragrant pink-white flowers that appear in midspring

Fragrant Cayuga snowball viburnum.

before leaves unfold. Evergreen to semievergreen.

 Fragrant snowball viburnum *(V. ×carlcephalum,* Zones 6 to 9) has loose, open growth 6 to 10 feet tall and wide. It produces sweetly fragrant white flowers in April or May.

 Korean spice viburnum *(V. carlesii,* Zones 5 to 7) has spicy sweet, pinkish-white flowers in late April to early May on a rounded, dense shrub 4 to 8 feet tall and 4 to 8 feet wide. Popular in northern gardens. Native to Korea.

 David viburnum *(V. davidii,* Zones 8 to 10) is a dense, large-leaved evergreen shrub 1 to 3 feet tall and 3 to 4 feet wide with metallic blue fruits. Native to China, it grows well in California gardens.

Arrowwood viburnum.

 Arrowwood viburnum *(V. dentatum,* Zones 3 to 8) is hardy and adaptable to many climates and harsh conditions. It has a dense habit with spreading branches, 6 to 15 feet tall and wide, and white flowers and blue-black fruits. Native from New Brunswick south to Florida and Texas.

Linden viburnum *(V. dilatatum,* Zones 5 to 8) is an upright, open shrub 8 to 10 feet tall and 5 to 8 feet wide with unpleasant-smelling white flowers in May and June. Its most outstanding season is September and October, when the bright red fruits ripen, often remaining effective into December. Plant in shrub borders, and grow several together to improve fruiting. Native to eastern Asia.

Burkwood viburnum.

Korean spice viburnum.

David viburnum.

Erie linden viburnum.

Judd viburnum.

Mariesii doublefile viburnum.

Chinese snowball viburnum.

Aurantiacum tea viburnum.

VIBURNUM *continued*

9'
8'

Judd viburnum (*V. ×juddii*, Zones 5 to 7) is similar to Korean spice viburnum but taller and more heat-tolerant.

10'
10'

Chinese snowball viburnum (*V. macrocephalum*, Zones 7 and 8) bears round, white balls of sterile flowers up to 8 inches across in late May to early June; they are the largest flower clusters of any viburnum. A dense, rounded shrub, it is semievergreen in southern areas and 6 to 10 feet tall and wide. In the northern part of its range, it needs protection from winter winds and must have well-drained soil. Native to China.

10'
10'

European cranberrybush (*V. opulus*, Zones 4 to 8) produces delicate, pinwheel white flowers, composed of sterile showy flowers on the outside of the cluster and fertile, less conspicuous flowers on the inside, in late May. Berrylike, bright red fruits are effective from September to November, accompanied by excellent fall color. It grows 8 to 15 feet tall and 10 to 15 feet wide. Susceptible to aphids, especially the snowball-flowered cultivar 'Roseum'. Native to Europe.

10'
14'

Doublefile viburnum (*V. plicatum* f. *tomentosum* 'Mariesii', Zones 5 to 8) is often considered the most beautiful of all deciduous flowering shrubs. It bears profuse, lacy pinwheel, pure white flowers gracefully arranged along horizontally tiered branches. It stands 8 to 10 feet tall and slightly wider with dark green foliage in summer and good fall color. Bright red fruits in late summer are attractive to birds. Excellent with broadleaf evergreens, as a focal specimen, for horizontal balance in upright shrub borders, against dark red brick, or with red flowers. It needs fertile, well-drained, moist soil for easy maintenance. 'Mariesii' and 'Shasta' bear the largest flower and fruit clusters. 'Pink Beauty' produces smaller deep pink flowers, and 'Shasta' has profuse, very large, white flowers and exceptional horizontal branching. Native to China and Japan.

10'
8'

Lantanaphyllum viburnum (*V. × rhytidophylloides* 'Willowwood', Zones 6 and 7) has large, leathery, semievergreen leaves on a shrub that reaches 8 to 10 feet tall and wide.

10'
8'

Tea viburnum (*V. setigerum*, Zones 5 to 7) is grown for its dramatic red fruit display on high, arching branches. It stands 10 to 12 feet tall and up to 8 feet wide. Tea viburnum works well when grown behind shorter shrubs, which cover the bare-bottomed stems responsible for its unusual, top-heavy but striking appearance.

8'
8'

Laurustinus (*V. tinus*; Zones 8 to 10) is an evergreen, upright, 6- to 12-foot-tall shrub for southern and West Coast gardens. It has dark green foliage, pink flowers turning to white, and bright metallic blue fruit. Dense, ground-hugging leaves make it good for screening, and it responds well to formal pruning. Adaptable to shade but flowers more in full sun.

10'
10'

American cranberrybush viburnum (*V. trilobum*; Zones 2 to 8) is a North American native similar to European cranberrybush but hardier and more resistant to aphids. 'Compactum' is a fine dwarf form with red autumn foliage.

Compactum European cranberrybush.

Willowwood lantanaphyllum.

Laurustinus Rubustum.

American cranberrybush viburnum.

OLD-FASHIONED WEIGELA

Weigela florida
wye-JEE-la FLOR-i-da

- Flowers in many colors
- Dark green leaves of medium texture
- Coarse and rangy
- Zones 5 to 8; some cultivars in colder zones

7'
8'

The floral display in late May and early June is outstanding. Some new forms, such as 'Wine and Roses', have good foliage. Native to northern China and Korea.

USES: Plant in the shrub border, in masses, and in groupings, where its form and texture are hidden when not flowering. Combine wiegela with abelia (*Abelia ×grandiflora*) and fothergilla (*Fothergilla*).
GROWTH RATE: Moderate.
CULTURE: Prefers well-drained soil and a sunny location but is adaptable and pest-free. Prune after flowering to clean up the shrub's appearance.
RECOMMENDED VARIETIES: *W. f.* var. *venusta* is hardy to Zone 4 with finely textured leaves and rosy pink flowers. 'Bristol Ruby' and 'Red Prince' have red flowers, and 'Red Prince' is the hardiest.

Pink Princess weigela.

YELLOW-ROOT

Xanthorhiza simplicissima
Zan-THOR-i-za SIM-pliss-ee-ma

- Brownish-purple flowers in spring
- Yellow-orange fall color
- Easy-to-grow ground cover
- Zones 4 to 8

2'
2'

Yellow-root is an easy-to-grow deciduous shrub, forming a uniform 2-foot-tall ground cover. Its oval to oblong leaves turn a beautiful yellow-orange in autumn. In spring, drooping clusters of tiny star-shaped, brownish-purple flowers on long spikes appear before leaves unfold.
USES: Stream banks, beside ponds, or in other wet areas; edging; under trees.
CULTURE: Plants tolerate a wide range of soils, but they grow most luxuriantly in humus-rich, moist but well-drained soil with a pH of 4.5 to 6. Part to full shade is also best for the plants. They withstand wet conditions and clay soil. Shear plants in early spring to promote lateral branching. Propagate by cuttings or division.

Yellow-root is a ground cover that develops brilliant red fall color.

ADAM'S NEEDLE

Yucca filamentosa
YUK-ka fil-a-men-TOH-sa

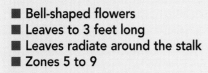

- Bell-shaped flowers
- Leaves to 3 feet long
- Leaves radiate around the stalk
- Zones 5 to 9

6'
3'

Striking architectural plant has narrow, stiff, arched, swordlike evergreen leaves and white flowers on a stout central stalk 3 to 8 feet tall. Native to the southeastern United States.
USES: Plant it in shrub borders, containers, desert gardens, or massed as a ground cover.
GROWTH RATE: Slow.
CULTURE: Adam's needle grows well in the hot, humid climate of the Gulf states, in the desert, and in average, well-drained garden soil. It needs excellent drainage. It does better in full sun and poor soils low in organic matter but can adapt to many soils and partial shade. Drought-tolerant.
RECOMMENDED VARIETIES: 'Golden Sword' leaves have green edges and yellow centers. 'Variegata' has cream-striped foliage. 'Bright Edge' leaves have cream edges and green centers.

Flower spikes of Adam's needle can reach 8 feet tall.

SELECTING
Woody Vines

Enveloped by a twining clematis, this quiet corner with a bench becomes a sanctuary.

A blooming wisteria transforms even the most ordinary patio.

The following guide of woody vines is full of information you'll need to grow healthy, beautiful vines. This isn't an encyclopedia of every vine known, but instead a carefully selected list of the most garden-worthy woody vines that are readily available. For a complete discussion of the information included in the individual vine entries, see page 202. For more on growing and selecting all types of vines, see Ortho's *All About Vines and Climbers*.

NOT TO WORRY

Do you remember how Sleeping Beauty's castle became covered and entwined with vines? Many people do. They worry about vines damaging structures and getting out of hand.

Selection is the key; it will bring joy rather than misery to your garden. By knowing how each vine grows, as well as how quickly, you can choose a vine that will be an asset rather than a problem.

Avoid damage to buildings by keeping rootlet-type vines away from wood structures and by making sure any masonry to be covered is in good condition. Do not use vines like wallpaper, to cover problems instead of fixing them. Be cautious in the use of vigorous climbers, and choose those whose ultimate size matches the structure on which they are growing.

Vigorous vines are useful in certain situations. Vigor, for instance, is a virtue when you have a four-story masonry wall to cover. Trumpet vine, Virginia creeper, and English ivy can be valuable in such a case. In most other cases, a less vigorous vine will need less maintenance.

How Vines Grow

Most vines need some type of structure to support their sprawling growth. When you select a structure, it is essential that you know how a vine grows, and its vigor, size, and weight, so you can select the right support. Vines grow in four different ways: twining, clinging by rootlets, clinging by tendrils, and climbing/sprawling. These growth habits are illustrated below, and each vine has its own ideal type of support. Trying to make a vine climb a structure not suited to it will only result in frustration. Vigorous vines need large, strong structures to support their mass. Petite vines can grow on light structures.

TWINERS wrap their stems around a vertical object. They grow on posts, chain-link fences, arbors, and lattices. Do not grow them on living trees because they can strangle and kill the tree.

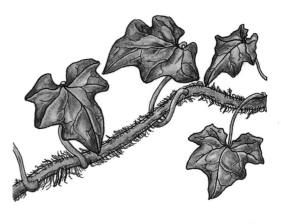

CLINGING ROOTLETS These plants have rootlets (some have adhesive discs) along the stem that attach to their support, such as a masonry wall, tree trunk, or rock pile. Some will grow on banks as a ground cover. They are not parasites and draw no nourishment from their support structure.

TENDRILS essentially reach out to attach to something. Tendrils are actually modified stems, but some vines (such as clematis) have modified leaves that also act as tendrils. Tendril vines cling well to shrubs, chain link, strings, netting, and thin lattice. A few vines have tendrils with adhesive tips. Some of these plants combine the qualities of tendril and rootlet vines.

CLIMBERS, SPRAWLERS These have lax stems that sprawl over other plants and can be tied to supporting structures. Even though they are often called climbers, they have no mechanism for climbing by themselves. Climbing and rambling roses are the best-known examples and usually need to be tied to their support.

Vines for Color

Long flower clusters of Multijuga Japanese wisteria open against new growth.

Red fruits and fall leaf color of American bittersweet.

Jackman Clematis at peak bloom in early summer.

Vines with showy flowers are a joy to use. They add luxuriant color and do not take up space. Some bloom with one brief burst of color; others blossom throughout the growing season. Trumpet honeysuckle blooms from May until October. Tropical vines such as mandevilla and golden trumpet (planted as annuals) bloom the entire summer. Three selections of clematis will give you spring-to-fall flowers: anemone clematis in spring, Jackman clematis in summer, and sweet autumn clematis in fall. With planning, flowers will span the seasons.

White, yellow, and orange shine at a distance against dark green and purple. White shows up on dark nights and is perfect near patios where you spend evenings.

Dark purples and blues add contrast to a bright border and complement yellows and oranges; purple shows off against the silver of conifers.

Bright colors are just what you need to show off flowers in a dark area.

Experiment with colors and combinations. If the flowers look appealing in a catalog, check to see if the vine will

VINES FOR SPRING BLOOM

Evergreen clematis (*Clematis cirrhosa* and *C. armandii*)
Anemone clematis (*Clematis montana*)
Golden clematis (*Clematis tangutica*)
Carolina jessamine (*Gelsemium sempervirens*)
Roses (*Rosa* spp.)
Wisteria (*Wisteria* spp.)

Leaves of star jasmine turn reddish with cooler temperatures of fall and winter.

'Cecile Brunner' rambler rose, in showy flower, scrambles over a sturdy arbor.

VINES FOR FRAGRANCE

Evergreen clematis *(Clematis armandii* and *C. cirrhosa)*
Anemone clematis *(Clematis montana)*
Sweet autumn clematis *(Clematis terniflora)*
Carolina jessamine *(Gelsemium sempervirens)*
Pink Chinese jasmine *(Jasminum polyanthum)*
Roses (some) *(Rosa* spp.)
Madagascar jasmine *(Stephanotis floribunda)*
Star jasmine *(Trachelospermum jasminoides)*
Wisteria *(Wisteria* spp.)

grow in your area, figure out what support it needs, then buy it. If the color doesn't seem to work, move it or replace it. In most cases, you'll love the effect; the "accident" is what makes gardening fun.

Plant vines with other plants that have similar flowers or fruit or with structures painted to emphasize color combinations, such as lavender and yellow, purple and rose, or purple and orange. Use these combinations in the garden. Mix vines, perennials, and shrubs together. Paint structures in colors that you like, and plant vines that contrast or match.

Climbing hydrangea shows golden yellow leaf color in fall.

Boston ivy in brilliant red fall color.

VINES FOR SUMMER BLOOM

Coral vine *(Antigonon leptopus)*
Cross vine *(Bignonia capreolata)*
Bougainvillea *(Bougainvillea* spp.)
Trumpet vine *(Campsis radicans)*
Jackman clematis *(Clematis* ×*jackmanii)*
Mandevilla *(Mandevilla* ×*amabilis)*
Climbing rose (some) *(Rosa* spp.)

Vines for Foliage and Late-Season Color

Star Showers Virginia creeper shows its pink-and-white-variegated leaves.

Leaves of aptly named Emerald 'n Gold wintercreeper euonymus have green centers and gold margins.

A fascinating garden is more than just flowers and foliage. And at the end of the growing season, when other colors pale, even those of autumn leaves, vines can be dramatic. They bring an upward-moving brightness to fall and winter.

Showy fruits

Probably the most famous vine for fruit is American bittersweet. It, or more often its weedy Asian cousin, is picked for autumn arrangements. Unfortunately, American bittersweet has become a rare plant in the wild. Growing it in your garden is one way to help increase its numbers. You'll need both a male and female plant for fruit to set.

Virginia creeper bears fruits that look like miniature Concord grapes. They are attractive, but what really sets them off are their red stalks. They won't cause you to slow down if you are driving by, but they are intriguing whenever you're close enough to walk near them.

Other fruits show off their form in interesting ways. Clematis seed heads resemble feathered headdresses, starting in the fall, then staying for early winter. Climbing hydrangea holds its old flowers and fruits through the winter, resembling dried floral arrangements.

Yellow and red fruits of Indian Brave American bittersweet.

Misty, a form of English ivy with variegated leaves.

Flowers and pom-pom-like seed heads of golden clematis provide several seasons of interest.

VINES FOR WINTER EFFECT

Trumpet vine *(Campsis radicans)*

Climbing hydrangea *(Hydrangea petiolaris)*

False climbing hydrangea *(Schizophragma hydrangeoides)*

Wisteria *(Wisteria spp.)*

Winter silhouettes

Winter is a wonderful time to appreciate the "bones" of vines. The bark of climbing hydrangea sheds to reveal papery, reddish-brown layers that become more beautiful as the plant ages. Old wisteria trunks twine around themselves in beautiful patterns, especially when outlined in snow. Boston ivy forms a flat, fine-textured tracery upon surfaces, especially in contrast to a yellow or ochre-colored masonry wall.

Evergreens

The presence of evergreens can help you get through the winter. Wintercreeper euonymus is one of the hardiest of the evergreen vines. Its cultivar 'Vegetus' climbs well and can eventually reach the top of a three-story building.

Some English ivy cultivars, such as 'Bulgaria' and 'Baltica', are nearly as hardy as euonymus. In far northern areas where they are borderline hardy, plant them

along a sheltered wall, and protect them from the winter sun. Some cultivars have yellow leaves; others have shapes that are distinctly different. Algerian ivy offers bolder leaves than English ivy, although it is not hardy north of Zone 8.

Overwintering birds seek the shelter of evergreens. A tree trunk covered by English ivy will be alive with winter bird sounds.

Red fall foliage and blue fruits of Virginia creeper.

In warm climates, evergreen clematis and creeping fig are good selections for evergreen vines. The clematis has shiny leaves and very showy, fragrant flowers. Creeping fig has small leaves and makes a fine-textured wall covering.

Autumn color

Autumn color is one of the joys of living in a climate with four distinct seasons. You usually think of trees when you think of fall color, but there are vines that are equally vibrant. They let you mix and match. Grow a vine with yellow fall foliage (climbing hydrangea) on the trunk of a tree with red fall color (pin oak, sour gum, sweet gum) for a trunk of yellow and a blaze of red or purple in the crown. Reverse the effect with the red of Boston ivy or Virginia creeper on a tulip tree.

EVERGREEN VINES

Cross vine *(Bignonia capreolata)*

Evergreen clematis *(Clematis cirrhosa* and *Clematis armandii)*

Wintercreeper euonymus *(Euonymus fortunei)*

Creeping fig *(Ficus pumila)*

Carolina jessamine *(Gelsemium sempervirens)*

Algerian ivy *(Hedera canariensis)*

English ivy *(Hedera helix)*

Akebia quinata
a-KEE-bee-a kwi-NAH-ta

Red-purple flowers of akebia are distinctive.

AKEBIA, CHOCOLATE VINE

- Beautiful leaves and chocolate-colored flowers
- Semi-evergreen, climbs by twining
- Vigorous, grows 10 to 15 feet per year
- Zones 5 to 9

Grown mostly for its refined, lovely foliage, akebia also produces subtle flowers that are showy up close, so plant it near a walkway where you are sure to pass it. The flowers appear early as the new leaves are unfurling, and they remain for several weeks. The dark green leaves are quite beautiful: Leaflets stay until late fall, when they turn brown, then drop.

USES: Best used where flowers and foliage can be viewed up close.

SITING AND CARE: Akebia thrives in sun or shade. It tolerates moisture but not flooding. Prune in late spring, just after flowering.

RECOMMENDED VARIETIES: There is a white-flowered selection called 'Alba'. Plant it against a dark house for contrast. Leaves of 'Variegata' have white markings, but it is not very vigorous. 'Shirobana' has fragrant white flowers.

Antigonon leptopus
an-tee-GOH-nun LEP-to-pus

Coral vine blooms in late summer.

CORAL VINE, CONFEDERATE VINE

- Coral pink flowers in late summer
- Deciduous, climbs by tendrils
- Vigorous, grows 10 to 15 feet in a season
- Zones 9 and 10 (will survive in Zone 8 but dies to the ground in winter)

Completely covering itself in rosy pink flowers, coral vine is a spectacular sight late in the season, when the showy effect of other plants is at a premium. It's easy to grow and is tolerant of difficult conditions. Native to Mexico.

USES: Coral vine is very vigorous and should be planted on lattice, chain-link fence, or other plants.

SITING AND CARE: This vine grows well in sunny spots and tolerates drought and hot, dry climates. Cut it back hard each spring (repeat in early summer if necessary) to control airy and profuse growth.

RECOMMENDED VARIETIES: 'Album' has white flowers; 'Baja Red' has deep rose-red flowers.

Aristolochia macrophylla (A. durior)
a-ris-to-LOK-ee-a mak-ro-FIL-la

Closeup of the namesake flower of Dutchman's pipe.

DUTCHMAN'S PIPE

- Bold foliage and unique flowers
- Deciduous, climbs by twining
- Vigorous, grows 10 to 15 feet in a season
- Zones 4 (southern part) to 7

This is one of the boldest-textured vines, with large (to 12 inches wide) and long, rounded dark green leaves. The flowers of Dutchman's pipe are the source of its common name. These fantastic purplish-brown flowers do look like macabre pipes. Native to the eastern United States.

USES: The flowers are small and hidden by the leaves, so plant it in a location that you will see from behind, as on a porch or next to a window. Grow it on a post, arbor, chain-link fence, or screened porch.

SITING AND CARE: Easy and adaptable, this is a vine that is virtually maintenance-free. It grows in sun or shade, needs adequate moisture, and is generally untroubled by pests. Its flowers are a favorite food of the rare pipe vine swallowtail butterfly larvae.

CROSS VINE

Bignonia capreolata
big-NO-nee-a ka-pree-o-LAH-ta

- **Fragrant, reddish-orange flowers**
- **Semievergreen to evergreen, climbs by tendrils with adhesive discs**
- **Grows quickly, 10 to 20 feet per year**
- **Zones 6 to 9 (south)**

From late spring well into summer, this southerner provides a massive, long-season display of red-orange flowers. The species is fragrant, although most varieties are not.

The tubular blossoms are very attractive to hummingbirds.

USES: Its tendrils wrap around other plants, onto netting and chain link. The adhesive discs at the tips of the tendrils allow the plant to climb tree trunks and masonry surfaces.

SITING AND CARE: Cross vine grows best in soil that has ample amounts of organic matter and moderate moisture. Blooms best in full sun. Protect the leaves from winter winds.

RECOMMENDED VARIETIES: 'Atrosanguinea' has reddish-purple flowers. 'Tangerine Beauty' is clear orange. 'Velcyll'—orange outside and yellow inside—is hardier.

Tubular red flowers of cross vine are a hummingbird magnet.

BOUGAINVILLEA, PAPERFLOWER

Bougainvillea glabra
boo-gan-VIL-lee-a GLA-bra

- **Spectacular flower bracts**
- **Evergreen; sprawls, so must be tied**
- **Rampant growth, 20 feet per year**
- **Zones 9 and 10, often grown as an annual or a container plant in the north**

This is one of the most famous of the subtropical vines. It is a greenhouse flower in the north and is popular outdoors in warm climates as a perennial. The plants produce flowers whenever the weather is hot.

The bracts surrounding the flowers provide the real show of color and remain attractive for up to a month. Native to South America.

USES: The colors are strong and often best surrounded by the green of other plants. Grow it on an arbor or spilling over a wall.

SITING AND CARE: Bougainvillea grows well in full sun with moderate moisture and good drainage. Watch out for the thorny stems. Aphids can be a problem.

RECOMMENDED VARIETIES: There are many cultivars (some are selections of the hybrid *B. ×buttiana)*, ranging in color from flamboyant pink to orange, yellow, and white. 'Raspberry Ice' has white and green leaves with red flowers.

Bougainvillea produces masses of flowers all summer.

AMERICAN BITTERSWEET

Celastrus scandens
sel-A-strus SKAN-denz

- **Fabulous display of fruits in autumn**
- **Deciduous, climbs by twining**
- **Vigorous, grows 10 to 15 feet per year**
- **Zones 3 to 8**

The red-orange fruit of bittersweet symbolizes autumn. The flowers are small and easily missed. Rare and endangered in much of the east, its Asian cousin (*C. orbiculatus*) is very invasive and weedy, often found in natural areas where it smothers and kills trees by girdling.

USES: American bittersweet is especially showy on an evergreen background. Plant on a large post, strong trellis, or chain-link fence. Include one male plant for every two or three females to ensure fruit production.

SITING AND CARE: American bittersweet grows in sun or shade, fruiting best in the sun. It tolerates a wide range of moisture. Cut stems dry well and remain showy all winter.

The American species fruits only at the tips of the shoots. Oriental bittersweet produces its fruits in clusters on side shoots.

Immature fruits of American bittersweet.

CLEMATIS (LARGE-FLOWERED HYBRIDS)

Clematis hybrids
KLEM-a-tis

- Stunning displays of large flowers and showy seed heads
- Deciduous; climbs by wrapping leaf stems around a structure and by twining
- Most grow 5 to 8 feet per year
- Most are hardy in Zones 4 or 5 southward to Zone 8

These big-blossomed vines always draw raves from guests. Unfortunately, clematis has an unwarranted reputation for being finicky and a challenge to prune.

USES: Because the large-flowered hybrid clematis are generally restrained in habit and light in weight, they are favorite choices to grow on other blooming plants, such as shrubs, small trees, and other vines. Try growing one on another plant, such as a spring-blooming tree peony. Match the colors; plant a pink clematis on a pink shrub. Or for a purple planting, use summer-blooming, purple-flowered Jackman clematis *(Clematis ×jackmanii)* on beautyberry *(Callicarpa bodinieri* 'Profusion') or Crimson Pygmy barberry. The clematis blooms during the summer, then the beautyberry takes over with purple fruit in fall. Plant a blue- or purple-flowered clematis next to an artemisia. The clematis will lounge all summer in the lush silvery leaves.

Jackman Clematis.

Nelly Moser Clematis.

SITING AND CARE: Clematis grows best with cool roots and leaves exposed to the sun, so plant the roots in the shade, and train the vine to grow into the light. Bury 2 to 3 inches of the stem; it will send out its own roots, increasing the odds of survival. Plant the vine on the north side of a shrub, tree, or tree stump. Heavy mulching with bark or wood chips also helps keep the roots cool. Good drainage and moderate moisture are important. Clematis is generally little troubled by pests, but wilt can be a problem. Additional balanced fertilizer each spring will help maintain or increase its vigor.

Clematis climbs by wrapping the stems of its leaves around a structure or plant, as well as by twining, and grows well on netting, chain link, and light trellises.

Prune a clematis to control growth, encourage flowering, and remove dead stems. Some clematis die back almost to the ground every winter. Wait till new growth starts in spring and remove everything dead. To encourage it to grow from the base, cut it off about 6 inches from ground level.

- **Prune after blooming:** If it blooms in spring, prune by midsummer. Winter pruning will remove flower buds. Plants that bloom in summer produce flowers on the current season's growth. Prune these anytime during the winter. Pruning after new growth starts will delay or prevent flowering. Just to make life interesting, some of the cultivars start blooming on old wood, then continue to bloom on the new growth. With these plants, avoid pruning except to shape the plant. If it becomes overgrown, cut back hard in winter.

RECOMMENDED VARIETIES: The following is a small sampling of the many cultivars available: 'Candida' has white flowers, yellow centers; 'Nelly Moser' has pinkish flowers with dark pink bands. 'Contesse de Bouchaud' has 5-inch-wide silvery rose flowers all summer long and blooms on new wood.

C. ×jackmanii produces violet-purple flowers on new wood in early summer and sporadically

Willy Alpine Clematis.

Scarlet Clematis.

Henryi Clematis.

Ville de Lyon Clematis.

throughout the summer. 'General Sikorski' has bluish-lavender flowers; 'Henryi', white; 'H.F. Young', large Wedgwood blue flowers; 'Miss Bateman', creamy white flowers with reddish centers; 'Niobe' has deep ruby flowers with yellow centers and blooms in late spring and into the summer on new wood. 'Pink Fantasy' is pink; 'Proteus', double flowers that look like mauve peonies; 'Ramona', large and lavender blue; 'Sugar Candy', pink with a deeper pink stripe and tolerant of partial shade; 'Sunset', large deep red flowers; 'Ville de Lyon', red flowers; 'Madame le Coultre', white flowers; 'Mrs. Cholmondeley', bluish-purple flowers and grows to 20 feet.

RELATED SPECIES: Species clematis are less well-known than their large-flowered hybrid cousins, but they are no less beautiful. Many produce large clusters of small flowers only once during the growing season. Some are quite fragrant, and some have attractive seed heads. Cultural requirements are the same as for the large-flowered hybrids, except many of the species tolerate shade.

Armand clematis (*C. armandii*, Zones 7 to 9) is an evergreen Chinese species with abundant, fragrant, showy white flowers above shiny dark green leaves. It blooms in early spring on old wood. It tolerates sun or light shade.

C. cirrhosa (Zones 8 and 9) is evergreen with drooping creamy white flowers in fall and winter.

Clematis ×durandii (Zones 5 to 8) is a beautiful hybrid that cannot climb on its own. Weave it through other plants or tie it to support structures. It has deep violet flowers produced in summer on new wood. It is best in full sun.

Grow pink anemone clematis (*C. montana* var. *rubens,* Zones 5 to 8) for a vanilla-scented profusion of pink flowers in spring. The new foliage of this Chinese plant is tinged bronze. Though dainty in appearance, the plant is vigorous enough to cover an entire wall (netting or string is needed). It is beautiful against brick or a gray stone. It tolerates light shade but is best in full sun. The species (*C. montana*) is rarely available but

has white flowers. 'Tetrarose' and 'Mayleen' have larger pink flowers. *C. montana* var. *wilsonii* blooms a week or so later than others with twisted cream-colored flowers.

The golden clematis species (*C. tangutica* and *C. orientalis,* Zones 3 to 8) have yellow flowers in summer and are native to Asia. The flowers point downward, resembling golden bells. Soon after flowering, the plants are covered in attractive feathery silver seed heads. Grow in full sun. The cultivars *C. o.* 'Bill Mackenzie' and 'Radar Love' have large flowers.

Scarlet clematis (*Clematis texensis,* Zones 4 to 8) is a Texas native with fascinating bottlelike, deep pink flowers and grayish-green leaves. The flowers are not large but definitely attract attention. Plant near a walkway so that the flowers are visible. It blooms in midsummer to autumn on new shoots. Plant it in full sun for best bloom. 'Gravetye Beauty' has crimson red flowers that are more erect and open than the species. 'Duchess of Albany' has beautiful, deep pink flowers that are more open and upright.

Italian clematis (*Clematis virginiana,* Zones 3 to 7) is the American virgin's bower, native to eastern North America. It is similar in effect to sweet autumn clematis, although less showy in bloom and less vigorous. Its small white flowers appear in late summer and early fall, in sun or shade.

Sweet Autumn Clematis.

Pink Anemore Clematis.

Euonymus fortunei
yew-ON-i-mus for-TOO-nee-eye

Wintercreeper euonymus can climb over buildings as well as trees.

WINTERCREEPER

- Showy orange fruits
- Evergreen (one of the hardiest), climbs by rootlets
- Generally slow growing, but vigor varies with cultivar
- Zones 5 to 9 (some cultivars hardy to Zone 4)

This cousin of bittersweet is a variable evergreen in northern regions (see page 164). Some plants produce showy, bittersweet-like orange fruits, which are poisonous.
USES: Best on masonry.
SITING AND CARE: Grow wintercreeper euonymus in full sun or shade with moderate moisture.
RECOMMENDED VARIETIES: Many varieties in a range of leaf colors and growth habits are available. 'Coloratus' turns purple in winter and is one of the hardiest (to Zone 4). 'Emerald Gaiety' and 'Albo-marginatus' have white-variegated leaves; 'Emerald 'n Gold' and 'Aureo-marginatus' have yellow variegation. 'Longwood' and 'Minimus' (also called 'Kewensis') have very small, dark green leaves. 'Vegetus' has bold leaves and produces ample quantities of attractive light orange fruit (hardy to Zone 4).

Ficus pumila
FI-kus PEW-mi-la

Creeping fig creates a tracery of small stems and leaves on a wall.

CREEPING FIG

- Small, neat dark green leaves
- Evergreen, climbs by rootlets
- Vigorous, grows 10 feet per year
- Zones 8 to 10

This relative of the edible fig is popular in the south outdoors, and as a conservatory plant in the north, for its small, dark, evergreen leaves that cling to the surface they climb on. Older plants sometimes produce fruit (inedible) on horizontal stems that bear larger leaves. Native to eastern Asia.
USES: Best used to climb rock or masonry. Can damage other surfaces.
SITING AND CARE: This plant prefers partial shade and moderate moisture. It is best to trim off horizontal shoots because neither the larger leaves nor the fruits are desirable. Shear back to keep from building up on itself.
RECOMMENDED VARIETIES: 'Minima' is a less vigorous selection with smaller leaves.

Gelsemium sempervirens
jel-SEM-ee-um sem-per-VI-rens

Carolina jessamine is a sweet-scented, colorful favorite in mild climates.

CAROLINA JESSAMINE

- Stellar evergreen with fragrant yellow flowers in early spring
- Climbs by twining
- Vigorous, about 10 to 15 feet per year
- Zones 8 to 10

Beloved in the south, this twining, blooming evergreen is beautiful, but all parts of the plant are poisonous. The showy, trumpetlike, fragrant yellow flowers appear in masses throughout the spring. The foliage tends to be sparse; occasional pruning will help the plant look fuller. The stems are cinnamon brown in color. Native to southeastern United States and Central America.
USES: Plant on chain-link fence, lattice, or posts.
SITING AND CARE: This vine grows in sun or shade with moderate moisture. It is little troubled by insects.
RECOMMENDED VARIETIES AND RELATED SPECIES: 'Pride of Augusta' ('Plena') has double flowers, which are showy longer than those of the species. Swamp jasmine (*Gelsemium rankinii*) is a nearly identical species, but flowers are not fragrant.

Hedera helix
HE-de-ra HE-licks

ENGLISH IVY

- Bold, evergreen leaves on a vigorous vine or ground cover
- Climbs with rootlets
- Zones 6 to 10 (Zone 5 for a few cultivars)

Goldheart English ivy.

Silver King English ivy.

Susan Gibbes English ivy.

This is the "true" ivy, with shiny, evergreen leaves. A vigorous grower, it serves equally well as a ground cover or a vine. There are two types of leaves. Juvenile foliage has five-lobed leaves on easily rooting stems. Ivy can stay in this juvenile stage for decades, never flowering or fruiting. Mature growth produces white clusters of flowers followed by blue-black fruit. Birds eat the fruit and spread the weedy seedlings.

USES: There are few structures it is unable to conquer (it will even grow on aluminum siding and glass blocks), but it's ideal on masonry, trees, or (with a little help) on lattice and chain link. Use the special leaf sizes and shapes where they will be noticed and add to the textural display. Yellow-and-white-variegated ivies brighten dark spots. The evergreen growth complements the straight trunk of trees such as tulip poplars, but it can strangle a tree if allowed to grow into the branches. Mix other vines with English ivy. Let ivy climb a tree, then plant a clematis to cling to the ivy if there is enough light. You'll have an evergreen background all winter, and the showy clematis flowers in summer. Ivy will grow as a ground cover wherever it has a chance. Interplant with bulbs, such as daffodils and snowdrops, to relieve the monotony of green. The dark ivy leaves set off bright yellow and white strikingly and hide dying bulb foliage.

SITING AND CARE: English ivy grows in sun or shade and tolerates drought. It roots easily wherever the stems touch the ground. Propagation is done simply by cutting shoots with preformed roots and planting the shoots directly where new plants are wanted. Mulch soil around cuttings, and don't let them dry out. New leaves will develop, indicating the plant is becoming established. Spring is the best time to take cuttings, before new growth starts, but it is possible throughout the summer and early fall. The milder the winter, the stronger this plant's vigor. Ivy is a staple of most southern gardens and is often cursed for being too vigorous. In the north, greater care is needed for successful planting. In the northern regions of Zone 6 (and in Zone 5), protect ivy from winter wind and sun. Otherwise, the leaves will "burn" (they will regrow). Regular pruning is needed on buildings to keep the new growth from invading windows and doors and from growing under siding and shingles.

RECOMMENDED VARIETIES AND RELATED SPECIES: In northern gardens, use only the hardiest cultivars. Any of the cultivars may "revert," or mutate back to standard green leaves. If a change in growth occurs, cut it off before it overtakes the original plant. 'Baltica', 'Bulgaria', 'Ogallala', 'Romania', and 'Thorndale' are the most cold-hardy selections. Use them for planting in Zone 5. 'Star' has five very pointed lobes and serves equally well as a ground cover and a vine; leaves are 2 inches long. 'Tomboy' has triangular leaves with rounded edges. It readily climbs and often blooms and produces fruit. 'Gold Craft' leaves are small (1 to 2 inches) and golden but tend to brown in winter. 'Goldchild' is not vigorous and doesn't climb well.

Algerian ivy (*Hedera canariensis,* also called *H. algeriensis*) has large (to 6 inches), smooth, evergreen leaves and is useful in Zone 9 (Zone 8 with protection) southward. It, too, forms a ground cover and climbs with rootlets.

Persian ivy (*Hedera colchica*) is similar to Algerian ivy but hardier (Zone 7). It produces bolder leaves than English ivy.

Parsley Crested English ivy.

Hydrangea petiolaris
hi-DRANG-gee-a pe-tee-o-LAH-ris

Rambling up a tree is the preferred habit of Climbing hydrangea.

CLIMBING HYDRANGEA

- **Creamy white flowers in late spring**
- **Deciduous, climbs by rootlets**
- **Slow-to-moderate growth rate**
- **Zones 5 to 7**

Creamy white flowers appear in late spring against a background of shiny deep green leaves. The flower clusters are lacy (sometimes described as lacecap), with large, four-sepaled blossoms surrounding a center mass of small flowers. They appear on 1- to 2-foot-long horizontal shoots and dry to an attractive tan. They are especially pleasant in winter when dusted with snow. In autumn, the leaves often turn bright yellow before falling. During the winter months, the peeling bark provides interest.

USES: Cover substantial masonry walls with this vine. It will clothe it with white flowers and turn a dull expanse into a floral masterpiece.

Climbing hydrangea can also be grown as a large shrub.

SITING AND CARE: Although it can grow in full sun, it thrives with at least a bit of shade. It requires average moisture and good drainage. Be patient with climbing hydrangea. Even if you purchase a blooming plant, the vine may put all its energy into leafy growth, and you may have to wait up to five years to see flowers. The wait is worth it, and the display will generously increase every year.

Japanese beetles can skeletonize the leaves, especially those in full sun. Shaded leaves seem of less interest to these pests. Little pruning is needed with climbing hydrangea, but prune it away from windows.

RECOMMENDED VARIETIES: 'Brookside Littleleaf' has small (1½ to 2 inches) leaves and is especially attractive trailing out of a container.

Jasminum polyanthum
jaz-MEEN-um po-lee-ANTH-um

Very fragrant, blush-pink flowers of pink Chinese jasmine appear over a long season.

PINK CHINESE JASMINE

- **Showy, fragrant pink flowers bloom over a long period**
- **Finely cut, narrow dark green leaves**
- **Deciduous to evergreen, grows by scrambling and twining**
- **Grows up to 15 feet tall**
- **Zones 9 and 10, also used in conservatories**

The very showy flowers (up to 3 to 4 inches wide) are produced over a long period, from late spring into autumn. It is very attractive against blues, grays, and blacks.

USES: Weave the stems into lattice or let them twine around supports. Train them up a south-facing wall or over an arch where you will appreciate the fragrance.

SITING AND CARE: Give the plant full sun and protection from the wind in colder areas. It is vigorous, tolerant of drought, and needs good drainage.

RELATED SPECIES: Winter-flowering jasmine (*Jasminum nudiflorum*) is another Chinese species. Its unscented yellow flowers appear sporadically throughout the winter and are set off against green stems. This plant is especially attractive cascading from a container or when trained upright and allowed to cascade down itself. Plant it with weeping forsythia to extend the effective bloom period. It is hardy in Zones 6 to 9. It cannot climb by itself and needs to be tied or woven to a support.

Winter-flowering jasmine.

Lonicera sempervirens
lah-NI-se-ra sem-per-VI-renz

TRUMPET HONEYSUCKLE

- Attractive flowers from spring until fall
- Deciduous, climbs by twining
- Slow-to-moderate growth rate, eventually reaching 10 to 15 feet
- Zones 4 to 9

This vine has the longest blooming season of any of the hardy climbers. Flowers open in midspring and continue putting on a show until they succumb to heavy frosts in autumn. Individual flowers are tubular and borne in showy clusters. They are not fragrant, but hummingbirds enjoy them. The flowers are followed by clusters of berries that are relished by other birds. The leaves are bluish-green, and the terminal leaf pairs tend to fuse together into one. Native to the United States.

USES: Plant a honeysuckle on an arch or an arbor, with a small shrub or a perennial at the base to hide the stems. Honeysuckle will also climb trellises, lattice, netting, chain-link fences, bamboo tripods, or even a single strand of rope. Place it where you will be able to observe the hummingbirds at a short distance without frightening them. It can also be grown as a ground cover.

SITING AND CARE: This vine tolerates shade but blooms best in the sun. It needs average moisture; avoid drought for best results. Aphids are a major nuisance.

RECOMMENDED VARIETIES: There are a number of selections of trumpet honeysuckle to choose for gardens. *Lonicera sempervirens* 'Sulphurea' and 'John Clayton' have yellow flowers, the latter being a newer selection that seems to be more floriferous and attractive. 'Magnifica' and 'Superba' have scarlet flowers; 'Cedar Lane' has long (to 2 inches), dark red flowers.

Superba trumpet honeysuckle.

Redgold honeysuckle is a hybrid with rich orange flowers.

Scarlet trumpet honeysuckle.

Goldflame honeysuckle.

Parthenocissus quinquefolia
par-then-o-SIS-us kwing-kwee-FO-lee-a

Leaves of Engelmannii Virginia creeper are smaller than the species.

Red leaves and blue berries of Virginia creeper make a stellar combination.

VIRGINIA CREEPER

- Trouble-free, vigorous native with good fall color
- Deciduous, sometimes climbs by tendrils that have adhesive discs
- Grows 5 to 10 feet per year
- Zones 3 to 9

Virginia creeper is commonly found in eastern forests, growing as a vine and as a ground cover. It offers bold leaves divided into five leaflets, each 4 to 5 inches long. Dark green during the summer, they turn a brilliant red (in the sun) in autumn. The flowers are inconspicuous, but the waxy blue-black fruit resembles small Concord grapes and are borne on red stalks. The fruit and stalks complement the autumn leaves and remain showy for several weeks after leaf drop. Birds crave the fruit.

USES: Use it to cover slopes and unsightly areas.

SITING AND CARE: Virginia creeper needs average moisture and grows in sun or shade. This tough climber grows almost anywhere and on almost anything, forming a solid mass of foliage. It wraps its tendrils around structures and plants, and with its adhesive discs at the tips of the tendrils, it climbs easily on rocks and masonry. It tolerates soil compaction and smog as well as seaside salt. Most gardeners feel it is too vigorous and not sufficiently showy for key garden areas. However, Virginia creeper is perfect for areas of low maintenance and low visibility. You can easily prune it to control overly vigorous growth. Simply cut unwanted shoots just above a leaf or a bud. The only pest problem is Japanese beetles, and these tend to attack only plants growing in the sun.

RECOMMENDED VARIETIES: 'Engelmannii' has smaller leaflets (4 inches) than the species but otherwise is very similar.

Parthenocissus tricuspidata
par-then-o-SIS-us tri-cus-pi-DAH-ta

Unmistakable marker of seasonal change: Green Showers Boston ivy in spring (left) and in fall.

BOSTON IVY

- Deep green leaves and neat habit
- Deciduous, climbs like a rootlet vine by tendrils tipped with adhesive discs
- Vigorous once established, grows 6 to 10 feet per year
- Zones 4 to 8

This "ivy" of the Ivy League covers the buildings of many northeastern United States universities and turns them into green boxes. Its color changes with the season: light green in spring, dark green in summer, and scarlet in fall. This is a flat growing vine. Its stems grow tight against a structure, with only individual leaves protecting out. Leaf width varies from 4 to 8 inches. Blue-black berries come on red stalks but become only apparent after the leaves fall. Birds consume the berries before winter arrives. Autumn color—peach to crimson—is best in full sun, becoming pale yellow in heavy shade. Plants cling with discs.

USES: Use it as a backdrop for summer flowers, especially reds, yellows, oranges, and whites.

SITING AND CARE: Grows in shade and tolerates drought. Reflected heat of south-facing masonry walls may inhibit new growth. In such cases, plant the vine on an adjacent east- or west-facing wall and allow it to climb into the sun. It is generally pest-free, although Japanese beetles may damage leaves in sun.

RECOMMENDED VARIETIES: 'Lowii' and 'Veitchii' have small (less than 3 inches) leaves. 'Beverley Brook' has leaves half the normal size. All three are significantly less vigorous than the species. 'Green Spring' and 'Green Showers' have glossy leaves up to 10 inches across. 'Purpurea' has reddish-purple leaves; 'Aurata' has yellow foliage marbled with green and red.

SILVER LACE VINE

Polygonum aubertii
Poh-LI-goh-num au-BERT-ee-eye

- Cascade of white flowers in late summer
- Deciduous, climbs by twining
- Grows to 10 to 20 feet a summer
- Zones 4 to 8

This vine brings bright white flowers to tired late-summer gardens. The individual flowers are small but are borne in a profusion of lacy clusters. The thin, arrowhead-shaped leaves have a fine texture and are small (less than 4 inches long). Native to western China.

USES: Silver lace vine will quickly cover a chain-link fence, netting, and shrubs.

SITING AND CARE: Grow this plant in sun or light shade. Give it average moisture; it tolerates drought. It blooms on new wood and can be cut back hard in spring. Occasionally, Japanese beetles will attack foliage.

A late-summer blanket of flowers covers silver lace vine.

CLIMBING AND RAMBLING ROSES

Rosa spp.
RO-za

- Stunning flowers
- Deciduous, scramblers need to be tied to supports
- Size varies with species and cultivar
- Many are hybrids
- Zones vary with species and variety

Grow these plants for their exuberant blooms. They are excellent cut flowers, and one shoot alone can produce a bouquet. These roses are actually shrubs with extremely long shoots. They have no mechanism other than thorns for climbing and need to be tied to structures. Roses with extra long stems are divided into two major divisions: ramblers and climbers.

- **Climbers** generally produce large-sized flowers, have stiff, thick stems, and are less vigorous than ramblers. Many will bloom heavily in early summer, then continue to flower the rest of the summer.
- **Ramblers** are vigorous growers, producing long, thin stems that are relatively easy to bend. Ramblers usually have small flowers in showy, dense clusters and tend to bloom only once a year, in early summer. Some ramblers produce attractive displays of fruit.

USES: Weave roses in lattice, obelisks, or wrought iron. Tie them to arches and to freestanding pillars. Train a vigorous rose upright, then allow it to cascade downward. Strong-growing ramblers tend to mound on themselves on top of an arbor, creating huge arches of blossoms.

Plant the Blaze climbing rose at the base of a post; tie main canes to it with twine.

American Beauty climbing rose graces arbor or pergola with its flowers.

CLIMBING AND RAMBLING ROSES

Multicolored Joseph's Coat comes from a disease-resistant plant.

Stems of Lutea banksian rose are thornless.

Limber stems of Hiawatha rose scramble over walls and fences.

SITING AND CARE: Plant roses in full sun and give them moderate moisture and good drainage. Train ramblers and climbing roses on any support to which they can be easily tied. Attach screw eyes to wooden walls or posts or drill holes into masonry and insert eyebolts for tying. Fasten the stems to the bolts with wire or green string. Training roses horizontally encourages the

production of flower buds. Do not let the canes become too entwined on something you have to paint regularly. You'll need to take the vines down before painting.

Plant a rambler at the base of small trees and train the shoots into the canopy. The rose will seek the sun, and within a year or two, the tree will fill with blossoms. Choose a tree with light shade, such as an old, unproductive apple tree. Or plant the rose next to a relatively young tree, and let the two grow old together.

All climbers and ramblers bloom on old wood for their first flush of flowers. The repeat bloomers also produce blossoms on new growth. Some with little vigor require little pruning. Vigorous ones will benefit from winter removal of old shoots because younger shoots will have more flowers.

Rambler roses bloom on old wood and therefore should not be severely pruned in winter. However, winter is the time to remove entire shoots where they have become crowded. Take out the oldest shoots, which will be the largest and colored brown and gray (young shoots tend to be green or red).

RELATED SPECIES: There are also some species roses used as climbers and ramblers. These are called "species" roses because they are naturally occurring species that have not been hybridized by humans. In areas where they are native, they scramble over other plants, usually on the edge of woods and in old, abandoned farm fields. Many of them make very attractive garden plants. Some of the best-known species roses are *Rosa banksiae, R. canina, R. laevigata, R. multiflora, R. rubiginosa, R. setigera,* and *R. virginiana.*

American Pillar rambling rose covers a series of arches.

Ghislaine de Feligonde is a hybrid multiflora rose.

Schizophragma hydrangeoides
ski-zo-FRAG-ma hi-drang-gee-OI-deez

FALSE CLIMBING HYDRANGEA

- White flowers create a wall of blossoms
- Deciduous, climbs by rootlets
- Once established, grows to 5 feet per year
- Zones 6 to 8

This vine looks like climbing hydrangea, and the two can be used interchangeably. It has showy white flowers and medium green leaves. False climbing hydrangea blooms about two weeks later than climbing hydrangea, so grow them together to extend the blooming season. Native to Japan and Korea.

USES: Grow false climbing hydrangea on tree trunks or masonry walls, or have it trail out of containers (it is root-hardy in containers outdoors to Zone 6).

SITING AND CARE: False climbing hydrangea grows in sun or shade. Give it moderate moisture.

Propagate by selecting stems already having rootlets. Cut these into 6-inch segments, and bury the lower two-thirds of the stems. Do this in early spring, and new plants will be rooted by midsummer. False climbing hydrangea is generally pest-free in the shade; Japanese beetles may attack plants growing in full sun.

RECOMMENDED VARIETIES: 'Moonlight' has gray-green foliage, which is significantly different in shape and color from the species. This foliage form is actually a juvenile trait. As the plant grows, it eventually sends out horizontal, mature shoots, with foliage a bit coarser and darker green. These shoots produce flowers.

False climbing hydrangea flowers while growing its way over a lattice screen.

Trachelospermum jasminoides
tra-kay-lo-SPERM-um jaz-min-OI-deez

STAR JASMINE

- A dense evergreen with fragrant flowers
- Evergreen; climbs by twining
- Vigorous, grows to 15 feet or more
- Zones 8 to 10

Tubular, creamy white flowers are star-shaped with an intense fragrance in late spring and early summer. Plant jasmine near a patio or anywhere you will enjoy it in the evening, when the flowers stand out due to their whiteness and fragrance. It is generally little troubled by pests. Native to China.

USES: Plant it on trellises, lattice, or chain-link fences. Use star jasmine (also called confederate jasmine) in a pot, trained on a cage of green mesh. This climber also serves as a ground cover and will blanket slopes.

SITING AND CARE: This vine does best in shade but will tolerate light sun. Provide moderate moisture with good drainage.

RECOMMENDED VARIETIES: 'Japonicum' leaves have white veins; its foliage turns bronze in autumn and winter. 'Minimum' has mottled leaves and a dwarf habit.

Flowers hang from star jasmine intertwined along the top of a fence.

Pinwheel-like flowers of star jasmine are intensely fragrant.

Wisteria floribunda
wis-TE-ree-a flo-ri-BUN-da

- Impressively long clusters of fragrant purple flowers in midspring
- Deciduous, climbs by twining
- Vigorous, grows up to 15 feet a year
- Zones 5 to 9

This Japanese native in full bloom is a memorable sight. It is one of the most beautiful of flowering vines, yet it can also be most challenging due to its vigor and strength. This is not a climber for weakly made structures. Many an arbor has collapsed under the twisting weight of wisteria. The fragrant flowers are bluish-violet, with cultivars varying from purple to pink to white. Individually small (less than 1 inch in length), the flowers are borne in pendant clusters from 8 to 24 inches long. The inedible fruits are thick, 6-inch-long, velvety green pods that resemble beans. The foot-long leaves have 11 to 19 leaflets, each about 3 inches long. They are unmarred by insects or diseases and form a dense

JAPANESE WISTERIA

screen throughout the summer. They turn pale yellow before dropping in autumn. The smooth, gray trunks become picturesque with age, sinuously wrapping around themselves. The trunk and leaf buds survive Zone 4 winters, but the flower buds do not. Native to Japan.

USES: Plant it on wrought iron and on large arbors and arches. This vine should be planted only on strong, maintenance-free structures; it will live for decades, and painting or rebuilding the structure will be difficult.

SITING AND CARE: Japanese wisteria needs full sun and moderate moisture for good flowering.

Getting a new wisteria to bloom can be a challenge, often requiring a wait of 5 to 10 years. Root pruning, withholding irrigation, and using only phosphate fertilizer (absolutely no nitrogen) may bring a reluctant wisteria into bloom. Seedlings seem to be especially slow to bloom, and there may be an advantage to buying a plant already of blooming age. Wisterias require frequent pruning to keep them within desired

Clusters of Japanese wisteria are long, and individual flowers open from the top down.

boundaries. Blossoms occur on spur shoots, which are short-side shoots off the main stems. Avoid removing them when pruning. Do major pruning right after flowering ends, plus one or two midsummer prunings of long shoots, cutting them back to the main part of the plant. In winter, do additional pruning to shape the plant, but avoid removing the spur shoots.

RECOMMENDED VARIETIES AND RELATED SPECIES: Two of the best cultivars are 'Macrobotrys' (also known as 'Longissima' and 'Multijuga'), with extremely long (to 36 inches) clusters of lavender-blue flowers; and 'Longissima Alba', with shorter white flower clusters up to 24 inches long.

Chinese wisteria (*Wisteria sinensis*) is a similar species and difficult to distinguish from Japanese wisteria except when in bloom. Chinese wisteria flowers appear before the leaves, in smaller clusters (6 to 12 inches long), and with the fragrant blossoms opening all at once. It is hardy to Zones 6 to 9 and generally has blue-violet flowers.

Relatively short flower clusters of American wisteria are attractive.

Flowers of Chinese wisteria come before leaves emerge, and flowers open all at once.

Resources

Arborvillage
P.O. Box 227
Holt, MO 64048
816/264-3911
e-mail: arborvillage@aol.com

Bovees Nursery
1737 SW Coronado
Portland, OR 97219
800/435-9250
www.bovees.com

Camellia Forest Nursery
9701 Carrie Rd.
Chapel Hill, NC 27516
919/968-0504
www.camforest.com

Carroll Gardens
444 E. Main St.
Westminster, MD 21157
800/638-6334
www.carrollgardens.com

Eastern Plant Specialties
Box 226
Georgetown, ME 04548
732/382-2508
www.easternplant.com

Forestfarm
990 Tetherow Rd.
Williams, OR 97544
541/846-7269
www.forestfarm.com

Gossler Farms Nursery
1200 Weaver Rd.
Springfield, OR 97478
541/746-3922

Greer Gardens
1280 Goodpasture Island Rd.
Eugene, OR 97401
800/548-0111
www.greergardens.com

Heirloom Roses
24062 NE Riverside Dr.
St. Paul, OR 97137
503/538-1576
www.heirloomroses.com

High Country Gardens
2902 Rufina St.
Santa Fe, NM 87505-2929
800/925-9387
www.highcountrygardens.com

Jackson & Perkins
1 Rose Lane
Medford, OR 97501
800/854-6200
www.jacksonandperkins.com

Louisiana Nursery
5853 Highway 182
Opelousas, LA 70570
337/948-3696
www.Durionursery.com

Mellinger's
2310 W. South Range Rd.
North Lima, OH 44452-9731
800/321-7444
www.mellingers.com

Musser Forests, Inc.
Route 119 North
P.O. Box 340
Indiana, PA 15701-0340
800/643-8319
www.musserforests.com

Plants of the Southwest
3095 Agua Fria Rd
Santa Fe, NM 87507
505/438-8888
Catalog $3.50
www.plantsofthesouthwest.com

Richard Owen Nursery
2300 E. Lincoln St.
Bloomington, IL 61701
309/663-9551
www.excitinggardens.com

Roses of Yesterday & Today
803 Brown's Valley Rd.
Watsonville, CA 95076
831/728-1901
www.rosesofyesterday.com

Roslyn Nursery
211 Burr's Lane
Dix Hills, NY 11746
631/643-9347
www.roslynnursery.com
Siskiyou Rare Plant Nursery
2825 Cummings Rd.
Medford, OR 97501
541/772-6846

The Fragrant Path
P.O. Box 328
Fort Calhoun, NE 68023
Catalog: $2.00.

Wayside Gardens
1 Garden Lane
Hodges, SC 29695
800/845-1124
www.waysidegardens.com

White Flower Farm
P.O. Box 50
Litchfield, CT 06759-0050
800/503-9624
www.whiteflowerfarm.com

Woodlanders Inc.
1128 Colleton Ave.
Aiken, SC 29801
803/648-7522
www.woodlanders.net

Yucca Do Nursery
P.O. Box 907
Hempstead, TX 77445
979/826-4580
www.yuccado.com

Index

Page numbers in **bold type** indicate main descriptions of plants or plant problems and generally include a photograph. Page numbers in *italic type* indicate additional photographs and illustrations.

METRIC CONVERSIONS

U.S. Units to Metric Equivalents			Metric Units to U.S. Equivalents		
To Convert From	**Multiply By**	**To Get**	**To Convert From**	**Multiply By**	**To Get**
Inches	25.4	Millimeters	Millimeters	0.0394	Inches
Inches	2.54	Centimeters	Centimeters	0.3937	Inches
Feet	30.48	Centimeters	Centimeters	0.0328	Feet
Feet	0.3048	Meters	Meters	3.2808	Feet
Yards	0.9144	Meters	Meters	1.0936	Yards
Square inches	6.4516	Square centimeters	Square centimeters	0.1550	Square inches
Square feet	0.0929	Square meters	Square meters	10.764	Square feet
Square yards	0.8361	Square meters	Square meters	1.1960	Square yards
Acres	0.4047	Hectares	Hectares	2.4711	Acres
Cubic inches	16.387	Cubic centimeters	Cubic centimeters	0.0610	Cubic inches
Cubic feet	0.0283	Cubic meters	Cubic meters	35.315	Cubic feet
Cubic feet	28.316	Liters	Liters	0.0353	Cubic feet
Cubic yards	0.7646	Cubic meters	Cubic meters	1.308	Cubic yards
Cubic yards	764.55	Liters	Liters	0.0013	Cubic yards

To convert from degrees Fahrenheit (F) to degrees Celsius (C), first subtract 32, then multiply by ⁵⁄₉.

To convert from degrees Celsius to degrees Fahrenheit, multiply by ⁹⁄₅, then add 32.

Ortho Complete Guide to Trees and Shrubs
Editor: Denny Schrock:
Contributing Technical Editors: Gary Kling, Michael D. Smith
Senior Associate Design Director: Tom Wegner
Assistant Editor: Harijs Priekulis
Copy Chief: Terri Fredrickson
Copy and Production Editor: Victoria Forlini
Photographer: Jay Wilde
Editorial Operations Manager: Karen Schirm
Managers, Book Production: Pam Kvitne,
    Marjorie J. Schenkelberg, Rick von Holdt
Contributing Copy Editor: Barbara Feller-Roth
Contributing Proofreaders: Mark John Conley, Juliet Jacobs,
    Mindy Kralicek, Terri Krueger
Contributing Illustrator: Mike Eagleton
Contributing Map Illustrator: Jana Fothergill
Indexer: Ellen Davenport
Editorial and Design Assistants: Kathleen Stevens,
    Karen McFadden

**Additional Editorial Contributions from
Art Rep Services**
Director: Chip Nadeau
Designers: lk Design
Illustrator: Dave Brandon
Bittersweet Lane LLC
Publishing Director: Michael MacCaskey
Editorial Art Director: Michele Newkirk

Meredith® Books
Editor in Chief: Linda Raglan Cunningham
Design Director: Matt Strelecki
Executive Editor, Gardening and Home Improvement:
    Benjamin W. Allen
Executive Editor, Gardening: Michael McKinley

Publisher: James D. Blume
Executive Director, Marketing: Jeffrey Myers
Executive Director, New Business Development:
    Todd M. Davis
Executive Director, Sales: Ken Zagor
Director, Operations: George A. Susral
Director, Production: Douglas M. Johnston
Business Director: Jim Leonard

Vice President and General Manager: Douglas J. Guendel

Meredith Publishing Group
President, Publishing Group: Stephen M. Lacy
Vice President-Publishing Director: Bob Mate

Meredith Corporation
Chairman and Chief Executive Officer: William T. Kerr

In Memoriam: E.T. Meredith III (1933–2003)

All of us at Meredith® Books are dedicated to providing
you with the information and ideas you need to enhance
your home and garden. We welcome your comments and
suggestions about this book. Write to us at:
    Meredith Corporation
    Meredith Gardening Books
    1716 Locust St.
    Des Moines, IA 50309–3023

If you would like to purchase any of our gardening, home
improvement, cooking, crafts, or home decorating and
design books, check wherever quality books are sold.
Or visit us at: meredithbooks.com

If you would like more information on other Ortho
products, call 800/225-2883 or visit us at: www.ortho.com

Thanks to
Rosemary Kautzky, Mary Irene Swartz

Photographers
(Photographers credited may retain copyright © to the listed
photographs.) L = Left, R = Right, C = Center, B = Bottom, T = Top

Liz Ball/Positive Images: 16R, 92TL, 124B; **Cathy Wilkinson Barash:**
203C; **Mark Bolton/Garden Picture Library:** 95BR, 168B; **Pat
Bruno/Positive Images:** 109C; **Gay Bumgarner/Positive Images:**
92TR, 97T, 132BR, 202C; **Brian Carter/Garden Picture Library:** 113T,
159B; **David Cavagnaro:** 8, 14R, 70, 81R, 82, 88R, 94TL, 98BR, 122R,
152B, 164T, 166C, 174TL, 181T, 183C, 189BR, 191TR, 191C, 195T, 198BR,
199CR, 202B, 204TL, 205BL, 208BL, 213BR; **Walter Chandoha:** 19BR, 90,
91, 136T; **Eric Crichton/Garden Picture Library:** 5T, 88L, 134T; **R.
Todd Davis:** 100TL, 103B; **Michael Dirr:** 110TR, 194BCL; **Catriona
Tudor Erler:** 15R, 16L, 73TT, 174B, 179B; **Ron Evans/Garden Picture
Library:** 7C, 97B; **Derek Fell:** 17, 18, 36L, 76B, 80B, 101C, 118T, 121B,
126B, 128C,135B. 136B, 146L, 151B, 155T, 157B, 162B, 172C, 180T, 180B,
184T, 185B, 190BL, 194TLC, 209B; **John Glover:** 10, 29, 79, 93B, 109B,
113TC, 114TL, 131L, 131TR, 133B, 142TL, 144-145B, 145B, 146-147T,
150T, 155C, 158C, 160TL, 160BC, 161T, 170T, 177T, 184B, 188TR, 188BC,
194TL, 195C, 202T, 207TC, 209CL; **John Glover/Garden Picture
Library:** 112T, 122L, 149B; **David Goldberg:** 19T; **Jerry Harpur:** 5B,
50BR, 144T, 157C, 196TL (Hakone Garden), 209T; **Marcus Harpur:**
102T, 119T, 166B (RHS Wisley), 181C (Edenbridge House, Kent), 191TCL;
Sunniva Harte/Garden Picture Library: 150B, 161B; **Neil
Holmes/Garden Picture Library:** 134B; **Saxon Holt:** 109T, 112B, 128T,
133T; **Horticultural Photography:** 108C, 120TR; **Jerry
Howard/Positive Images:** 23C, 94BR, 96T, 167CR; **Rosemary Kautzky:**
2-3, 11, 58B, 103C, 106B, 111T, 111B, 114TR, 115TR, 116C, 129T, 144BL,
169C, 196TR, 203B, 211T; **Donna & Tom Krischan:** 28TR, 138B, 189TC,
190BR, 193TR, 194BR, 205TL; **Andrew Lawson:** 51B, 110TL, 111C,
120TL, 130BR, 135T, 137C, 137B, 147T, 153T, 163B, 176C, 183B, 185C,
193B#2, 204TR, 209CR, 213BL; **Janet Loughrey:** 50TL, 58T, 84B, 99C,
107T, 114BL, 114BR, 116T, 118C, 119C, 141B, 142B, 149T, 155B, 159T,
162C, 165T, 175B, 178T, 189TR, 204BL, 204BR, 205BR, 214T; **Charles
Mann:** 25, 99T, 102B, 104B, 115B, 118B, 129B, 132BL, 141C, 150C, 203T;
John Miller/Garden Picture Library: spine; **Clive Nichols:** 64T (Vale
End, Surrey), 95TL, 98TL, 130BL, 137T (Englefield House, Berkshire),
139T (Hillier Gardens, Hampshire), 154C, 156T, 169B, 182T, 191TL,
193B#1, 194TRC (Hearns House, Oxfordshire), 194BL, 198TL, 199B;
Clive Nichols/Garden Picture Library: 154B; **John Parker/Positive
Images:** 100C; **Jerry Pavia:** 7TR, 9, 14L, 19BL, 20L, 21, 22C, 23L, 23R,
26, 73B, 92BL, 92BR, 95TR, 96B, 101T, 104C, 107B, 108T, 110B, 113B,
117T, 117B, 123T, 125B, 127B, 129C, 131BR, 139C, 140T, 142TR, 143T,
152C, 153C, 153B, 156B, 158T, 165C, 166T, 170B, 171C, 173BL, 173BR,
174TR, 176T, 177C, 178C, 178B, 181B, 182B, 183T, 185T, 186BC, 187BR,
190T, 190TCL, 190CR, 190BC, 193B#4, 200TR, 200B, 206T, 206C, 207TL,
208T, 210T, 210BR, 212TR, 212BL, 214BL, 214BR; **Ben Phillips/Positive
Images:** 89BR, 198BL, 201TL, 201TR, 210BL; **Ann Reilly/Positive
Images:** 172T, 175C, 187TR; **Howard Rice/Garden Picture Library:**
20R, 68T, 124C, 138T, 159C, 193B#3, cover; **Richard Shiell:** 7B, 81L, 99
inset, 104T, 113BC, 115TL, 117C, 120B, 126C, 127C, 128B, 130T, 136C,
146BR, 147B, 148, 152T, 156C, 163C, 165B, 177B, 182C, 184C, 186BL,
188BL, 188BR, 189BL, 191B, 198TR, 210C; **Pam Spaulding/Positive
Images:** 123C, 172B; **Peter Symcox/Positive Images:** 186R; **Michael S.
Thompson:** 12, 15L, 22L, 22R, 28B, 30T, 35TL, 54B, 59T, 62B, 69, 76T,
78T, 89BL, 93T, 94TR, 94BL, 95BL, 98TR, 99B, 100B, 100TR, 100BR, 101B,
103T, 105, 106T, 106C, 107C, 108B, 109 inset, 112C, 116B, 119B, 121C,
122C, 123B, 124T, 125T, 125C, 127T, 132TL, 132TR, 133C, 134C, 135C,
139B, 140C, 140B, 141T, 143B, 145T, 147C, 151T, 154T, 160BL, 161C,
162T, 163T, 164C, 164B, 168T, 168C, 169T, 171T, 171B, 173T, 176B, 179T,
180C, 184CB, 187BL, 187BC, 188TL, 189TL, 193TL, 194TR, 194BCR, 195B,
199TL, 200TL, 201B, 205TR, 206B, 208BR, 211C, 211B, 212TL, 212TC,
212BR, 213T; **Rick Wetherbee:** 167CL; **Justyn Willsmore:** 24R, 50BL,
59B, 93C, 98BL, 102C, 121T, 126T, 138C, 151C, 157T, 158B, 160TR,
160BR, 167TL, 167B, 175T, 179C, 186T, 192T, 207TR, 207B